HOME ENVIRONMENT AND VALUE DEVELOPMENT

By

Dr. Sudha Rani Upadhyay

Lecturer

J. T. College

Allahabad

DISCOVERY PUBLISHING HOUSE

NEW DELHI

First Published - 2003

Reprinted - 2015

ISBN: 978-81-7141-714-8

Home Environment and Value Development

Published by:

DISCOVERY PUBLISHING HOUSE PVT. LTD.
4383/4B, Ansari Road, Darya Ganj
New Delhi-110 002 (India)
Phone: +91-11-23279245, 43596064-65
Fax: +91-11-23253475
E-mail: discoverypublishinghouse@gmail.com
sales@discoverypublishinggroup.com
web: www.discoverypublishinggroup.com

Printed at:
Infinity Imaging Systems
Delhi

Preface

India is passing through a phase of transition. Revolutionary change is visible in entire pattern of life. Old values have tumbled down and new are still in the state of flux. Social life is marred with unresolved tensions, conflicts and violence. Adult support for youth's search for identity is lacking and guidelines for accepted behaviours are blurred and contradictory. Worship of false values and false heroes has become the order of the day. A double moral standard is the reality which is no healthy setting for our younger generation. This state of value crisis and uncertainty has led to high incidence of stress and weakening of moral and human values, which in turn is creating many serious conflicts, social and ethical. This is high time, when we should think about the ways and means to check this deterioration of moral and human values.

It is in this pathetic contextual reality, researcher feels that parents, teachers and students need to understand the effects of stress in home, society, school and self on development of moral judgement and various values. It is also essential to analyse the dynamics of various aspects of home environment on moral judgement and values. The present study. 'Effects of Stress and Home Environment on Girl's Moral Judgement and Values' is an humble attempt to help parents and to some extent teachers in their efforts to enhance the development of moral judgement and values among girls.

This research work was supervised by Dr. K.S. Misra, Reader, Department of Education, University of Allahabad. I had the privilege of being initiated into research under his able guidance. His constructive criticism, fertile imagination, discriminating taste in educational research, invaluable advice and his inspiration which was contributed generously and thoughtfully has much to do with the completion of this venture. I wish to record my special thinks and high sense of gratitude to Dr. Misra.

I am extremely grateful to Prof. R.S. Pandey, Head, Department of Education, University of Allahabad, Prof. Janak Pandey and Prof. R.K. Naidu, Department of Psychology who encouraged me from time to time by giving their valuable advice and suggestions in completion of this thesis.

I shall be failing in my duty, if I do not acknowledge Dr. Deepa Punetha, Lecturer, Dept. of Psychology, University of Allahabad, for her kind cooperation and constant encouragement at various stages of this work.

I express my gratefulness of Dr. Yoganand Sinha, Lecturer, Department of Psychology, University of Allahabad, who willingly extended his help and expertise on matters related to analysis of data.

My special thanks are to the librarians of N.C.E.R.T; N.E.P.A; J.N.U., Delhi University, New Delhi, Department of Education; Department of Psychology; General library, University of Allahabad, Bureau of Psychology and M.L.N. Medical College, Allahabad for the facilities and cooperation they provided to me.

Deep appreciation is expressed to all the principals who allowed me to collect data, teachers who extended their cooperation and the students who willingly and cheerfully provided the data.

A special note of profound indebtedness is due to my young children, Shobhita and Harsh, parents, in-laws, relatives and friends who cheerfully supported my long hours of preoccupation with the finalization of this thesis. I would like to express my gratitude to my husband Dr. R.K. Upadhyaya, Lecturer, Department of Defence and Strategic Studies, University of Allahabad, for his constant inspiration, encouragement and love which enabled me to reach upto this stage in my career.

I am thankful to Mr. Shashi Bhushan Pandey and Mr. Ravi Prakash Gupta for taking interest in typing out this manuscript and Mr. Bharat Bhushan Varshney for getting the copies Xeroxed.

Finally, warmest thanks to all those who rendered help in carrying out this investigation.

Sudha Rani Upadhyay

Contents

1

Introduction

Adolescence is a distinct and important period in the life cycle of the individual. It is seen as developmental stage between childhood and adulthood in which there is psychosocial moratorium. It is a stage of transition. Adolescents are in a state of tension and strain. Adolescent is exposed to many life events, often originating within the family over which he or she has little control (Coddington, 1972). On the other hand, adolescence compared with earlier ages, is characterized by a more active interaction with the environment (Scarr & McCartney, 1983). In fact, it is widely accepted that one of the hallmarks of the adolescent years is the experimentation with diverse behaviours and roles and often painful tendency to create stressful experiences (Weiner, 1980) that is the experience of self-generated (Controllable) negative events (e.g. school suspension, running away from home etc.).

Simons and Rosenberg, (1973) regarded the period of 12-14 years as stress age. Adolescent students face critical situations where they have to adjust to varying environments satisfying both personal and social needs, The adjustment is made through the process of interaction between the person and the environment. Discrepancies between what a person desires or expects from the environment and what he actually gets make him feel stress. Students, are usually exposed to several stress producing situations.

Sources of Stress: Their Taxonomy

Life experiences include several kinds of vague, indistinct novel, or traditional expected stressors which pose great difficulties for individuals. Their anxiety over impending future events, lack of feedback on effectiveness of coping endeavours or growing realization of one's failure in dealing with life situations which are faced successfully by others often lead to painful and disturbing stress. Any life event may be stressful if it causes changes in and demands readjustment of an average person's normal routine. Researchers have been usually concerned with life stress or stressful life events (Dohrenwend & Dohrenwend, 1974) examination stress assessed as test anxiety, (Spielberger, Gonzalez, Taylor, Alagaze & Anton, 1978) and organizational/occupational stress (Cooper & Payne, 1978; 1980; Pareek, 1981). Several researchers have classified different sources of stress. Lazarus and Cohen. (1977) have considered three general classes of stressors. The first, cataclysmic phenomena refers to sudden, unique and powerful single events or clusters of related occurrences affecting large numbers of people. Many of these have been studied, including natural disaster (Baker & Chapman, 1962; Sims & Baumann, 1974) and relocation (Fried, 1963; Schulz, 1976).

A second class of stressors includes those powerful events but affiliative and socially comparative behaviours have been identified as styles of coping with a focused, specific threat (McGrath, 1970; Schachter, 1959) and social support has been shown to moderate the effect of stress (Cobb, 1976). These events include response to illness, death or significant loss (Greene, 1966; Parkers, 1972; Hackett & Weisman, 1964) or losing one's job (Kasl & Cobb, 1970).

Lazarus and Cohen refer to the third group of stressors as 'daily hassles', that is, those stable and repetitive problems encountered in daily life. Many of these are more chronic, including job dissatisfaction (Kahn & French, 1970;

Frankenhaeuser & Gardell, 1976), neighbourhood problems (Harburg, Erfrut, Chaperi, Nauenstein, Schull & Schork, 1973) and commuting (Singer, Lundberg, & Frankenhaeuser, 1978). Crowding, especially that encountered in one's neighbourhood, in transportation setting and in residential buildings, may also be considered to be chronic or often repeated stressors (Epstein, 1981). The cumulation of instances of unwanted contact and loss of control appears to be responsible for stress and withdrawal that have been observed (Baum & Valins, 1977).

Baum et. al., (1982) advised to distinguish between physical and psychological stressors. According to them physical agents such as pollution, climate, and temperature have direct effect on us. Stress response can be evoked by changes and challenges that are experienced in daily life by disruption of one's habits (eg., by crowding or unpredictable noise) or culturally governed mores, by obstacles and hindrances placed before us through malfunction of social systems, or by deprivation or loss experienced in life. In short, a noxious agent may be anything from a virus to a vicissitude.

Stressors in Students Life

Sources of stress lay both in person and in environment. The degree of threat is limited by the strength of the motive or motives whose gratification is endangered (Lazarus, 1966). Individual differences exists in needs of students. A discrepancy between demands and individual's opportunities to meet those demands (McGrath, 1970) is not enough alone to cause stress. Stress arises when satisfaction of needs is endangered, and it is necessary and difficult for the individual to act.

During adolescence, students face the problem of identity. They have to experiment with variety of roles and formulate values and ideals for themselves. They express a ripening need for independence and autonomy by moving away from parents to peer group, while, at the same time, retaining dependence on the family as a stable anchor point for resolution of many important issues. As Douvan and Adelson, (1966) suggest that during this period, the youngster must synthesize earlier identifications with personal qualities and relate them to social opportunities and social ideals. When this synthesis fails, stress arises. According to Hamilton, (1979) major potential sources of strain reside in each person's systems of needs and goals. Rotter, (1966) is of the view that where affiliation and achievement needs are not adequately met, adoptive coping processes may be unavailable. The biological changes that occur during adolescence, and consequent need for the person to cope with morphological and physiological developments and to come to terms with growing heterosexual interests also generate stress. Conflict between id, ego and super ego and confrontation of internal processes (instinct, drives and internalized societal values), cause stress among the adolescent students.

The school system in India, according to Ramanujam, (1993) is highly competitive, rigid, unimaginative, complex which makes absolutely no allowances for individual variation. The child has to adjust with arbitrarily established criteria of academic competence. His worth is assessed on the basis of his school performance. His acceptance by his parents, his status among his siblings, his relationship with the peer group and finally his self image are determined on the basis of school performance. His individual tastes, his special aptitudes and his freedom of choice has no meaning. Feather, (1975) found that high-school students saw their schools as emphasizing values concerned with achievement, competence, rules of conduct and responsibility. The more the students own value priority differ from those they attribute to their schools, the more dissatisfied they were the aspects of school environment. Sharma, (1972) showed elevations in state anxiety with the approaching examinations. On several occasions demands exceed the person's capacity. This situation may result in stress leading to sense of inadequacy and inferiority. Ramanujam, (1993) in his clinical work found the children of school age as inhibited and diffident. They had distorted perceptions of environment, confusion as regards status at home and very poor self image. They perceived psychological testing as examination and equated whole set-up with school.

A student spends about 25 percent of his time working in educational setting. Stress is conceptualized as an outcome reflecting the lack of congruence between individual needs and goals with the opportunities and constrains afforded by the school setting. A student may experience stress if his or her past classroom setting experience her differs substantially from the current situation. Ahrentzen et.al., (1982) are of the view that need for achievement and the related concept of competition/cooperation, will also interact with environmental characteristics. Students with high achievement motivation and/or competitive drive placed in a classroom setting that emphasize group learning and cooperation would experience stress. The same would apply to students with low achievement needs who are placed in highly competitive classrooms. According to them persons differ in the amount of stimulation desired from the environment. Some people prefer unpredictable life-styles whereas others are attracted to the more routine. They believe that this sensation or arousal seeking tendency will interact with the setting the person is in and that stress will result if there is incongruence. Hyman, Zelikoff and Clarke, (1988) concluded that children may be more at risk than adults in relation to stressors in society over which they have relatively little control.

Another source of stress lie in 'social isolation'. It ranges from 'maternal deprivation' to 'peer group rejection'. The adolescent is assumed to move away from the family to peer-group, in order to borrow strength and identification. Difference between his value systems and those of peers creates a stressful situation inducting fear of peer group rejection.

In adolescence infantile ties are reawakened. While moving more and more to peer group. Adolescent is dependent on family as a stable anchor point for the resolution of many important issues. Cohesive relationship have positive effect on the well being of adolescents. Srivastava and Singh, (1979) highlighted the importance of the parents personality, especially that of mother, in producing psychosomatic stress disorders in children to a very large extent. The role of undesirable parental models, death of parents, or demanding, strict and disciplinarian parents in causing psychosomatic stress disorders has been documented by Chaturvedi, (1983). Coby, Kamp, Paul, Arrihdell and William, (1991) found that depression was associated with less parental affection and more parental control. The study revealed that various types of phobic disorders were related to a parental child rearing style of less affection and more control as compared to healthy control. Burrera & Garrison, (1992) found depression negatively related to family and parental support. It showed that disturbance in important supportive attachment has special significance for the experience of depressive symptoms by adolescents. Luther and Quinlan, (1993) have evidence to show that high self critical depressive tendencies were associated with intrusive mothers and fathers. However, higher self critical tendencies were found among women with neglectful mothers who were low, both in care and over protectiveness.

One of the features of modern Indian society is the rapid breakdown of traditional values and the transitional character of its social, political and economic structure. According to Sinha, (1962) this phenomena of transition has been taken to underline the general incidence of high anxiety which has been observed among the Indian students population. In such a period of rapid change, the problem of identity confusion is intensified by the breakdown of traditional values and traditional roles where the adult support for youths search for identity is lacking and where the guidelines for accepted behaviours get blurred and contradictory. Intensified form of such confusion results in variety of psycho-social disorders. Carstairs and Kapur, (1976) found evidence to show that socia-cultural and economic changes induce stress and mental disorders in rural community. Chatterjee, (1978) has discussed the role of environmental situation like military aggression, economic conditions, industrialization and social change as possible stressors leading to psychosomatic illness.

Moderators of Stress

People differ greatly in their interpretation of stressful situations and in their choice of coping styles. An important question concerns the nature of those variables that may determine which individuals are likely to be most adversely affected by the life change and which are not. Several researchers have pointed to the role of moderator variables. These may be drawn from within the person or from the environment and include at least five categories: health/energy/morale, problem solving skills, utilitarian resources, general and specific beliefs and social network.

Role of Health, Energy and Morale

If a person is weak, frail, sick, tired or depressed his coping effectiveness is reduced and he is more likely to be adversely affected by the stressful events where as healthy and robust person can withstand stressful transactions. The same crisis that healthy person survives may destroy the weak. Several researchers (Hamburg et. al., 1953; Visotsky et. al., 1961; Hamburg & Adams, 1967; Andreason et. al., 1972; Dimsdale, 1974; Bulman and Wortman, 1977) suggested that people with robust health and high morale are capable of managing surprisingly well the severe life crisis.

Role of Problem Solving Skills

These include the ability to search for information to analyses situations for the purpose of identifying the problem, to generate alternative courses of action, to weigh alternatives with respect to desired or anticipated outcomes, and to select and implement an appropriate plan of action (Janis, 1974; Janis and Mann, 1977). These skills may have moderating effect on stress.

Role of Utilitarian Resources

Resources such as money, tools instructional manuals, special training programmes, social agencies etc., greatly increase the coping options available to a person in stressful transactions. These resources significantly help in moderating the effect of stress. Socio-economic status is correlated positively and strongly with nearly all kinds of positive adoptional outcome, including health, morale and social functioning (Syme & Berkman, 1976).

Role of General and Specific Beliefs

Bandura, (1977) has emphasized that the belief in self-efficacy reduces the effect of stress. According to Rotter, (1966) and Lefcourt, (1976) self-efficacy is related conceptually to locus of control variable. It seems sensible to assume that persons who believe that they can master most demands and threats by doing what is needed or by discovering what to do and how to do it are less likely to be threatened or to feel helpless or hopeless in stressful transaction.

Belief systems whether positive or negative, can theoretically vary from the most broad or general, in which virtually every environmental context is a challenge or a threat, to narrower instances in which this or that situation or class of situations in challenging or threatening.

Belief system enable people to create meaning out of like, even out of damaging experiences. According to Naidu, (1983) the profile of high stress tolerators indicate that they generally think positively about themselves and others and believe in existence of God. Pandey, (1990) studied the differential vulnerability of stress. She found that non-attachment helped individuals to maintain positive health status in the face of stressful life events. Sethumadhavan, (1992) found responsible people have less health problems specially the psychological strain.

Role of Social Support

Social networks and support systems have attracted growing interest in stress research, behavioural medicine, and social epidemiology (Antonovsky, 1972); Nuckolls et. al., 1972; Cassel, 1976; Cobb, 1976; Berkman, 1977; Kaplan, Cassel and Gore, 1977;), Social support from significant others is of major importance in coping with important life events and social support can reduce of eliminate the adverse consequences of these events upon health or well being (Cohen & wills, 1985; Coyne & Downey, 1991; Sarason, Sarason & Pierce, 1990). However, findings on the role of support in alleviating stress are sometimes contradictory and difficult to interpret. Mechanic, (1962) and Friedman, et. al., (1963) noted that there are stress situations in which family members exacerbate stress or block coping rather than help. Hiller and Swindle, (1983) suggested that the relationship between support and adjustment to stress may be due to differences in social competence rather than to stress buffering effects of support. According to Andrews et. al., (1978) and LaRocco & Jones, (1978) social support may not be beneficial on all occasions. A lot of social support may sometimes be cognised as intrusions only to exacerbate distress. Tripathi, Caplan and Naidu, (1986) found that parental support in interaction with social support acceptance did not minimize strains which were caused due to poor performance in examination.

Social support can be regarded as an extremely valuable potential source of moderating stress. Pearlin, (1975) suggest that social relations function as real safety valves and vehicles of escape for individuals. However, the most common view according to Thoits, (1986) is that support promotes adjustment to stress by providing assistance with appraisal and coping processes.

Role of Family in Development of Students

The parent-child relationship is unique among human ties. Although it embodies many of the features of any close relationship companionship, affection, interdependence of action sequences, some degree of meshing of goals, and the potential for considerable conflict. Family is an important agency of socialization. It caters the primary needs of protection, food, housing and clothing for the child. They also determine how the young children will spend their time. The parents also act on behalf of the children when they are not yet competent to act for themselves. But it is the parental role as educator and supporting individual that has been the primary focus for the developmental psychologist's interest. Parental behaviour supports children's learning to inhibit behaviour that would be irritating or injurious to others and at the same time fosters the acquisition of the positive behaviour that society demands, including helpfulness and thoughtfulness toward others, self-reliance, acceptance of responsibility, and the acquisition of skills that will support successful adult functioning. Thus parent-child interaction is instrumental in social moral and cognitive development of the child (Maccoby & Martin, 1983).

A variety of parenting dimensions have been identified as described in preceeding paragraphs. However, because of the differing methods theoretical approaches and developmental foci, there has been no general consensus on the most significant axe along which to compare parents. According to Maccoby & Martin, (1983) early studies on techniques of discipline tended to be classified under two major headings, power assertive discipline including physical punishment, yelling, shouting, forceful commands and threat and love oriented discipline including showing disappointment, isolation, withdrawal of love, praise, contingent giving of affection and reasoning.

Analysis of parental variables by Baldwin and his colleagues, (1955) revealed a major warmth/ cold dimension, but two other orthogonal dimensions, democracy/autocracy and emotional involvement/detachment emerged neither of which closely corresponded to the restrictive permissive dimension. Democratic parenting reflected the degree to which the parents merely communicated information regarding the requirements of real world. Democratic parenting include parental efforts to justify their actions or policies. According to Baldwin, (1955) when the parents make himself the source of control upon the child, he is following an authoritarian technique and when he merely communicates to child the rules that exists, he is following a democratic technique.

Parker and colleagues, (Parker, Tupling & Brown, 1979) identified two dimensions caring and empathetic versus rejecting or indifferent and secondly an overprotection dimension that involves encouraging dependency, controlling, intruding and infantilizing.

Following the early factor-analytic studies, the control versus autonomy (or restrictive versus permissive) dimension also began to break down and be redefined. Studies based on children's reports of their parent's child-rearing attitudes and behaviour differentiated two dimensions; psychological autonomy giving versus psychological control arousing guilt or instilling anxiety and firm versus lax control (Burger & Armentrout, 1971; Schacter, 1965).

Baumrind's (1967) conceptualization of parenting employed representing the intersection of two dimensions. Parental demandingness and parental responsiveness. Pulkkinen, (1982) differentiated among parents according to whether they were child centred or parent centred.

Maccoby & Martin, (1983) presented two dimensional classification of parenting. The fourfold picture included, authoritarian-autocratic patterns, indulgent-permissive pattern; authoritative-reciprocal pattern and indifferent uninvolved pattern.

In Authoritarian-autocratic pattern, parent's demands on their children are not balanced by their acceptance of demands from their children. Although it is understood that children have needs that parents are obliged to fulfil, power assertive parents put strict limit to the allowable expression of these needs. Parents attach strong value to the maintenance of their authority and suppress any effort that their children make to challenge it. When children deviate from the parental requirements, fairly severe punishment (often physical) is likely to be employed. The parents classified as authoritarian may very in degree and weighing of its component.

Indulgent-permissive pattern suppose that permissiveness is a relative matter as any parent who is functioning in any degree in the parental role exercises some control over the children.

The Authoritative-reciprocal pattern recognizes the rights of both parents and children. Children are required to be responsive to parental demands and parents reciprocate by accepting their children's reasonable demands and point of view, thus encouraging child's independence and individuality. The Indifferent-uninvolved pattern reveals a relationship by very low parental involvement. Parents will tend to orient their behaviour primarily to the avoidance of inconvenience, parental function may be greatly reduced any only functional relationship survives.

Hoffman, (1980) reviewed the discipline research done mainly in 1950's and 1960's and organised it around three broad types of discipline-power assertion, love withdrawal, and induction.

The power assertive parents manage the child by physical force or control over the child's material resources. Children's compliance to parental commands is based on fear of punishment rather than child's inner resources like guilt, shame, punishment, dependency or respect. Non power assertive parents may use love withdrawal technique to gain control over child's undesirable behaviour. Using love withdrawal technique parents simply give direct but non-physical expression to his anger or disapproval of the child behaviour engaging in some undesirable behaviour. Like power assertion, love withdrawal has highly punitive quality. It is not based on the fear of punishment but it poses ultimate threat of separation or abandonment. Another technique adopted by the parents is 'induction'. Parents promote discipline through reasoning and discussion. They may directly appeal to conformity inducing agents within the child. The effectiveness of induction is based on helping the child to understand the problem involved, to comprehend his own resources and controlling his own behaviour accordingly.

Misra, (1981) studied ten dimensions of parent-child inter-action. These dimensions were control, protectiveness, punishment, conformity, social isolation, reward, deprivation of privileges, nurturance, rejection and permissiveness. These dimensions can influence the development of values and moral judgement among girls. Some of these aspects of home environment may also moderate the effects of stress. Studies in the area of socialization refer psychological theories about how the learning proceeds. Jennigs and Niemi, (1974) mention observational learning, reinforcement and psychoanalytic theory, and cognitive-developmental theory as important frameworks for understanding socialization; Baumrind (1975) adds two other processes that may be important in understandings adolescent identity, namely, reciprocal role assumption and psychological reactance.

The family has been regarded as the prime agent of socialization for preadult and a lot of evidence now exist to show that children will resemble their parents in some of their social and political orientations and behaviours (Acock

& Bengtson, 1976; Bengtson & Star, 1975; Jennigns and Niemi, 1974; Feather, 1975; Feather, 1978; Kandel & Hesser 1972; Thomas 1971; Troll Neugarter & Kraines, 1969)-though there are variations among studies in the degrees of resemblance obtained. Some observers have preferred to focus on discontinuities between parents and their children and to interpret these in terms of intergenerational conflict and rebellion (Feuer, 1969), while others have argued that development of student ideology (Block, 1972; Kraut & Lewis, 1975). In a perceptive review or research on adolescent socialization Campbell, (1969) argued that family structures, endure through the entire period of adolescence—as residential, affectional, and companionship units. The ties between parents and children remain close throughout the adolescent years. The positive orientation toward parents does not diminish, and may indeed increase, during adolescence. The parents and the parent child relationship are both important influences on the adolescence. These influences help in development of values and moral judgement.

Origin of Problem and its Statement

Stress has adverse effects on physical well beings of the individuals. Numerous negative life events are reported before the onset of the diseases like, coronary heart disease (Hinkle, 1974; Bhargava, Sharma and Agrawal, 1982), alcoholism (Rangaswami, 1983); ulcerative colitis (Chakraborty, Shah & Parikh, 1983; Khurana, 1983) breast cancer (Christopher, 1979), Carcinoma in various parts of body (Udupa, 1980), pulmonary tuberculosis (Gupta and Srivastava, 1983) and psychiatric disorders (Saxena, Dubey, Sundaram and Chawala, 1983 Rao and Namalvar, 1976; Chattopadhyay & Dasm 1983).

Stress has been found to produce adverse effects on development of students' personality cognitive abilities, adjustment and achievement. Ansari, Sampurna, Udupa and Agrawal, (1979) showed that patient with stress disorders had a high level of anxiety as well as stronger achievement motives than controls. Chaturvedi found that patient with stress disorders tended to the aloof, pessimistic tenderminded apprehensive and had indisciplined self-concepts. Compas, (1987) reviewed that cross sectional studies have found consistent, although, modest correlation of stressful events with psychological behavioural and somatic problems. Colby, & Golib, (1988) examined depression associated deficit in sensory and short term memory and found, while sensory memory was intact in depressed, short term memory processing was impaired. Singh & Kang, (1977) found individuals under stress lacking in proper social behaviour and adjustment. Feg. (1992) studying life stress and psychological adjustment among American, Asian-American and Asian foreign graduate students found well documented relationship between negative life stress and psychological maladjustment.

At present our society is facing value crisis. Students face several moral and valued dilemmas and they find themselves ill equipped to solve them. This may add to students stress and their inability to cope with stress. It is quite possible that stress might have influenced the development of values and moral judgement among the girls. Social learning theory, psychoanalytic theory and person environment-fit theory clearly point to the effectiveness of parents in influencing the development of moral judgement and values. Studies have shown that home environment can facilitate or inhibit the development of values and moral judgement. Parent-child interactions can moderate the effects of stress on development of values and moral judgement. The present research has been undertaken to find answers to the following questions:

1. Does stress influence values and moral judgement among girls?

2. Is stress related to values and moral judgement?
3. Is home environment related to values and moral judgement?
4. Do girls differing with respect to stimulation in home environment differ in their values and moral judgement.

The problem of the present study may by stated as "Effects of stress and home environment on girl's moral judgement and values."

Objectives of the Study

The main objectives of the present study were:

1. To find out relationship between stress and values.
2. To find out relationship between stress and moral judgement.
3. To find out relationship between home environment and values.
4. To find out relationship between home environment and moral judgement.
5. To find out whether girl's experiencing different levels of stress in their values.
6. To find out whether girls experiencing different levels of stress differ in their moral judgement.
7. To find out whether girls perceiving different levels of stimulations in home environment differ in their values.
8. To find out whether girls perceiving different levels of stimulation in home environment differ in their moral judgement.
9. To study the prominent and other values of stressful students.

Besides the above mentioned main objectives following subsidiary objectives were also achieved:

1. To study the distribution of scores on various values of girls.
2. To study the distribution of scores on ten dimension of home environment as perceived by girls.
3. To study the distribution of scores on overall moral judgement as well as various items of the moral judgement questionnaire.
4. To study the distribution of scores on stress.

Theoretical Background

Moral development is viewed as one aspect of socialization, with socialization meaning the process by which children learn to conform to the expectations of the culture in which they grow up. In the case of moral values, children not only learn to conform, they also internalize these standards and thereby accept the standard as correct and as representing their own personal values.

The Cognitive Developmental Theorists

Piaget and Kohlberg claimed that internalization occurs in a series of fixed, qualitatively distinct stages whose end product, which is achieved if at all in adolescence, is a universal sense of justice or concern for reciprocity among individuals. Each stage is viewed as a homogeneous type of moral questioning and evaluate issues. Moral reasoning strategy or conceptual framework designed to answer moral reasoning within a stage is thus consistent across different moral problems and situations. Each stage builds upon, reorganizes, and encompasses the preceding one and is, therefore, more comprehensive, providing new perspectives and criteria for making moral evaluations. The content of moral values is postulated as not playing an important role in defining a stage.

Cognitive developmental theorist claims that all persons, regardless of social or cultural background pass through the stages of moral development. Movement from one stage to the next results from a restructuring of the preceding stage. Thus an emerging stage develops out of its predecessor, a synthesis of the old and new. Each individual works out its own synthesis rather than adopting readymade one provided by the culture. The individual should pass through all preceding stages before he can move to next one. Although the particular age at which the stage appears is influenced by environment and level of cognitive development, either of which can advance or retard—and in the extreme even preclude—the appearance of a stage, the stages will appear in the same order for all individuals, all cultures.

The essence of morality according to Piaget, (1932) includes both the individual's respect for the rules of social and his sense of justice, that is concern for reciprocity and equality among individuals. Piaget's theory is based on the developmental shift of these two aspects of morality—from respect and submission to authority, to self-government and control.

Piaget's two stages were derived from the attitudes expressed by children towards the origin, legitimacy and the alterability of rules in the game of marbles as well as the response to the stories, where children have to judge the act of others.

Pigets first stage is stage is referred as moral realism, morality of constraints or heteronomous morality. In this stage, children view rules as sacred and unalterable. They tend to view behaviours as absolutely right or wrong and think that everyone views them in the same way. They believe that acts should be judged on the basis of the magnitude of its consequences rather than by intention behind these acts.

Belief in immanent justice seem to be another characteristic of this stage. He believes that violation of social norm will be followed by physical accident or misfortunes willed by God or any inanimate object.

Piagets' second stage of moral development, is the stage of autonomous morality, the morality of cooperation or reciprocity. This stage is generally attained at late childhood or at early adolescence. They realize that the society in which they live is based on co-operation, mutual respect and equality. Social values and norms are not absolute. They can be modified in response to human needs. The child at this stage gives up moral absolutism and recognizes possible diversity in views of right and wrong. While judging on action as right or wrong, the stress is laid on intentions as well as on consequences. They feel that punishment should be reciprocally related to the misdeed through restitution or direct retaliation by the victim rather than be painful, arbitrary or administered by authority. While the heteronomous child defines duty and obligation largely in terms of obedience to authority, the autonomous child defines it more in terms of conforming to peer expectations, considering their own welfare, expressing gratitude for the past favour and affections and above all, putting oneself in the place of others.

Piaget claims that both maturation and environmental influence play a role in the transition from one stage to another. Moral growth requires that the child gives up egocentricism and realism and develop a concept of self as distinct from others who have their own independent perspectives about events. This shift occurs in interaction with peers beginning in childhood and extending into adolescence.

While stressing the overriding importance of peer interaction, Piaget also made clear that the parent's child-rearing practices might also play a significant role in moral development. Parent's according to Piaget, generally tend to be authoritarian in their practice and as a result help consolidate the child's natural tendency towards heteronomy. On the other hand, if they provide an environment of mutual help and understanding for the child, in which he can reciprocate with them, this would increase the likelihood of moral autonomy taking root. Parent can contribute to the young child's movement towards autonomy by burdening him with fewer demands and anticipating and creating conditions that prevent misdeeds and thus minimize the child's punishment experience. It seems clear, if parents and other authorities could overcome their natural tendencies to relate heteronomously to child and if the interaction between them is mutual and reciprocal, this will foster rather than hinder their moral growth.

Kohlberg's stage schema and research it stimulated, has more direct relevance to adolescent moral thought. In developing his stages Kohlberg attempted to retain best of Piaget's analysis and to fit it into more refined comprehensive and logically constructive framework. In Kohlberg's system, growing up in moral judgement consists of advancing through three levels of development, from a premoral or reconventional level to one that involves conforming to society's conventions and finally to a top level that transcends convention and is based on personal self-accepted moral principles. This top level is sometimes called post conventional or autonomous. Each level contains two stages.

The first major process of moral development is premoral level were the control of conduct is external. This level is divided into two stages. The first stage is called obedience and punishment orientation while the second is naive hedonistic and instrumental orientation. At initial stage children obey rules to avoid punishment. The actor is judged wrong if it is punished. To them, right means obeying those in authority. There is only objective responsibility present alongwith egocentrism that gives difference to superior power or prestige dominated by a trouble avoiding perspective. At the second stage, child looks upon right action as instrumentally satisfying his self needs and only occasionally those of others. Values are relative to each actors needs and perspective. He manifests an unsophisticated egalitarianism and orientation to exchange and reciprocity. Emphasis is on conventional role conformity due to social reward. Preconventional children, according to Kohlberg, (1981, 84) have instrumentalistic or authority oriented understanding of morality.

The conventional level of morality is usually dominant in later childhood. It is defined as maintaining the social order and conforming to the expectations of others. Control of conduct is external in the sense that the standard conformed to, are the rules and expectations held by significant others by virtue of personal attachment or delegated authority. However, the motivation is largely internal. The child takes the role of significant others and respects their judgement. Thus the personal reactions of authority serve as cues to rightness or wrongness of an act, hence to the moral virtue of the actor.

This level is again subdivided into two stages. Stage three manifests itself by seeking approval through pleasing and assisting others. Kohlberg, therefore, calls it the Good-Boy, Nice-Girl orientation stage. Generally the child conforms mainly to avoid disapproval and dislike by others and tries to please and help others. In judging others, intentions are considered.

Kohlberg terms his stage four as authority and social order maintaining orientation. Person does one's duty, shows respect for authority and maintains social order for its own sake. He believes that virtue must be rewarded.

The third level morality of self-accepted moral principal, characterizes adolescence, though many people never attain it. Morality is defined in terms of conforming to shared or sharable standards, rights or duties. Person acknowledge, the possibility of conflict between two socially accepted standards and tries to reach at rational decision between them. Control of conduct is internal. The standard conformed to have internal source and the decision to act is based on an inner process of thought and judgement concerning right and wrong. This level is divided into two stages.

Contractual and legalistic orientations is Kohlberg's fifth stage of moral growth and development. The stage is based upon the recognition and acceptance of democratize laws with the recognition of arbitrary starting point of agreement being important to person. Law is generally the ultimate criterion of the right. Whenever, there is a conflict between the individual and law or contract, though there may be sympathy for the former. The latter prevails because of its greater functional rationality for society.

The last stage of moral development is the conscience or principle orientation. In stage six morality is based upon individual principles relative to broadly general and logically ethical principles of justice, reciprocity, equality and human dignity. The orientation is not only to actually ordained social rules but also to the principles of choice as they involve appeal to logical consistency, reasoning and universality. The individuals orientation is to the conscience as a directing agent of the person, and to mutual respect and trust. Conduct is controlled by internalized ideals that exerts pressure towards action which seem right, regardless of reaction of others. If the individual acts otherwise self-condemnation or guilt results. Though, aware of the importance of law and contract moral conflict is generally resolved in terms of broader moral principles.

Kohlberg claims that the developmental stages, he has identified are universal, integrated and invariant. According to him, the development of moral reasoning would follow the same invariant sequence in all cultures and lead towards the same ultimate level of development, representing, universal ethical principles. However, the rate of development and highest stage reached can show systematic differences. Kohlberg data, (1958) suggest that most of the people do not go beyond stage 3 and 4.

The moral stages, according to Kohlberg, also reflect a sequence of successive changes in role taking ability. The ability to take another person's perspective is seen as having special significance in transition from premoral to conventional morality (from stage 2 to 3). Role taking experiences provide the individual with different perspective and thus instigate cognitive conflict. The resolution is sought through modification of existing moral structure. Thus, he views movement from one moral stage to next as largely a natural outgrowth of cognitive development whereas the environment provides the raw materials upon which cognitive processes operate.

According to Kohlberg, participation in all groups—whether with peers or authority figures—provides the individual with direct experience in taking alternative roles.

This provides first-hand, knowledge about working of sociomoral world. Kohlberg views some forms of social participation especially stimulating to moral development because they provide many stage-appropriate opportunities for role taking and gaining understanding of the social order. Other forms, which lack these opportunities or which arouse inhibiting anxieties, will retard progress through the moral stages and perhaps even fix the individual permanently at an early stage. However, greater role adaptation according to Kohlberg is promoted by families that encourage sharing in decision, awarded responsibility to the child, pointed out consequences of action to others, communicated within the family group and exhibited emotional warmth.

Psychoanalytic Theory

Psychoanalytic account of conscience development, worked, out primarily for males, claims that young child is subjected to many frustration due to parents intervention and other physical factors. Due to these frustration, the child develops hostility towards parents, specially against father. Anxiety over anticipated punishment, especially withdrawal of love and abandonment by parents, the child repress both hostility and erotic impulse towards mother. To gain mastery over the anxieties and repression and seek affections from the parents children adopt rules and prohibitions emanating from parents. Whenever they violate these prohibitions, guilt occurs. In order to avoid guilt experience, children try to act always in accordance with incorporated parental prohibitions. They control their impulse to act on the contrary by creating defence mechanism. By about five to six year, these basic process of conscience formation are complete. These process are solified during childhood.

During adolescence, hormonal changes at puberty and associated drives and emotional state disrupts the impulse control achieved during latency periods. Solnits, (1972) suggests that in adolescence the infantile ties to the parents are reawakened. The hold of childhood superego is weakend. This creates a vacuum. The individual.is compelled either to find new mature grounds for moral stances or erect defenses to ward of uncontrollable impulse and keep earlier control system intact.

Thus psychoanalytic theory focusses on moral motivation rather than moral thought. It lays stress on anxiety and repression. Psychoanalytic theory puts great stress on the importance of parents. Stressing the motivational rather than cognitive aspect of morality, it has provided the main theoretical inspiration and overall direction for most research on the role of parental practices in shaping and determining moral character.

Social Learning Theory

In social learning theory a child's, conscience on moral values are not inborn. The infant arrives in the world amoral. Then by the same modelling and conditioning principles that produce all of her other beliefs, child gradually acquires values and capacity for self-control and self-direction. In other words, her character is learned, not inherited.

Investigations cited by Bandura, (1962, 65 and 68) support his contention that the development of self-control or conscience is heavily influenced by the models children observe and by patterns of direct reinforcement that they encounter, such as disciplinary measures used by parents and teachers. The degree to which the child resists the temptation has been most readily affected in experimental situation by how immediately the model in the situation is rewarded or punished. The characteristics of the model also influence how likely it is that the child will adopt the modelled self-control or lack of it, with the greatest influence exerted by model who are capable, successful and prestigious.

Bandura and MacDonald, (1963) argue against generality of moral development noting the marked inconsistency and specificity of moral behaviour. He suggested that modelling of socializing agent is sufficient to explain moral development and judgement. Consistency in moral development is observed in children only when parental model exhibit consistency in moral conduct across a variety of situations.

Hoffman's Model of Morality

Another theoretical approach focusses on the role of empathy and its developmental transformations in moral development. Empathy is defined as a vicarious emotional response to another person's feeling or situation. It provides motivational base for moral action.

Hoffman claimed that a neural basis for empathy exists and that it may have always been part of man's biological makeup. Hoffman, (1976, 1978) proposed a theoretical model for the ontogenetic development of empathy, its transformations, and its implications for moral development. According to him empathy has three components: an affect arousal component, a cognitive component and a motivational component. The conception of empathy based morality stresses importance of the integration of young adolescent's capacity for empathic arousal, with their newly emerging cognitive awareness of other's as well as themselves as individual. The perceived contrast between other's well being and one's own is seen as producing a potential force towards moral action.

Expectancy Value Theory

Feather, (1962) argued for an interactionist approach to the analysis of behaviour, for an approach that is neither situation specific or person specific but that attempts to account for a person's behaviour in terms both the particular situation to which he is exposed and the relatively stable personality characteristics that he brings with him to the situation. This approach is called expectancy-value theory, (Feather, 1959).

Feather has differed from Rokeach, for he has been more concerned with investigating values and value systems within a general theoretical framework that emphasizes a person's adaptation to the various environments to which he may be exposed and his attempts to resolve discrepancies between his own personal characteristics and commensurate environmental characteristics perceived to be present in the immediate situation. It was assumed that persons tend to seek environments that best fit their own personal characteristics and that they are more likely to feel happy and satisfied with such environments than would be the case if there was a significant degree of mismatch.

Theory of Cognitive and Behavioural Change

Person's values provide him with a comprehensive set of standards to guide actions, justification, judgements, and comparison of self and other and to serve need for adjustment, ego defence, and self actualization. All these diverse functions converge into a single overriding, master function namely to help maintain and enhance one's total conception of oneself. Self conceptions include all one's cognition, conscious and unconscious, about one's physical image; intellectual and moral abilities and weaknesses; socio-economic position in society; national regional ethnic, racial and religious identity; the sexual, generational, occupational, marital, and parental roles that one plays in society; and how well or poorly one plays such roles. This conception of the self is not necessarily a positive one. Every person attempts at the very least to maintain and, in so far as, possible to enhance whatever self conception he has managed to develop as a result of socialization.

According to Rokeach, (1973) since the total belief system is a functionally interconnected system, a change in any part of it should affect other parts and should moreover affect behaviour. The more central part affected by an induced change, the more enduring and far reaching should be its effect, not only on other parts of cognitive system but also on behaviour. Thus, an induced change in self-conceptions which is claimed to take place as a result of various experiences (such as therapy, ineligious conversion, hypnosis, psychesurgical thought control, and brain washing) should lead to changes in terminal and instrumental value, in functionally related attitudes, and in behaviour. An induced change in a particular terminal value should lead to a systematic changes in other terminal values in the hierarchy, functionally related instrumental values, functionally related attitudes, and behaviour and should ultimately affect self-conceptions as well.

According to Rokeach, (1973) this theory of cognitive and behavioural change suggests that under certain conditions values may be easier to change than attitudes. If a person's values are in fact standards employed to maintain and enhance self-conceptions, then a contradiction between values and self-conceptions can be most effortlessly resolved by changing the less central values. A value that contradicts self-conceptions is more likely to undergo change than an attitude that is discrepant with persuasive communications or behaviour. According to Rokeach, (1973) a value should undergo enduring change if maintenance or enhancement of self-conception is at stake, and its having undergone change should lead to systematic changes in other related organizations within the belief system and should then culminate in behavioural change. This theory suggest that any change in self conception leads to change in values. Changes in self-concept may cause stress.

The feeling of dissatisfaction can arise over issues concerning morality and competence (Bramel, 1968), and more or less human strivings for goodness and greatness (Rokeach, 1964). The more the discrepancy between self-conception and performance, the more it will be experienced as a state of dissatisfaction. A person who experiences such states as anxiety, internal conflict, dissatisfaction, self-alienation, alienation from society, or confusion over self-identity may be suffering from some affective state of self-dissatisfaction. According to Rokeach, (1973) the person in such a state, will be motivated to remove the source of the self-dissatisfaction by modifying one or more of the components of his belief system so that all the components are more compatible with self-conceptions.

Hypothesis

Following hypotheses were tested in order to achieve various objectives of the study:

1. Stress[1] is negatively related to values[2].
2. Stress is negatively related to moral judgement[3].
3. Protectiveness, conformity, reward, nurturance and permissiveness are positively related to values.

4. Control, punishment, social isolation, deprivation of privileges and rejection are negatively related to values.
5. Protectiveness conformity, reward, nurturance, and permissiveness are positively related to moral judgement.
6. Control, punishment, social isolation, deprivation of privileges and rejection are negatively related to moral judgement.
7. Girls experiencing different levels of stress do not differ in their values.
8. Girls experiencing different levels of stress do not differ in their moral judgement.
9. Girls perceiving different levels of stimulation[4] in home environment do not differ in their values.
10. Girls perceiving different levels of stimulation in home environment do not differ in their moral judgement.

Definition of Terms

VALUES

Value appears as a basic concept in theories that have emerged from sociology, political science, education, social psychology and anthropology. It also have secure place in historical analysis, philosophy and religion. The study of societal values has a long history in sociology and anthropology (Kluckhohn & Strodtbeck 1961) and the study of individual values has similarly long history in psychology (Allport, Vernon & Lindzey 1960). The cross cultural study of both societal and individual values, however, is relatively recent (Feather, 1975; Hofstede, 1980; Zavalloni, 1980).

In both disciplines values are inferred constructs (held collectively by societies and individually by persons). Kluckhohn, (1951) defined the term values as conception held by an individual, or collectively by members of a group of that which is desirable and which influences the selection of both means and ends of action from among available alternatives. This complete but rather complex definition has been simplified by Hofstede, (1980). According to him values refer to "a broad tendency to prefer certain states of affairs over others". Values are usually considered to be more general in character than attitudes, but less general than ideologies.

The value of a societal system, according to Parson, (1968) are, the conceptions of the desirable type of society held by the members of the society of reference and applied to the particular society of which they are members. The same applies to other types of social systems. A value pattern then defines a direction of choice, and consequent commitment to action.

According to Williams, (1979) a value system is an organized set of preferential standard, that are used in making selections of objects and actions, resolving conflicts, invoking social sanctions, and coping with needs or claims for social and psychological defenses of choices made or proposed. Values are components in the guidance of anticipatory and goal-directed behaviour; but they are also backward looking in their frequent service to justify or explain past conduct.

Perhaps the best known and most widely used approach to studying values in psychology is that of Rokeach. Rokeach, (1973) defined values as belief. He classified value into prescriptive or proscriptive beliefs rather than as descriptive or evaluative beliefs. Prescriptive or proscriptive beliefs are those wherein some means or end of action is judged to be desirable or undesirable. In this he agrees with Williams, (1968) who argues that more important usage of the term for the purposes of analyses in social science is likely to be one in which values are defined as criteria or standards held by people that affect the evaluative acts in which they are involved. For Rokeach, values are very general, transcendental relatively enduring beliefs wherein some means or end of the action is judged to be personally or socially desirable in relation to opposite or converse. For example, a person might believe that equality is preferred to inequality or that it is preferable to behave honestly rather than dishonestly.

Further, Rokeach classified that the beliefs defining values may refer either to modes of conduct or to end-states of existence, to means or to ends. The values referring to mode of conduct are called instrumental value. They are further subdivided into two kinds, one having moral focus and other concerning competence. Moral values and competive values may conflict. Thus a person may experience conflict between being honest and being polite, or being ambitious and being helpful or so on. Terminal values refer to end-state of existence, which include such concepts like equality, freedom, world of peace, inner harmony. Rokeach suggests that there are two kinds of terminal values, those having a personal focus such as salvation and inner harmony and those having a social focus such, as world of peace true friendship among people.

Rokeach assumes that the number of values relating to goal or "end-state of existence" (the terminal values) is likely to be very small. He identified 18 terminal values namely: A comfortable life, an exciting life, a sense of accomplishment, a world at peace, a world of beauty, equality family security, freedom, happiness, inner harmony, mature love, national security, pleasure, salvation, self-respect, social recognition, true friendship and wisdom.

The number relating means or "modes of conduct" (the instrumental values) is likely to be rather larger, but still much less than many thousands of specific beliefs or attitudes that a person has at any one time. Rokeach, identified 18 instrumental values namely: Ambitions, broadminded, capable, cheerful, clean, courageous, forgiving, helpful, honest, imaginative, independent, intellectual, logical, loving, obedient, polite, responsible and self-controlled. Both terminal and instrumental values occupy central positions in the total system of a person's beliefs and attitudes and changes in them are likely to have widespread effects throughout the system and on behaviour.

Feather, (1975) conceived value and value system in terms of a general theory of abstract structures. Abstract structures are residues or summaries of past experience and they are formed as a person copes with the influx of information from both social and physical environments. A value may be seen as a particular kind of abstract structure that involves a general concept-like behaving responsibly (a mode of conduct) or freedom (an end-state of existence). This concept has a structural properties and involves a network of association which may take different forms for different peoples.

A value system may be conceptualized as a more complex type of abstract structure, one in which various general concept that have affective and normative significance are ordered along a continuum of importance.

For the purpose of this study values refer to enduring prescriptive or proscriptive beliefs that relate to specific mode of behaviour or end-states of existence preferred to an opposite mode of behaviour or end-states of existence. Rokeach, (1973) has also defined values in similar way.

Stress

The world around us is changing so rapidly that sometimes it seems difficult to keep peace with changes and adjust according to changing situations. There are numerous moments in life where we find ourselves unable to take any decision. It becomes difficult to acquire a balanced and satisfactory equilibrium of mind leading to state of "stress".

The term stress has evolved over the past several decades, to encompass a large variety of phenomena and is used in a number of different ways. Even in scientific literature, stress is used in three distinct ways. It is first used to refer to an event or to any environmental stimulus that causes a person to feel tense or aroused. In this sense, stress is something external to the person. Second, it is used to refer a subjective response to what is going on. In this sense stress is the internal mental state of tension or arousal. It is the interpretative, emotive, defensive and coping process occurring inside the person. Such processes may promote positive growth or produce mental strain. In its third stage, stress is, as the physical reaction to the body to demand or damaging intrusions. Demand promotes a natural arousal of body to a higher level of activity, which can be positive and health promoting. Selye, (1936) viewed it analogous to the immune system's response to an invading germ and defined it as the reaction of the organism to some sort of outside threat. According to him any external event or any internal drive which threatens to upset the organismic equilibrium is stress. The organism is reactive and little cognition is involved in the model. Later on, Selye, (1956) attempted a broader concept of stress, with his description of General Adoption Syndrome, with the stages of alarm, resistance and exhaustion, but at heart it remained a reactive model emphasizing throughout that stress consists of nonspecific consequences of any stressor. Research done with this conceptualization was the sort that followed the medical tradition of animal models, using physical and physiological stressors and measuring physiological and endoctrinological changes as indications of stress.

In contradiction, a second tradition of stress research can be considered to be transactional. Stress is defined as the outcome of interaction between the organism and environment. The general approaches taken by Lazarus, (1966) and Leventhal, (1970) are examples of this type of work. In the transactional model an event in the environment is considered to be a stressor only if the organism's appraisals of it, and of its own resources, suggest that it is threatening or disturbing. Research done in this tradition tend to be human oriented and uses psychological measures, both for how the subject evaluates the stress and in terms of subjects reaction to it.

The stress can be defined rationally by reference to both the person and the environment (Coyne & Lazarus, 1980; Holroyd & Lazarus, 1982; Lazarus & Lavnier, 1978). According to this view stress is said to occur in face of "demands that tax or exceed the resources of the system" or, to put it in a slightly different way, demands to which there are no available or automatic adoptive responses, Which is in contrast to definition of stress phrased either solely in terms of occurrence of events consensually regarded us stressful (Holmes & Masuda, 1974) or solely in terms of responses that are sometimes consequences of stress, such as physiological mobilization (Selye, 1976), cognitive disruption (Horowitz, 1976) or behaviour disorganization.

Stress requires a judgement that environmental and/ or internal demands tax or exceed the individual's resources for managing them. Cox & Mackay, (1981) defined stress as involving for stages: Demand, reception, response and perceived consequences. Cox then added fifth process, feedback, which can occur at any stage.

Following Cox and Mackay, (1981), Chalmers, (1981) noted that "the experience of stress is balance or imbalance resulting from the interaction of the four components: Internal needs and values, external environmental demands and constraints, personal resources or capabilities and external environmental supplies and supports.

For the purpose of this study, stress has been defined as a perceptual phenomenon arising from a comparison between the demands on the person and his ability to cope.

Cox, (1978) also defined stress in the same way. Thus stress occurs when there are demands on the person which tax or exceed his/her adjustive resources. This draws support from the views of Lazarus and his associates.

Home Environment

For the purpose of present study, home-environment has been considered to be a measure of "the quality and quantity of social, emotional, and cognitive support that has been available to the child within the home since early childhood." This definition is quite similar to definition of 'Home stimulation' by Caldwell et.al., (1975). Index to this environment is to be provided by subjects composite scores on ten dimensions of home environment which measure home environment characteristic in terms of parental child rearing behaviour. The operational definition of these characteristics are as follows:

1. **Control:** It indicates the "autocratic atmosphere in which many restrictions are imposed on children by the parents in order to discipline them.
2. **Protectiveness:** It implies "prevention of independent behaviour and prolongation of infantile care."
3. **Punishment:** It includes physical as well as affective punishment to avoid the occurrence of undesirable behaviour.
4. **Conformity:** It indicates parent's directions, commands or orders with which child is expected to comply by action. It refers to "demands to work according to parents' desire and expectations."
5. **Social Isolation:** It indicates use to isolation from beloved parents family members for negative sanctions.
6. **Reward:** It includes material as well as symbolic rewards to strengthen or increase the probability of desired behaviour.

7. **Deprivation of Privilege:** It implies controlling children's behaviour by depriving them of their rights to seek love, respect and childcare from parents.

8. **Nurturance:** It indicates "existence of excessive unconditional physical and emotional attachment of parents with the child, parents have keen interest in and love for the child.

9. **Rejection:** It implies "conditional love recognizing that the child has no rights as a person, no rights to express his feelings, no rights to uniqueness, and no right to become autonomous individual."

10. **Permissiveness:** It includes, "provisions of opportunities to child to express his views freely and act according to his desire with no interference from parents.

REFERENCES

1. Refers to overall stress, and stress in the areas of home, school, society and individual.
2. Refers to 40 values namely: A comfortable life, an exciting life, a sense of accomplishment, a world of peace, a world of beauty, equality, family security, freedom, happiness, innerharmony, mature love, national security, pleasure, salvation, self-respect, social recognition, true friendship, wisdom, equality, power, social justice, ambitious, broadminded, capable, cheerful, clean, courageous, forgiving, helpful, honesty, imagination, independent, intellectual, logical, loving, obedient, polite, responsible, self-control and self-determination.
3. Refers to overall moral judgement, moral judgement exhibited with respect to twelve items of Moral Judgement Questionnaire.
4. Refers to each dimension of home environment namely: control, protectiveness, punishment, conformity, social isolation, reward, deprivation of privileges, nurturance, rejection and permissiveness.

2

Review of Related Researches

It is necessary that a researcher must take advantage of the knowledge that has accumulated through rational-logical analysis and empirical enquiry. The past is to be discussed to view a problem in a proper perspective so that a researcher may streamline his efforts to solve the problem. Keeping in view the objectives of the present research, numerous relevant studies pertaining to moral judgement, home environment and values have been surveyed. The present chapter deals with those studies that are related to the problem of this study. The studies have been organized in four clusters.

1. Studies related to instrumental and terminal values;
2. Studies on moral judgement in relation to home environment;
3. Studies on values in relation to home environment;
4. Studies on moral judgement in relation to stress.

Studies Related to Instrumental and Terminal Values

Feather, (1970) conducted study to find out whether student's educational choice is related to his value concept. Sample consisted of 463 first year university students.

Kruskal-Wallis one-way analysis of variance was used for analysis. Results showed that students in sciences ranked being ambitious, responsible, and self-controlled as more important in their priorities. Students in humanities ranked a world of beauty and being imaginative and intellectual as more important in their priorities. These differences suggest that students enrolling in science courses were more interested in materialistic values, in competence and achievement and in controlling impulses, than were in students enrolling in the humanities. The later were relatively more concerned with aesthetic values and with values involving imagination and the world of ideas. Social science students tended to be intermediate. In regard to general sex difference, males assigned more importance to pleasure, wisdom and being imaginative and logical and less importance to a world of peace, family security and being honest than did females.

Feather, (1972) conducted value fit-adjustment study on 15-17 year old secondary school students of 19 schools in Adelaide. Tools used were Rokeach Value Survey, and modified version of Cornell Job Description Index (J.D.I) to measure students satisfaction with aspects of the school situation. There was indeed a tendency for satisfaction scores and happiness rating to be positively related to the degree of similarity between a students own values and those he attributed to the school. Nearly all the correlations were positive and many of them were statistically significant. He concluded, that, although the evidence supported the hypothesis of positive relationship between the value match and school adjustment, the correlations were quite low.

Rokeach, (1973) compared United States of America, Canada, Australia and Israel college men. Results showed that American college men care relatively more for a comfortable life, social recognition, and being ambitious and care less for being helpful than do Canadian, Australian and Israeli college men. They generally place a higher value on being ambitious than on being capable. Israelies place highest importance to a world at peace, and national security. They placed generally lower value on freedom and being independent and higher value on being helpful, clean, polite, obedient, and self-controlled. Christian values salvation and forgiving were placed at the bottom. The value that most notably distinguishes Australians from Americans. Canadians and Israelies is true friendship. Australians ranked equality, sense of accomplishment, wisdom, being broadminded and cheerful as higher. They rank family security, happiness and intellectual lower than do the other three groups. Canadian students generally place a lower value on a sense of accomplishment and wisdom, and on being ambitious and capable. Canadian college men also seem to care less than the other three groups about being self-controlled, polite, and obedient. Instead, they rank relatively higher aesthetic values and values that emphasize love, peace of mind, personal happiness, honesty and independence.

Beech and Schoeppe, (1974) obtained information from pupils in New York City Public schools about their value systems using Rokeach's Value Survey Children from grades 5, 7, 9, and 11 were tested (Corresponding to ages 11, 13, 15, and 17 year's respectively). Half of the respondents came from the middle-class and half from lower-class schools. Boys and girls were represented in approximately equal numbers for each grade and the results were presented separately for each sex. As far as the girls were concerned, the result showed that certain values were regularly ranked high or low in importance across all grades. Thus a world at peace and freedom were consistently among the first four terminal values and salvation was consistently ranked lowest in importance on the average. Among the instrumental values, being honest and loving consistently ranked very high in relative importance at all age levels, while being imaginative and logical were consistently ranked very low. The following values increased in relative importance for the girls from fifth grade: a sense of accomplishment, equality, inner harmony, self-respect, social recognition, wisdom, being ambitious, being broadminded, being independent, being logical, and being responsible. The following values decreased in relative importance: a comfortable life, an exciting life, a world of beauty, family security, pleasure, salvation, true friendship, being cheerful, being helpful, being honest, being obedient, and being polite.

Feather & Collins, (1974) conducted study of values with reference to students differing in educational choice. Ss were studying at the Mitchell CAE in Bathurst, New South Wales in three main programmes, namely, business administration, teacher education, and general studies. Rokeach Value Survey was used. Results showed that students in business administration ranked a comfortable life, social recognition and being ambitious as much more important than did those in other two programmes. Teacher education and general studies students assigned more importance to a world at peace, mature, true friendship and being honest and loving than did students in business administration. These effects occurred irrespective of whether the respondents were male or female. As regard to sex difference; males in general tended to rank a comfortable life, pleasure and being imaginative as relatively more important than did females; females ranked inner harmony, self-respect, wisdom and being forgiving and loving as relatively more important than did males.

Feather, (1974) Studied the values of students in co-educational and single sex state high schools. The results of the analysis showed that there was no significant differences between the co-educational and single-sex schools in the relative importance assigned to particular terminal values by either boys or girls for either self or school rankings. Both, boys and girls from single sex school ranked being clean as higher in relative importance than did the students from co-educational schools. This was true for both self and school rankings. Girls in the single-sex schools saw their school as placing more emphasis on being helpful and polite than did girls in co-educational schools. They also saw their schools as assigning less importance to being intellectual and logical. The main effects of the sex composition of a school (co-ed versus single-sex) emerged from the analysis, were found only in regard to instrumental values and then, with the exception of being clean, only for the girls and only for the perceived school values.

Feather and Rudzites, (1974) compared value systems of second generation immigrant Latvians born in Australia with Australian children having Australian parents, using Rokeach Value Survey. Sample included both girls and boys with mean age for Latvian group 15.22 years and for Australian 15.69 years. The Latvian group consisted of attenders and non-attenders. Result showed that the respondents were similar on the own average value systems, irrespective of whether respondents were Latvians or Australians and this similarity was more pronounced for terminal than for the set of instrumental values. Among the terminal values, respondents from all three groups ranked a world at peace, freedom, happiness, and true friendship as among the most important values and national security, pleasure and salvation as among their least important values. Among the instrumental values, respondents from all the three groups ranked being honest broadminded, responsible, and loving as among their most important values and being imaginative and obedient as among least important. Comparison for the perceived value and the actual value showed discrepancy. Latvians assigned greater importance to the following values for their Australian peers than the Australians did themselves in their own ranking a comfortable life, an exciting life, pleasure, and being imaginative and lower importance to family security, inner harmony, salvation, wisdom, and being forgiving. The Australian respondents assigned greater importance to the following values for New Australian peers than both groups of Latvians did themselves in their own rankings, social recognition and being courageous and lower importance to exciting life and wisdom.

Feather and Hutton, (1974) applied the Rokeach Value Survey (R.V.S) to compare Australian and Paupa students in New Guinea. Paupa students belong to number of different educational institutions of Paupa New Guinea. The average age of respondents in these institutions ranged from 17.79 to 20.69 years. There were four times as many males as females in the sample. The sample consisted of 1116 students. The Australian sample consisted of 1408 students belonging to secondary schools, 404 students of Flenders University and 506 from Mitchell CAE. Results of the study indicated that among terminal values Paupa New Guinea students gave much higher priorities to a world at peace, equality, national security, salvation, social recognition and comfortable life than did the Australian students, and they assigned much less importance to happiness, inner harmony, self-respect, a sense of accomplishment, mature love, and a world of beauty than did the Australians. Among the instrumental values, the Paupa New Guinea students assigned higher importance to being helpful, obedient, and polite, and much lower importance to being loving, self-controlled, broad-minded, independent and logical than did the Australians.

Feather, (1975) conducted two extensive surveys in 1972 and other in 1973, both involving Rokeach Value Survey. In each survey parents were tested alongwith children who were 14 years old or more. The mean age for parents was 40's. The mean age for children was around 18 years. The result showed that there was value congruence as well as value discrepancy when the average value system of parents were compared with those of their children. The similarity coefficients based on the aggregate data were all positive, but they vary in size. Daughter were more similar to their parents than the sons were, although the resemblance were moderated by socio-economic status. Both Parents and children rank values, such as a world at peace, happiness, wisdom, honest and responsible high in importance and values, such as pleasure, social recognition, salvation, obedient and imaginative, low in importance. The children assigned relatively more importance than their parents to such values as excitement and pleasure, equality and freedom, a world of beauty, close companionship with others, and a broadminded and imaginative stance towards the world.

The purpose of the study by Dwivedi. (1980) was to find out if there is any difference between value preference of students belonging to high and how socio-economic status, using Rokeach value Survey and SES index developed by R.P Verma and P.C. Saxena. It was found that in terminal values a comfortable life, an exciting life, a world of peace, freedom, pleasure and social recognition were ranked higher by students from low socio-economic status whereas the happiness, mature love, self-respect and wisdom were ranked higher by the students of high economic status. In instrumental values ambition, cheerfulness, cleanliness, courage, intelligence were ranked higher by the students of low SES whereas in helpfulness, affection, responsibility and self-control the students of high SES were higher.

Rokeach, (1973) studied values as social indicator of the quality of life in America. He studied 18 terminal and 18 instrumental values by sex, income, education, race, age and religion. He concluded that some values were uniformly considered to be the most and least important by Americans of both sexes. At the top of terminal hierarchy for both sexes were, a world at peace, family security and freedom and at the bottom was, an exiting life, and then pleasure, social recognition, and a world of beauty. At the top of instrumental value hierarchy for both sexes were honest, ambitious and responsible and at the bottom were imaginative, obedient, intellectual and logical. Concerning sex differences, 12 out of 18 terminal values and 8 out of 18 instrumental values discriminate significantly between American men and women. The largest terminal value differences, was found for a comfortable life, which men rank fourth on the average (composite rank order) and which women rank thirteenth, the largest instrumental value difference was found for imaginative. Men also place a significantly higher value than did women on an exciting life, a sense of accomplishment, freedom, pleasure, social-recognition, capable, ambitious, imaginative and logical. Women value significantly more than did men, a world at peace, happiness, inner harmony, salvation, self-respect, wisdom, cheerful, clean, forgiving and loving. Considering the income differences 9 to 18 terminal and 11 of the 18 instrumental values showed significant differences associated with being poor or rich. The instrumental value clean best distinguished the poor from rich. The next value was a comfortable life, other terminal and instrumental values that were noted to be more characteristic of the poor than of rich were salvation, true friendship, being cheerful, forgiving, helpful, obedient and polite. In contrast, values more characteristic of affluent were a sense of accomplishment, family security, inner harmony, intellectual and logical. The poor were religious than the rich, more other-directed and conforming to traditional values less concerned with taking responsibility and with the security of family and more motivated by a desire for affiliation with members of one's own sex than a desire for love with members of opposite sex. The poor differ from the rich by placing a lower value on competence, intellectual and self-actualization values. The pattern of results found for Americans differing in education is essentially the same as that found for Americans differing in income. Of all 36 values equality showed the greatest difference between black and white. Average black Americans ranked himself as more ambitious than the average white Americans.

Atleast 30 out of the 36 values showed significant age differences either in the adolescent or national sample or in both samples. The general impression gained from data was one of continuous value change from early adolescence through old age with the presence of several generation gaps rather than just one.

Ng, et.al., (1982) carried out an extensive survey of the ethnic-cultural group in nine East-Asian and Pacific countries using modified Rokeach instrument. Instead of ranking procedure, the rating procedure was used; and four additional value items were incorporated into the questionnaire. Main and interaction effects of the ethnic-cultural and sex factors were assessed. Highly significant main and interaction effects were found. Discriminant function analysis revealed two dimensions that maximally discriminated the country samples. The first function "reflects on the negative pole, societal-oriented values that emphasize the submission of self to a hierarchical society (obedient, polite) and the country (national security) and on the positive pole, self-oriented values with a strong `dionysian tendency' (that is, self-indulgence, and self-satisfaction). The second function `reflects, on the positive pole, self-oriented values, which (unlike their counterpart of function 1) emphasize the cultivation of inner strength; and on the 'negative pole, materialistic-oriented values (comfortable life, Equity)". New Zealand, Tasmania and Japan were found at Dionysian end of the function one Paupa Niugine', Malay and India were found at the societal-oriented end of the function one. Results pertaining to second discriminant function showed Japan at a greater value distance from the other two highly developed countries (Tasmania and New Zealand) than from any one of the less developed countries. Of four value items incorporated in the survey, all except self-determination correlated significantly with at least one discriminant function. They suggested that social power, social justice and equity should be retained in future surveys.

Punetha, et.al., (1987), were of the view that while the British literature on multilingualism has invoked value differentials not only between Asian immigrant groups and the host culture but also amongst the former, no empirical evidence actually exists. Hence, an extended Rokeach Value Survey was administered to three Asian groups (Hindus, Muslims and Sikhs) and to a British indigenous sample; the bilingual immigrants were offered a choice of the questionnaire in their own ethnic tongue or in English. Canonical variate analysis showed large intergroup value differentials with language choice having an effect for all Asian groups (greatest for Sikhs and least for Hindus). Immigrants choosing English had a value position intermediate to the indigenous group and the Asians choosing their ingroup tongue. Family security and honesty were ranked highly by all groups (that is except for Sikhs regarding the former value in their own language and the latter one in English). Social justice and happiness were ranked highly by the indigenous group and by Asian Ss in English, and salvation, power and imagination were ranked lowly by all groups. The three highest rank values for the indigenous sample were happiness, honesty and freedom, family security was ranked first by Sikhs in English, and by Hindus irrespective of language choice. The highest ranked value for Muslims in English was social justice with self-respect and freedom ranked second and third respectively. For Muslims who chose their ethnic tongue, self-control and clean were ranked joint first, and responsible third. The two highest ranked values for the Sikhs who chose their ingroup language were honesty and responsible.

Schwartz and Bilsky, (1987, 1990) have extended the Rokeach tradition. In a study of the thirty-six values in a number of societies (Australia, Finland, Germany, Hong Kong, Israel, Spain, and the United States) seven distinct motivation domain emerged in all societies; achievement, enjoyment, maturity, prosocial, restrictive conformity, security, and self-direction; an eight (social power) existed only in Hong Kong. Some value oppositions were evident in all societies. The opposition between prosocial and achievement values and the opposition between achievement and security values were quite evident. Some value compatibilities were also present in all societies (for example, restrictive conformity, prosocial, and security).

Studies on Moral Judgement in Relation to Home Environment

Hoffman, (1970) summarized data from eight studies and found that power-assertive child rearing techniques are associated with low scores on measures of conscience. Internal moral judgements as distinct from internal one's, were more common among children whose mothers used power assertion infrequently. In another study (1970), he found that love withdrawal have only weak and inconstant relationships with indices of children's moral development.

Hoffman, (1971) conducted study to see if identification plays any role in moral development. The identification scores of seventh-grade children, were based on the extent to which they consciously admired and strived to emulate their parents. Few significant relationships are obtained. Farther identification related positively to conformity rules, internal moral judgement, and salience of moral values in boys, and to conformity to rules in girls. Mother identification related to conformity to rules in boys. Neither mother nor father identification related significantly to the major moral internalization indice, guilt confession, and acceptance of blame.

Bearison and Cassel, (1975) investigated the child's ability to take the perspective of another person in a communication game, and related this ability to aspects of child rearing. Children whose mother were more given to use of person-oriented (regulatory statements that draw attention to the feeling, thoughts, needs or intentions of the mother, the child or a third person, who may be affected by the child's actions) argument rather than position-oriented (referring to rules or statues) were more successful in taking the perspective of another person in a game that required them to do so.

Saraswathi, (1978) conducted Study to find out the relationship between various maternal disciplinary practices as reported by children and the development of moral judgement, to determine the most effective disciplinary techniques for the internalization of morality, social class and sex difference if any in perceived maternal disciplinary practices in a subgroup of boys and girls. Major findings suggested a trend of negative correlation between maternal power assertion and moral maturity scores (MMS) of children, and positive correlations between maternal induction and moral maturity scores of children. The correlation was, however, clearly significant only in case of upper middle class girls and approached zero in case of working class boys. The pattern of relationship between love withdrawal and MMS was neither clear nor consistent in terms of direction. There was high usage of a mixed pattern of discipline i.e., use of both power assertion and induction. Upper middle class children whose mothers were perceived as using such a mixed mode of discipline scored significantly higher in MMS than those who perceived their mothers as using predominantly power assertion. Power assertion was the predominant mode of discipline in both social classes. The highest usage both in terms of frequency as well as intensity (beating, physical assertion of power) was reported by the working class boys.

Bandyopadhyay, (1981) conducted study to adopt Piaget's stories and study the growth of moral judgement with age, and examine the effects of intelligence, socio economic conditions, sex, type of school and parental discipline on moral judgement. Sample consisted of 440 children of both sex, age group 6-11 years. Major findings indicated that moral judgement grew with age and the relation was appreciably linear. Of seven areas of moral judgement, girl showed more maturity than boys in three areas viz., attitude towards justice, equality and authority, and collective responsibility. In three areas, viz moral realism, imminent justice and guilt, there was no sex bias, but in efficacy of punishment, girls gave less mature responses than boys. Children showed more mature moral judgement where both parents adopted the same form of discipline (love oriented or power assertion). The greater the divergence between the parents, the lesser was the development of moral judgement.

Garg, (1983) conducted study to find out the main effect of parental disciplinary practices and social class on personality needs, moral judgement and problem solving ability of children belonging to age group of 10-15 years and to study the interaction of these variables while they influenced personality needs moral judgement and problem-solving ability. A poor mode of parental control promoted in greater magnitude, the moral judgement of the children in comparison with strict and moderate modes of parental disciplinary practices. Children of 12-13 years had significantly better ability to solve problems and moral judgement in comparison with children of 10-11 or 14-15 years.

Singh, (1983) ventured to study moral judgement is relation to prolonged deprivation and parental attitudes. The variables studies in relation to moral judgement were prolonged deprivation, three types of parental attitudes-possessive, dominative and ignoring, demographic variables-sex, area, birth order, age, educational status of fathers, income and type of school. The sample consisted of 350 children studying in fifth grade and belonging to the age range of 9 to 12 years. A significant positive correlation was obtained between father's attitude to possessiveness and children's moral judgement, father's attitude of domination was found to be unrelated to children's moral judgement. No significant correlation was obtained between father's ignoring attitude and children's moral judgement.

Sethi and Gupta, (1984) conducted study to find out the relationship of children's moral judgement level to their perception of their mother's child rearing attitudes. Subjects in the study were 60 boys and 72 girls ranging from 9 to 11 years in age and studying in classes spread over 5th to 7th standards. The analysis of data revealed that the boys with high moral judgement perceived their mothers to be accepting and loving but less intrusive and non-enforcing. The girls with high moral judgement also perceived their mother as accepting and loving, but controlling and enforcing as well. Perception of maternal rejection and hostility was associated with low moral judgement in both boys and girls.

Bhargava, (1986) studied moral developmental trends among children from the concrete operational stage (8+ to 11+ years) to formal operational stage (12+ to 13+ years). He examined variables of home and educational environment in relation to moral judgement at the concrete operational stage and formal operational stage. He also studied the sex differences in moral judgement with respect to its development in 8+ to 15+ year age group. Findings of the study suggested that there was significant development of moral judgement from one age to next successive age group. The measures of home variables i.e., parental acceptance, parental avoidance, family relationship, moral attitude of parents and socio-economic status were positively related with moral development at concrete and formal operational stage.

Studies on Values in Relation to Home Environment

Horn and Knott, (1971) suggest that the parents of activist more than other parents of the same generations were influenced by freudian theory. They used inductive discipline. They gave reasons for the kinds of behaviour they wanted from the child and the punishment they administered. They rarely used spanking or other forms of corporal punishment. They encouraged their children to express themselves truly and to take responsibility.

Block Hann and Smith, (1969) has identified a subgroup of activist who rejected parental values. This subgroup engaged in considerable protesting, but unlike other activists, showed little interests in social service activities (e.g. tutoring, hospital, Volunteer work) and frequently described their relationship with their parents as involving conflict, anger, criticism, tension and the absence of warmth, intimacy and appreciation.

Burton, (1972) demonstrated that under certain condition parent may communicate to their children that when success and honesty are in conflict it is more important to succeed than to be honest.

Pattnaik. A., (1987) studied the relationship between home environment and values of the secondary girl students. It was found that the Control aspect of home environment is positively related with social and knowledge values; protectiveness aspect of home environment is positively related with religious, aesthetic and health values but negatively related to social and family prestige values; punishment aspect of home environment is positively related with aesthetic value but negatively related with democratic values; conformity aspect of the home environment is positively related with religious, aesthetic and health values but negatively related with social and family prestige values; social isolation aspect of home environment is negatively related with aesthetic value; reward aspect of home environment is positively related to religious, democratic, aesthetic and health values but negatively related with social knowledge, power, and family prestige values; deprivation of privilege aspect of home environment is positively related with power value; nurturance aspect of home environment is negatively related to family prestige value; rejection aspect of home environment is positively related to social, power and family prestige value but negatively related to religious, democratic, aesthetic and health value; permissive aspect of home environment is positively related with social, knowledge and family prestige value but negatively related with aesthetic and economic value.

Studies on Moral Judgement in Relation to Stress

Stress creates cognitive and emotional disorders. When these disorders are caused by other factor, they may produce stress.

Sigman, & Erdynast, (1988) studied interpersonal understanding and moral judgement in adolescents. This study concerns with moral judgement of adolescents suffering from emotional and cognitive disorder. In present study 10 male and 10 female (19.9 years, I.Q. 40-109) for behavioural and congitively disturbed adolescents were included. Ss who were socially engaged showed higher level of moral judgement and inter personal understanding than socially withdrawn Ss. Severely of disturbance and intelligence level are unrelated to measures of social and moral understanding. It is concluded that social evolvement is critical for the development of social and moral judgement.

Hoffman, (1963) generalized on the basis of empirical research that moral orientation based on the fear of external detection and punishment is associated with relatively frequent use of discipline techniques physical punishment and material deprivation, which have been called power assertive discipline. A moral orientation characterized by independence of external sanctions and high guilt is associated with relatively frequent use of non-power assertive discipline—sometimes called psychological, indirect or love-oriented discipline.

Analysis of Studies

Study by Sigman & Erdynast, (1988) indicates that stressors may not be related to social and moral understanding. Hoffman, (1963) gathered evidence to prove the differential effects of love-oriented and power assertive disciplinary practices on moral orientation based on fear of external detection and punishment or independence of external sanctions and high guilt.

The problem of the effect of parent-child interaction i.e. home environment has attracted the attention of many researchers in India and abroad. The studies point to the importance of some dimensions of patenting like, power assertion, avoidance, ignoring, punishment, hostility, rejection, punishment and possessiveness. Results of Hoffman, (1970) and Saraswathi, (1978) reveal negative relationship between power assertion and moral development as measured in terms of internality of moral judgement or moral maturity. Hoffman, (1970) found weak and inconsistent relationship between love withdrawal and moral judgement. However, Bhargava, (1988) reported positive relationship between moral development and avoidance. Singh, (1983) could not find any significant relationship between father's ignoring and moral judgement. Hoffman, (1971) Provided evidence to show positive relationship between conformity and internal moral judgement. Bearison and Cassel, (1970) showed the positive role of person-oriented child-bearing on development of moral judgement. Studies by Sarswathi and Bandyopadhyaya, (1981) have yielded results to indicate positive relationship between induction and moral maturity. They also provided evidence to show the effectiveness of mixed mode of discipline emphasizing the use of induction as well as love withdrawal. Garg's, (1983) Study has indicated that less control in home environment is more conducive to the development of moral judgement than strict/moderate control. Sethi and Gupta, (1980) and Bhargava, (1986) have found that acceptance and love oriented patenting is positively related to moral judgement. Rejection and hostility has been found to be associated with low moral judgement (Sethi & Gupta, 1984), Bandyopadhyaya, (1981) pointed to the fact that punishment is associated with less morally mature responses.

Studies by Horn and Knott, (1971); Block, Hann and Smith, (1969); Burton, (1972); and Patnaik, (1987) have shown the importance of home environment on development of values. Patnaik has found the control, protectiveness, punishment, conformity, social isolation, reward, depravation of privileges, nurturance 'rejection' and permissiveness aspects of home environment differentially related to moral judgement.

Rokeach's Value Survey is being extensively used for measuring values, instrumental and terminal, in many studies during the recent times. Studies have shown differences in the values of students differing with respect to sex (Rokeach, 1973; Feather & Collins, 1974; Feather, 1974), educational choice (Feather, 1970, Feather & Collins, 1974), nature of schools (Feather, 1974), culture as represented by belongingness to different countries (Feather & Hutton 1974; Feather & Rudzitis, 1974; Ng, et. al., 1982; Punetha, et. al., 1987; Schwartz & Bilsky, 1987, 90) and social class (Rokeach, 1973; Beech & Schoeppe, 1974; Feather, 1975; Dwivedi, 1980).

Present Study

Analysis of various studies shows that home environment can influence the development of values and moral judgement and our understanding of the dimensions of home environment that may facilitate or inhibit the development of various instrumental and terminal values as measured by Rokeach's value survey (Original or adopted versions) is far from being definite. The present study is an attempt in this direction. Stress appears to adversely affect the development of various values and moral judgement. But no significant scientific investigation has been undertaken to verify this hypothesis based on various theories as mentioned in the first chapter. The present study may be a modest beginning in this direction.

3

Design of Research

The second chapter embodies description of the studies related to the present one. The present chapter includes the description of the method adopted for conducting the present study, selection of sample, tools used, data collection procedure and the statistical techniques adopted for analysing the data.

Method of Study

The present study is descriptive research. The study aim to investigate the effect of stress and home environment on values and moral judgement. It is a causal-comparative and correlational study.

Population and Sample

The girl students of class IX of Allahabad city constituted the population of this study.

Four girls intermediate colleges were randomly selected from the list of colleges of girls intermediate colleges situated in Allahabad city for the purpose of data collection. The tools were administered on all girls studying in class IX irrespective of their curriculum, socio-economic status, intelligence, and academic achievement. The initial sample for the present study consisted of 468 girls. The incomplete data sheets were eliminated. So, 436 girls constituted the final sample of the study. This was a cluster sample.

Table 3.1: Schools and sample size for the study

S. No.	School	N
1.	D. P. Girls Intermediate College, Allahabad.	114
2.	St. Anthony's Convent Girls Intermediate College, Allahabad.	108
3.	Mary Wana Maker Girl's Intermediate College, Allahabad.	110
4.	Jagat Taran Girl's Intermediate College, Allahabad.	114
	Total	**436**

Variables in the Study

The present study attempts to explore the effect of stress and home environment on moral judgement and values. Hence, the two major independent variables of this study are - Stress and Home Environment. The major dependent variables are - Moral Judgement and Values.

Tools Used

Suitable tools pave the way for successful accomplishment of the objectives of the study and the collection of pertinent data. The selection of tools for a particular study depends upon various considerations such as objectives of the study, the amount of time at disposal of the researcher, availability of suitable tests, personal competence of the researcher, techniques of scoring and interpretation and the like. Taking these factors into consideration, the following tools were selected for use by the researcher.

1. Stress Scale for Students constructed by K. S. Mishra and S. P. Pandey was used for measuring stress.
2. Home Environment Inventory prepared by K. S. Mishra was used for measuring ten dimensions of home environment.

3. Moral judgement questionnaire constructed by S. K. Pal and K. S. Mishra was used for measuring moral judgement.
4. Hindi version of adopted Rokeach Value Survey by Ng. et. al., (1982) was used for measuring 40 values of girls.

Stress Scale for Students

It was developed by K. S. Mishra and S. P. Pandey. It measures the frequency of exposure to various stressors. It measures stress in four areas of life, namely: home, school, society and self.

This stress scale contains 60 items. Five options namely always, very often, many times, sometimes and never are given. Out of these five, students has to give one response showing the frequency of his/her exposure to the given stressors.

There is no time limit for the administration of this tool but students can complete it in about 40 to 50 minutes. Split half reliability coefficients for the total score was .95. for home, society, school and individual areas these values were .83, .75, .92 and .82 respectively.

Home Environment Inventory

This inventory was developed by K. S. Mishra to measure students perception of their home environment.

It consists of 100 items which are arranged in a random manner. It provides quantitative measures of 10 dimensions of home environment namely: control, protectiveness, punishment, conformity, social isolation, deprivation of privileges, rejection, permissiveness, nurturance, and reward.

Content validity has been determined on the basis of opinions expressed by parents and experts. Intrinsic validity coefficients are significant .05 level and range from .16 to .74. Split half reliability coefficient for various subtests in the inventory range from .73 to .95.

ROKEACH VALUE SURVEY (E. V.)

Rokeach Value Survey (1967) as extended by Ng. et. al., (1982) was used to measure forty values of girls studying in Hindi medium schools. These values are: A comfortable life, an exciting life, a sense of accomplishment, a world of peace, a world of beauty, equality, family security, freedom, happiness, inner harmony, mature love, national security, pleasure, salvation, self-respect, social recognition, true friendship, wisdom, equity, power, social justice, ambitious broadminded, capable, cheerful, clean, courageous, forgiving, helpful, honesty, imagination, independence, intellectual, logical, loving, obedient, polite, responsible, self-control and self determination.

This adapted test differed in two important ways from traditional Rokeach Value Survey. Four additional value (Self-determination, Social power, Social justice and Equality) were included for the reason that they would be relevant to some of the countries under going rapid political and economic change. Secondly, instead of asking the respondents to rank order the values, they were asked to rate each value on nine point scale of importance. The decision to replace the ranking procedure by rating procedure was based on a consideration of the latters relatively greater psychosomatic benefits for crass cultural research (Ng, 1981). Amongst these, the most critical one is the problem of interdependence associated with ranked data. Within one set of values, the ranks are interdependent and are, therefore, void of measuring outside the given set. Results obtained through the ranking procedure in one study can become part of a cumulative body of knowledge if, and only if, the same set of values, no more and no less, is used and continued to be used in subsequent studies. This appeared to be a unrealistic strategy for cross cultural research. Studies by Feather, (1975); More, (1975) and Rankin and Grube, (1980) have shown that the rated data and the ranked data given by the same set of respondents fare equally well in terms of rank order correlation test retest reliability, construct validity, convergent and discriminant validity. As far as the prediction of attitudes is concerned rated data are slightly superior. On the other hand, the rating procedure is more susceptible to social desirability and is less intrinsically motivating for the respondent, but has the advantage of greater ease and speed in the completion of R.V.S.

The English version of the value questionnaire (consisting of 36 R.V.S value items plus self-determination, social power, social justice and equity), together with instruction on how to indicate the answers on nine point scale of importance, was translated into the written language commonly used by the respondents. For India, translation was done in Hindi. The translation was done through back/double translation. This tool is internationally recognized one and is considered very useful for the further surveys, particularly, when the survey's includes countries experiencing rapid social change. The tool measures the values of individual ranging from age 11 years to 90 years.

Moral Judgement Questionnaire

It has been developed by S. K. Pal and K. S. Mishra. It requires students to think of their decisions or behaviours in twelve moral dilemmas based on situations related to children's life and given justifications for their response. These dilemmas are:-

1. Halfcost ticket
2. Lost examination question paper
3. Mischievous students' group
4. Dilemma of friendship
5. Obtaining fruits without payment
6. Broken chair for the teacher
7. Act of a ball.
8. Unclaimed money

9. Improper action and friendship
10. Demand for killing by a beautiful girl
11. Dishonestful honesty
12. Sympathy of a thief friend

Test-retest reliability of the Moral judgement Questionnaire is .7186. Construct validity was established by studying the relationship of overall moral judgement to cognitive abilities. The correlation ranged from .3848 to .5650.

Collection of Data

Extended version of Rokeach's Value Survey, Moral Judgement Questionnaire, Stress Scale and Home Environment Inventory were administered on the sample subjects. The purpose of administering the four tools was explained and the instructions printed on the tools were read by the researcher. Students also went through the instructions simultaneously, then, they responded to various items of various tools. Scoring was done in accordance with the procedure prescribed for the respective tools.

While responding to items of the stress Scale, girls gave five responses namely, (1) Never, (2) Sometimes, (3) Many times, (4) Very often and (5) Always.

For a tick in the box 1- Never- no score was awarded. For a tick in box 2 related to 'sometimes' 1 score was awarded. For a tick in the box 3 related to 'often' a score of 2 was awarded.

For a tick in the box 4 related to 'very often,' a score of 3 was awarded. For a tick in the box 5 related to 'Always' score of 4 was awarded. Every item belonged to a certain category A, B, C, or D and so the scores on items related to each of the four areas of stress were added together to get a score on each of the four categories which were then added together to get a composite stress score.

While responding to Home Environment Inventory items girls chose one of the five responses namely: Never, least, sometimes, often, mostly. They were assigned scores of 0, 1, 2, 3, and 4 respectively. The hundred items belonged to ten dimensions and therefore scores on items belonging to each dimension were added together to get score for each of the ten dimensions of home environment namely, control, permissiveness, nurturance, reward, conformity, rejection, punishment, protectiveness, social isolation and deprivation of privileges.

While responding to moral judgement questionnaire, the girls gave their judgement on twelve moral dilemmas of questionnaire. The researcher evaluated the answers of the students who were assigned 1,2,3,4,5, or 6 stages. Scores for twelve moral dilemmas were treated separately and all the categories were added to get the total moral judgement score.

Students responded to each of the 40 values of an extended version (40 items) of Rokeach's Value Survey on 9-point scale (Ng. et al., 1982). Girls rated each of the 40 values, according to the importance of that value for themselves. I stood for the least important value, while 9 stood for most important value.

Each of the 40 values were namely: A comfortable life, an exciting life, a sense of accomplishment, a world of peace, a world of beauty, equality, family security, freedom, happiness, inner harmony, mature love, national security, pleasure, salvation, self-respect, social recognition, true friendship, wisdom, equity, power, social justice, ambitious, broadminded, capable, cheerful, clean, courageous, forgiving, helpful, honesty, imagination, independent, intellectual, logical, loving, obedient, polite, responsible, self-control, and self-determination.

Analysis of Data

For determining the normal distribution of scores on dependent and independent variables skewness and

Kurtosis were computed. Means and standard deviation were also computed in order to describe the pattern of scores on different variable.

Kendall Rank correlation Coefficient was computed to find out the relationship of stress, overall as well as that related to four areas, with each of the 40 values and twelve items of Moral Judgement Questionnaire and over all moral judgement.

Kendall Rank Correlation coefficient was computed to find out the relationship of each of the ten dimensions of home environment with each of the 40 values and twelve items of Moral Judgement Questionnaire and overall moral judgement.

Kruskal Wallis one way analysis of variance was used to find out whether girls experiencing high/moderate/low stress differ with respect to various values and moral judgement (12 items and overall moral judgement).

Kruskal Wallis one way analysis of variance was used to find out whether girls experiencing high/moderate and low level on each of the ten dimensions of home environment differ with respect to various values and moral judgement (12 items and overall moral judgement).

1. Mann-Whitney 'U' test with correction for ties was used for comparing high/moderate/Low stressful girls on various values and moral judgement. This test was computed only when Kruskal Wallis test yielded significant results.
2. Mann-Whitney 'U' test with correction of ties was computed for comparing high/moderate/Low girls on each of the ten dimensions of home environment on various values and moral judgement. This test was computed only when Kruskal Wallis test yielded significant results.

4

Results and Discussion

The present study was conducted to find out whether home environment affect values and moral judgement among girls. Data on values, moral judgement, stress and home environment was collected from 436 girls. Analysis of the data was done by using Kruskal Wallis one way ANOVA, Mann-whiteny U-Test and Kendall's Rank coefficient of correlation. The present chapter embodies the description of results of analysis pertaining study of distribution of scores on various variables and testing of various hypothesis.

Study of Distribution of Scores on Stress

Table 4.1: Values of mean, SD, Kurtosis and Skewness for stress

S. No.	Variable	Mean	S.D.	Kurtosis	Skewness
1.	Stress in home	10.569	7.089	0.846	1.062
2.	Stress in school	10.183	6.395	1.614	1.174
3.	Stress in society	28.099	12.538	1.979	1.179
4.	Stress in self	12.658	5.968	–.419	0.453
5.	Overall stress	61.509	27.355	1.596	1.085

Mean rank shown in table 4.1, for stress in home, school, society, self and overall stress are 10.569, 10.183,

28.099, 12.658 and 61.509 respectively, Kurtosis values for distribution of scores on stress in home, school, society. Self and overall stress are .846, 1.614, 1.979, –.419, and 1.596 respectively. Distribution of scores on stress in home, school, society and overall stress are platykurtic and distribution of score for stress in self is leptokurtic.

Skewness values for stress in home, school, society, self and overall stress are 1.062, 1.174, 1.179, .453 and 1.085 respectively. So the distributions of stress scores are positively skewed.

Distribution of Scores on Various Aspects of Home Environment

Table 4.2: Values of mean, SD, Kurtosis and Skewness for various dimensions of home environment

S. No.	Variable	Mean	S.D.	Kurtosis	Skewness
1.	Control	18.984	6.238	–.392	.010
2.	Protectiveness	26.695	6.892	–.322	–.356
3.	Punishment	22.665	6.077	.182	.071
4.	Conformity	29.080	5.903	.718	–.649
5.	Social isolation	10.330	6.264	.176	.561
6.	Reward	28.745	6.674	1.447	–1.015
7.	Deprivation of privileges	8.255	5.168	.213	.650
8.	Nurturance	22.216	6.364	.037	–.511
9.	Rejection	9.337	5.508	–.196	.396
10.	Permissiveness	16.399	5.274	.268	.254

The table 4.2 shows mean rank for ten dimension of home environment namely: Control, protectiveness, punishment, conformity, social isolation, reward, deprivation of privileges, nurturance, rejection and permissiveness are 18.984, 26.665, 22.665, 29.080, 10.330, 28.754, 8.225, 22.216, 9.337 and 16.399 respectively.

Kurtosis values for the distribution of scores on control, protectiveness, punishment, social isolation, deprivation of privileges, nurturance, rejection are: .392, –.322, .182, .213, .037, and –.196 respectively. Distribution of scores for control, protectiveness, punishment, social isolation, deprivation of privileges, nurturance and rejection are slightly leptokurtic. Distribution of score on conformity .718, reward 1.447 and permissiveness .268 are slightly platykurtic.

Table 4.2 shows Skewness values for distribution of scores for ten dimension of home environment. Skewness values for distribution of scores for control, punishment, social isolation, deprivation of privileges, rejection and permissiveness are .010, .071, .561, .650, .396, .254 respectively. Thus distribution of scores on deprivation of privileges, social isolation and rejection are positively skewed. Values for distributions of scores for protectiveness, conformity, reward and nurturance are –.356, –.649, –1.015 and –.511. They indicate negative skewness of respective distributions.

Distribution of Scores on Values

Table 4.3 shows Mean, Standard Deviation, Skewness, Kurtosis for the values namely: A comfortable life, an exciting life, a sense of accomplishment, a world of peace, a world of beauty, equality, family security, freedom, happiness, inner harmony, mature love, national security, pleasure, salvation, self-respect, social recognition, true friendship, wisdom, equity, power, social justice, ambitious, broadminded, capable, cheerful, clean, courageous, forgiving, helpful, honesty, Imagination, independent, intellectual logical, loving, obedient, polite, responsible, self-control and self-determination are 4.640, 5.805, 7.188, 7.778, 7.725, 7.124, 7.495, 7.443, 7.282, 6.037, 6.135, 7.732,

6.837, 5.787, 7.663, 7.642, 8.204, 7.766, 7.399, 6.252, 7.718, 7.218, 6.835, 7.399, 7.321, 8.268, 7.459, 7.151, 7.369, 8.014, 6.195, 7.255, 7.151, 6.275, 7.401, 7.876, 7.360, 7.433, 7.005, 7.606 respectively.

Kurtosis values for distribution of score on values: A comfortable life, a world of peace, a world of beauty, family security, national security, self-respect, social recognition, true friendship, wisdom, social justice, ambitions, clean, courageous, helpful, honesty, independent, intellectual, loving, obedient, polite, responsible, self-determination are .856, 2.445, 1.147, .311, 2.055, 1.259, .386, 5.621, 1.335, 2.304, .536, 7.046, .561, .657, 3.720, .365, .542, .456, 2.087, 1.356, .598, .717 respectively are platyturtic. Kurtosis values for distribution of scores on values namely: An exciting life, a sense of accomplishment, equality, freedom, happiness, inner harmony, mature love, salvation, self-respect, equity, power, broadminded, capable, cheerful, forgiving, imagination, logical, self-control are lepokurtic.

Table 4.3 shows skewness values for each of the 40 values. They range from –.120 to –2.554. They show that distribution of scores for most of the values is negtively skewed.

Table 4.3: Values of Mean, SD, Kurtosis and Skewness for various values

S. No.	Variable	Mean	SD	Kurtosis	Skewness
1	2	3	4	5	6
1.	A comfortable life	4.640	1.894	.856	–.120
2.	An exciting life	5.805	2.554	–1.032	–.299
3.	A sense of accomplishment	7.188	1.921	–.033	–.842
4.	A world of peace	7.778	2.164	2.445	–1.864
5.	A world of beauty	7.725	1.744	1.147	–1.373
6.	Equality	7.124	2.283	.214	–1.067
7.	Family security	7.495	1.773	.311	–1.031

(Table Contd...)

(Table 4.3: Contd...)

1	2	3	4	5	6
8.	Freedom	7.443	1.833	.139	−1.034
9.	Happiness	7.282	1.885	−.095	−.861
10.	Inner harmony	6.037	2.262	−.543	−.367
11.	Mature love	6.135	2.159	−.363	−.414
12.	National security	7.732	1.818	2.055	−1.578
13.	Pleasure	6.837	2.021	−.440	−.526
14.	Salvation	5.787	2.245	−.540	−.279
15.	Self-respect	7.663	1.770	1.259	−1.328
16.	Social recognition	7.642	1.684	.386	−1.084
17.	True friendship	8.204	1.500	5.621	−2.330
18.	Wisdom	7.766	1.702	1.335	−1.421
19.	Equity	7.399	1.810	.091	−.937
20.	Power	6.252	2.121	−.341	−.389
21.	Social justice	7.718	1.794	2.304	-1.577
22.	Ambitious	7.218	2.042	.536	−1.091
23.	Broadminded	6.835	1.994	−.485	−.536
24.	Capable	7.399	1.636	.048	−.889
25.	Cheerful	7.321	1.839	−.122	−.847
26.	Clean	8.268	1.448	7.046	−2.554
27.	Courageous	7.459	1.790	.561	−1.093
28.	Forgiving	7.151	1.856	.081	−.851
29.	Helpful	7.369	1.843	.657	−1.110
30.	Honesty	8.014	1.590	3.720	−1.918
31.	Imagination	6.195	2.193	−.488	−.406
32.	Independent	7.255	1.940	.365	−1.023
33.	Intellectual	7.151	1.889	.542	−.978
34.	Logical	6.275	2.050	−.510	−.393
35.	Loving	7.401	1.819	.456	−1.065
36.	Obedient	7.876	1.550	2.087	−1.518
37.	Polite	7.360	1.990	1.356	−1.342
38.	Responsible	7.433	1.828	.598	−1.120
39.	Self-control	7.005	1.976	.075	−.831
40.	Self-determination	7.0606	1.855	.717	−1.223

Distribution of Scores on Moral Judgement

Table 4.4: Showing values of Mean, SD, Kurtosis and Skewness for various items of moral judgement and overall moral judgement

S. No.	Variable	Mean	S.D.	Kurtosis	Skewness
A.	Total moral judgement	36.638	5.684	.761	–.458
B.	Items of M.J.Q.				
1.	Half cost ticket	3.209	.987	–.704	–.659
2.	Lost examination question paper	3.257	.916	–.428	–.621
3.	Mischievous student's group	2.803	.710	.750	–.705
4.	Dilemma of friendship	3.124	.775	.165	–.575
5.	Obtaining fruits without payment	3.154	.983	–.384	–.676
6.	Broken chair for the teacher	3.195	.791	.170	–.781
7.	Act of ball	2.729	.937	–.884	–.043
8.	Unclaimed money	2.422	.765	.354	.977
9.	Demand for killing by a beautiful girl	3.252	1.163	–.440	.484
10.	Dishonestful honesty	3.273	.759	–.394	–.470
11.	Sympathy of a thief friend	2.780	.890	1.212	.761
12.	Improper action and friendship	3.440	.912	–.556	–.874

Mean rank values shown in table 4.4 for total moral judgement and for each of the twelve items of moral judgement are 36.638, 3.209, 3.257, 2.803, 3.124, 3.154, 3.195, 2.729, 2.422, 3.252, 3.273, 2.780, and 3.440 respectively kurtosis values for distribution of scores on total moral judgement is .761. Value of kurtosis for the twelve items range from –.884 to 1.212. Skewness values for various items of moral judgement questionnaire range from –.874 to .977. These values show that the distribution of scores for most of the items of moral judgement questionnaires are negatively skewed and lektokurtic.

Formation of Criterion Groups

Mean and standard deviation for scores on overall stress as well as stress in home, school, society and self areas; and ten dimensions of home environment namely: Control, protectiveness, conformity, social isolation, reward, deprivation of privileges, nurturance, rejection and permissiveness were computed. Girl obtaining high scores (mean +1 SD) on an independent variable were included in the High Criterion Group (HCG) while those getting scores less than (Mean –1 SD) on a particular variable were included in the Low Criterion Group (LCG). Remaining girls were included in Moderate Criterion Group (MCG). The cut-off scores for the fifteen variables have been given in table 4.5. Krushkal-Wallis one-way Analysis of variance was used for comparing HCG, MCG and LCG on various dependent variables. Between group comparison were done by using Mann Whitney U-test. Result have been given in section 4.6 and 4.7.

Table 4.5: Cut off scores for high and low criterion groups for independent variables

Sl. No.	Variable	Cut off score for	
		HCG	LCG
1	2	3	4
1.	Overall Stress	88.86	34.16
2.	Stress in home	17.658	3.480
3.	Stress in society	16.578	3.788
4.	Stress in school	40.637	15.561
5.	Stress in self	18.622	6.694
6.	Control	25.222	12.746
7.	Protectiveness	33.587	19.803

(Table Contd...)

(Table 4.5: Contd...)

1	2	3	4
8.	Punishment	29.742	17.588
9.	Conformity	34.983	23.177
10.	Social isolation	16.594	4.066
11.	Reward	35.419	22.071
12.	Deprivation of privileges	13.423	3.087
13.	Nurturance	28.580	5.852
14.	Rejection	14.845	3.829
15.	Permissiveness	21.673	11.125

HCG = High criterion group
LCG = Low criterion group

Study of the Effect of Stress on Values

RESULTS

It was hypothesized that "Girls experiencing less, moderate and high stress, in home, do not differ from one another in values."

Table 4.6 present result of Kruskal Wallis one way ANOVA for values for girls experiencing different level of stress low, moderate and high. Observation of chi-square values show that out of 40 values, six values are significant. Five values are significant at .05 level and one value is significant at .01 level. This allows acceptance of the hypothesis with respect to 34 values. This means that girls experiencing low, moderate and high level of stress in home do not differ from one another on 34 values namely: A comfortable life, an exciting life, a sense of accomplishment, a world of peace, equality, family security, freedom, inner harmony, mature love, national security, salvation, self respect, social recognition, true friendship, equity, power, social justice, ambitious, broadminded, capable, cheerful, clean, courageous, forgiving, honesty, independent, intellectual, logical, loving, obedient, polite, responsible, self-control and self-determination.

Table 4.6: Mean ranks and chi-square values showing difference on various values among girls experiencing low/moderate/high level of stress in home

S. No.	Values	Level of Stress			Chi-Sq.	Sign.
		Low[1]	Moderate[2]	High[3]		
1	2	3	4	5	6	7
1.	A comfortable life	227.86	212.43	238.04	3.7192	.1557
2.	An exciting life	235.47	214.72	221.44	1.3926	.4984
3.	A sense of accomplishment	230.18	219.91	202.51	1.7672	.4133
4.	A world of peace	229.67	221.87	194.12	4.3937	.1112
5.	A world of beauty	240.82	222.03	184.22	8.3136	.0157*
6.	Equality	234.68	218.64	204.52	1.9936	.3691
7.	Family security	219.18	217.16	223.96	.1846	.9118
8.	Freedom	217.46	220.08	212.25	.2446	.8849
9.	Happiness	259.82	222.16	167.92	19.0959	.0001**
10.	Inner harmony	236.00	210.50	239.99	4.5374	.1034
11.	Mature love	203.33	222.70	212.17	1.4105	.4940
12.	National security	223.48	217.68	218.08	.1217	.9410
13.	Pleasure	259.18	211.41	216.73	7.4813	.0237*

(Table Contd...)

(Table 4.6: Contd…)

1	2	3	4	5	6	7
14.	Salvation	234.98	212.47	231.96	2.5922	.2736
15.	Self-respect	224.72	216.29	223.29	.3856	.8246
16.	Social recognition	229.72	219.18	206.20	1.2708	.5297
17.	True friendship	230.85	220.75	198.17	3.4723	.1762
18.	Wisdom	241.90	220.28	191.15	6.1566	.0460*
19.	Equity	248.66	215.20	208.42	4.2931	.1169
20.	Power	239.59	218.69	200.24	3.2060	.2013
21.	Social justice	223.25	221.01	203.31	1.4123	.4935
22.	Ambitious	203.96	223.76	206.88	2.0444	.3598
23.	Broadminded	218.86	217.84	221.19	.0428	.9788
24.	Capable	239.91	216.52	209.72	2.1951	.3337
25.	Cheerful	233.82	216.69	213.97	1.0852	.5812
26.	Clean	229.90	217.87	211.91	.9802	.6126
27.	Courageous	219.57	221.79	202.83	1.4043	.4955
28.	Forgiving	244.53	212.62	223.43	3.4027	.1824
29.	Helpful	248.06	218.61	193.57	6.2987	.0429*

(Table Contd...)

(Table 4.6: Contd...)

1	2	3	4	5	6	7
30.	Honesty	233.92	216.02	216.69	1.2564	.5335
31.	Imagination	188.62	228.68	197.44	7.4848	.0237*
32.	Independent	240.96	216.27	209.96	2.3951	.3019
33.	Intellectual	245.86	213.55	218.12	3.3473	.1876
34.	Logical	214.62	223.69	198.40	2.4226	.2978
35.	Loving	239.58	219.03	198.70	3.5845	.1666
36.	Obedient	245.18	217.54	200.79	4.6131	.0996
37.	Polite	237.14	220.76	192.96	4.5532	.1026
38.	Responsible	233.43	218.11	207.92	1.4096	.4942
39.	Self-control	215.26	219.44	216.93	.0693	.9659
40.	Self-determination	232.39	216.00	218.27	.9523	.6212

1N = 57
2N = 310
3N = 69
*Significant at .05 level
**Significant at 0.1 level

Significant values of Chi-squre were found for six values namely: A world of beauty, happiness, pleasure, wisdom, helpful and imagination. These values allow partial rejection of the null hypothesis. This allows us to infer that girls experiencing low, moderate, and high level of stress in home differ from one another with respect to six values.

Further analysis was done by using Mann-Whitney. 'U' test, Results are shown in tables 4.7 to 4.12.

Table 4.7 shows that mean rank for girls experiencing low and moderate stress are 197.67 and 181.49 respectively. The mean rank for less stressful girls is not significantly different from that for moderately stressful girls (Z = –1.1520, P >.05). This indicates that no significant difference exist between less and moderately stressful girl on value named a world of beauty.

Table 4.7: Mean ranks, U-values & Z-values showing differences on 'a world of beauty' values among girls experiencing different levels of stress in home

S. No.	Level of stress	N	Mean rank	U-value	Z-value	P
1.	LSG	57	197.67	8056.0	–1.1520	.2493
	MSG	310	189.49			
2.	LSG	57	72.15	1473.5	–2.5874	.0097**
	HSG	69	56.36			
3.	MSG	310	194.04	8823.0	–2.4435	.0145*
	HSG	69	162.87			

* Significant at .05 level

** Significant at .01 level

Mean rank for less stressful girl is 56.36. The mean rank for low stressful girls is higher than that for highly stressful girls (Z =–2.5874, P < .01). This lead to infer that girls experiencing low level stress give more importance to a world of beauty value than the girls experiencing high level of stress. Mean rank for moderately stressful girls is 194.04 mean rank for highly stressful girls is 162.87 . The difference between the two groups is significant (Z = –2.4435, P < .05). This allows to infer that moderately stressful girls consider a world of beauty value more important than the highly stressful girl.

Table 4.8 shows that mean rank for less stressful girls is 211.19. Mean rank for girl experiencing moderate stress is 179.00. The mean rank for less stressful girls is higher than mean rank of moderately stressful girls (Z = –2.2130, P < .05). It means that value happiness is viewed more important by the less stressful girls than the girls who are moderately stressed. Mean rank for the girls experiencing

Table 4.8: Mean ranks, U-values & Z-values showing differences among less/moderate/highly stressful girls (in home) on 'happiness' value

S. No.	Level of stress	N	Mean rank	U-value	Z-value	P
1.	LSG	57	211.19	7285.0	–2.2130	.0269*
	MSG	310	179.00			
2.	LSG	57	77.62	1161.5	–4.1182	.0000**
	HSG	69	51.83			
3.	MSG	310	198.66	8010.0	–3.3917	.0007**
	HSG	69	151.09			

* Significant at .05 level
** Significant at .01 level

low level of stress is 77.62 and mean rank for highly stressful girls is 51.83. The mean rank for less stressful girl is grater than the mean rank for highly stressful girls (Z = 1161.5, P < .01). Inference can be drawn that girls experiencing low stress give more preference to value happiness than the girls experiencing high level of stress. Mean rank for moderately stressful girl is 198.66. Mean rank for highly stressful girls is 151.09. Mean rank for moderately stressful girls is higher than that for the girl experiencing high stress (Z = –3.3917, P < .01). This indicates that the two groups very significantly on value named happiness. In comparison to girls experiencing high stress, moderately stressful girls give more importance to value happiness.

Table 4.9 shows that mean rank for less stressful girls is 217.90. Mean rank for the girls experiencing moderate stress is 177.77. Mean rank or less stressed girls is higher than moderately stressed girls (Z = –2.7250, P < .01). This

Table 4.9: Mean ranks, U-values and Z-values showing differences among girls experiencing less/moderate and high stress in home on 'pleasure' value

S. No.	Level of stress	N	Mean rank	U-value	Z-value	P
1.	LSG	57	217.90	6902.5	–2.7250	.0064**
	MSG	310	177.77			
2.	LSG	57	70.28	1580.0	–1.9869	.0469*
	HSG	69	57.90			
3.	MSG	310	189.15	10430.5	–.3333	.7389
	HSG	69	193.83			

* Significant at .05 level
** Significant at .01 level

means that pleasure values is more prominent among girls experiencing less stress than those who are moderately stressed. Mean rank for less stressful girls is 70.28. Mean rank for girls under high stress is 57.90. Mean rank for less stressed girls is greater than that for highly stressed girls (Z = –1.9869, P < .05). This indicates that value pleasure finds an important place among girls experiencing less stress than the girls under high stress. Mean rank of 189.15 and 193.83 are for moderately stressful and highly stressful girls respectively. The mean rank for moderately stressful girls is not significantly different from that for highly stressed girls (Z = –.3333, P > .05). This permits us to infer that moderately stressful and highly stressful girls do not vary from each other on pleasure value.

Table 4.10 shows that mean rank for less stressful girls is 199.15. Mean rank for moderately stressful girls is 181.21. Mean rank for less stressful girls is not significantly different from that for moderately stressful girls (Z = –1.2781, P > .05). This indicates that less stressful and moderately stressful girls do not differ significantly from each other on value named wisdom. Mean rank for less stressed girls is 71.75. Mean rank of highly stressed girls is 56.68. Mean rank of less stressful girls is greater than that for highly stressed girls (Z = –2.4676, P < .01). This allows to infer that girls experiencing less stress give more importance to value wisdom than the girls experiencing high stress. Mean rank for moderately stressful girls is 194.57. Mean rank for the highly stressful girls is 169.47. Mean rank for less stressful girls is not significantly different from that for highly stressful girls (Z = –1.8506, P > 0.5). This indicates that no significant difference exist between less stressful and highly stressful girls on value named wisdom.

Table 4.11 shows that mean rank for less stressful girls is 205.32. Mean rank for girls experiencing moderate stress is 180.08. The difference between the mean rank of the two group is not significant (Z = –1.7186, P > .05). This indicates that no difference exists between girls experiencing

Table 4.10: Mean ranks, U-values and Z-values showing differences among girls experiencing low/moderate/high level of stress in home on 'wisdom' value.

S. No.	Level of stress	N	Mean rank	U-value	Z-value	P
1.	LSG	57	199.15	7971.5	–1.2781	.2012
	MSG	310	181.21			
2.	LSG	57	71.75	1496.0	–2.4676	.0136**
	HSG	69	56.68			
3.	MSG	310	194.57	9278.5	–1.8506	.0642
	HSG	69	169.47			

* Significant at .05 level
** Significant at .01 level

Table 4.11: Mean ranks, U-values and Z-values showing differences among girls experiencing low, moderate and high stress in home on 'helpful' value

S. No.	Level of stress	N	Mean rank	U-value	Z-value	P
1.	LSG	57	205.32	7620.0	–1.7186	.0857
	MSG	310	180.08			
2.	LSG	57	71.75	1496.5	–2.3984	.0165*
	HSG	69	56.69			
3.	MSG	310	194.03	9444.5	–1.5736	.1156
	HSG	69	171.88			

* Significant at .05 level
** Significant at .01 level

low level and moderate level of stress in home. Mean rank for the less stressed girls is 71.75. Mean rank for highly stressed girls is 56.69. Mean rank for less stressful girls is greater than the mean rank for highly stressful girls (Z = –2.3984, P < .05). It indicates that low stressful girls, in comparison to highly stressful girls, give more importance to value named helpful. Mean rank for moderately stressed girls is 194.03 while the mean rank for highly stressful girls is 171.88. The mean rank for moderately stressed girls is not significantly different from that for highly stressful girls (Z = –1.5736, P > .05). This allows to infer that both moderately and highly stressed girls do not differ significantly from each other.

Table 4.12 shows mean rank for less stressful girls is 155.58. Mean rank for moderately stressful girls is 189.23. The Mean rank for moderately stressful girls is greater than that for less stressful girls (Z = –2.2507, P < .05). The inference can be drawn that moderately stressful girls excel

Table 4.12: Mean ranks, U-values and Z-values showing differences among girls experiencing less/moderate/high stress in home on 'imagination' value

S. No.	Level of stress	N	Mean rank	U-value	Z-value	P
1.	LSG	57	155.58	7215.0	–2.2507	.0244*
	MSG	310	189.23			
2.	LSG	57	62.04	1883.5	–.4159	.06775
	HSG	69	64.70			
3.	MSG	310	194.95	9159.0	–1.9103	.0561
	HSG	69	167.74			

* Significant at .05 level
** Significant at .01 level

less stressful girls on imagination value. Mean rank for less stressful girls is 62.04. Mean rank for highly stressed girls is 64.70. Mean rank for less stressful girls is not significantly different from that for girls experiencing high level of stress (Z = –.4159, P > .05). Inference can be drawn that less and highly stressed girls do not vary from each other on imagination value. Mean rank for moderately stressful girls is 194.95. Mean rank for highly stressed girls is 167.74. Mean ranks for moderately and highly stressed girls do not differ from each other (Z = –1.9103, P > .05). This indicates that there exists no significant difference among moderately and highly stressed girls on imagination value.

It was hypothesized that "girls experiencing less, moderate and high stress in society do not differ significantly from one another in values".

Table 4.13 presents results of Kruskal Wallis one way ANOVA for values among girls experiencing less/moderate/high stress in society. Observation of chi-square values shows that out of 40 values only six are significant. Three values are significant at .05 level and three values are significant at .01 level. So the null hypothesis stands acceptable with respect to 34 values. This means that girls experiencing low, moderate and high level of stress do not differ from one another on 34 values namely: A comfortable life, an exciting life, a sense of accomplishment, world of peace, a world of beauty, family security, freedom, inner harmony, mature love, national security, pleasure, salvation, self respect, social recognition, equity, power, social justice, ambitious, broadminded, capable, cheerful, clean, courageous, honesty, imagination, independent, intellectual, logical, loving, obedient, polite, responsible, self-control and self-determinantion.

Significant values of chi-square were found for six values, namely: Equality, happiness, true friendship, wisdom, forgiving and helpful. These values lead to partial

Table 4.13: Mean ranks, and chi-square values showing differences on various values among girls experiencing low/moderate/high stress in society

S. No.	Values	Level of Stress			Chi-Sq.	Sign.
		Low[1]	Moderate[2]	High[3]		
1	2	3	4	5	6	7
1.	A comfortable life	213.41	218.26	223.73	.2482	.8833
2.	An exciting life	205.34	222.19	208.28	1.2168	.5442
3.	A sense of accomplishment	245.37	216.94	206.47	2.8990	.2347
4.	A world of peace	242.28	219.29	195.93	4.8287	.0894
5.	A world of beauty	242.14	218.22	201.93	3.0967	.2126
6.	Equality	256.88	218.46	189.32	8.3384	.0155*
7.	Family security	232.55	213.87	233.21	2.0397	.3607
8.	Freedom	201.59	221.70	213.85	1.2359	.5390
9.	Happiness	274.58	218.75	174.13	18.0514	.0001**
10.	Inner harmony	227.91	214.26	234.60	1.6772	.4323
11.	Mature love	187.61	222.46	220.39	3.2591	.1960
12.	National security	212.39	214.93	242.81	3.0747	.2150
13.	Pleasure	240.67	218.33	202.43	2.5892	.2740

(Table Contd...)

(Table 4.13: Contd...)

1	2	3	4	5	6	7
14.	Salvation	219.08	218.23	219.52	.0066	.9967
15.	Self-respect	239.95	214.56	223.72	2.0300	.3624
16.	Social recognition	257.24	213.74	215.00	5.5271	.0631
17.	True friendship	250.59	218.20	195.57	7.0675	.0292*
18.	Wisdom	260.23	217.34	192.88	8.8103	.0122**
19.	Equity	231.04	214.63	230.18	1.4046	.4954
20.	Power	216.40	223.03	195.22	2.6175	.2702
21.	Social justice	228.22	216.89	219.90	.3920	.8220
22.	Ambitious	233.21	221.35	191.55	3.8377	.1468
23.	Broadminded	237.03	213.33	232.74	2.4507	.2937
24.	Capable	254.63	213.38	218.97	4.6175	.0994
25.	Cheerful	253.36	214.29	214.93	4.2936	.1169
26.	Clean	220.23	217.69	221.65	.0885	.9567
27.	Courageous	229.68	218.75	208.54	.8081	.6676
28.	Forgiving	264.17	210.50	227.48	8.1310	.0172*
29.	Helpful	268.28	214.60	201.77	9.2258	.0099**

(Table Contd...)

(Table 4.13: Contd...)

1	2	3	4	5	6	7
30.	Honesty	251.05	217.28	200.26	5.5602	.0620
31.	Imagination	214.64	219.97	213.39	.1950	.9071
32.	Independent	227.59	215.76	226.59	.6913	.7078
33.	Intellectual	243.82	214.68	220.07	2.2930	.3177
34.	Logical	217.25	221.19	204.66	.9119	.6338
35.	Loving	238.93	219.30	198.46	2.9737	.2261
36.	Obedient	256.73	214.79	209.59	5.6469	.0594
37.	Polite	239.51	214.72	223.20	1.8079	.4050
38.	Responsible	241.90	216.71	210.42	2.9673	.3539
39.	Self-control	247.65	215.71	211.50	2.9653	.2270
40.	Self-determinantion	237.57	213.91	229.14	2.2409	.3261

1 N = 46
2 N = 330
3 N = 60
* Significant at .05 level
** Significant at .01 level

rejection of null hypothesis. This allows to infer that girls experiencing low, moderates and high level of stress differ from one another with respect to six values. Further analysis was done by using Mann-Whitney U test. Results are shown in table 4.14 to 4.19.

Table 4.14 shows that mean rank for less stressful girls is 217.62. Mean rank for girls experiencing moderate stress is 184.44. Mean rank for less stressful girls is greater than that for moderately stressful girls ($Z = -2.0573$, $P < .05$). This indicates that less stressful give more preference to value named equality than moderately stressful girls. Mean rank for less stressful girls is 62.76. Mean rank for girls under high stress is 46.40. The former is significantly greater than the latter ($Z = -2.8729$, $P < .01$). This allows to infer that equality value finds dominant place among girls experiencing low level of stress in society, than that of girls who are under high level of stress. Mean rank for moderately stressed girls is 199.52. Mean rank for highly

Table 4.14: Mean ranks, U-values and Z-values showing differences among girls experiencing low/moderate/high level of stress in society on 'equality' value

S. No.	Level of stress	N	Mean rank	U-value	Z-value	P
1.	LSG	46	217.62	6250.5	–2.0573	.0397*
	MSG	330	184.44			
2.	LSG	46	62.76	954.0	–2.8729	.0041**
	HSG	60	46.40			
3.	MSG	330	199.52	8575.0	–1.7330	.0831
	HSG	60	173.42			

* Significant at .05 level
** Significant at .01 level

stressed girls is 173.42. The former is not significantly different from the latter (Z = –1.7330, P > .05). This indicates that moderately and highly stressed girls do not differ from each other on equality value.

Table content of table 4.15 shows that mean rank for less stressful girls is 231.53. Mean rank for girls experiencing moderate stress in 182.50. The former is greater than the latter (Z = –.33.0067, P < .01). This indicates that girls perceiving moderate stress in society give less importance to happiness than the girl perceiving less stress. Mean rank for less stressful girls is 66.54. Mean rank for highly stressful girls is 43.5. Mean ranks of the two group differ significantly from one another (Z = –4.0360, P < .01). This indicates that girls experiencing low level of stress give more importance to happiness value than the girls experiencing high level of stress. Mean rank for the girls experiencing moderate stress in society is 201.75 mean rank for girls experiencing high level of stress is 161.13. Former is greater than the latter

Table 4.15: Mean ranks, U-value and Z-value showing differences among girls experiencing less/moderate/high stress in society on 'happiness' value

S. No.	Level of stress	N	Mean rank	U-value	Z-value	P
1.	LSG	46	231.53	5610.5	–3.0067	.0026**
	MSG	330	182.50			
2.	LSG	46	66.54	780.0	–4.0360	.0001**
	HSG	60	43.50			
3.	MSG	330	201.75	7838.0	–2.6662	.0077**
	HSG	60	161.13			

* Significant at .05 level

** Significant at .01 level

(Z = –2.6662, P < .01). This allows to inter that girls, experiencing moderate stress excel highly stressed girls on happiness value.

Table 4.16 shows that mean ranks for low stressful girls is 213.48. Mean rank for moderately stressed girls is 185.02. Former is significantly greater than the latter (Z = –2.0044, P < .05). This means that girls experiencing low stress in society give more importance to true friendship value than the highly stressful girls. Mean ranks for less stressful girls is 60.61. Mean rank for girls experiencing high stress is 48.05. Mean ranks for the two group differ significantly from one another (Z = –2.5441, P < .01). This indicates that less stressful girls give more preference to true friendship than those experiencing high stress in society. Mean rank for the moderately stressful girls is 198.68. Mean rank for girls experiencing high stress is 178.02. Mean ranks of both the groups do not vary significantly from each other (Z = –1.5341, P > .05). This

Table 4.16: Mean ranks, U-values and Z-values showing differences among girls experiencing less/moderate/high stress in society on 'true friendship' value

S. No.	Level of stress	N	Mean rank	U-value	Z-value	P
1.	LSG	46	213.48	6441.0	–2.0044	.0450*
	MSG	330	185.02			
2.	LSG	46	60.61	1053.0	–2.5441	.0110**
	HSG	60	48.05			
3.	MSG	330	198.68	8851.5	–1.5341	.1250
	HSG	60	178.02			

* Significant at .05 level
** Significant at .01 level

allows to infer that moderately stressed and highly stressed girls give nearly equal importance to true friendship.

Table 4.17 shows that mean ranks for less stressful girls is 220.75 and mean rank for moderately stressful girls is 184.00. The former is significantly greater than the latter ($Z = -2.3385$, $P < .05$). This allows to infer that girls experiencing less stress in society give more importance to wisdom are moderately stressful. Mean rank for girls experiencing less stress is 62.98. Mean rank for the girls experiencing high stress is 46.23. Mean rank for the less stressful girls is higher than that for highly stressful girls ($Z = -3.0134$, $P < .01$). So, girls experiencing less stress in society have more preference for wisdom than the girls experiencing high stress. Mean rank for moderately stressed girls is 198.84 and mean rank for highly stressed girls is 177.14. Value of ($Z = -1.4695$) is not significant at .05 level. This means that moderately and highly stressful girls do not differ from each other on importance given to wisdom.

Table 4.17: Mean ranks, U-values and Z-values showing differences among girls experiencing less/moderate/high stress in society on 'wisdom' value

S. No.	Level of stress	N	Mean rank	U-value	Z-value	P
1.	LSG	46	220.75	6106.5	–2.3385	.0194*
	MSG	330	184.00			
2.	LSG	46	62.98	944.0	–3.0134	.0026**
	HSG	60	46.23			
3.	MSG	330	198.84	8798.5	–1.4695	.1417
	HSG	60	177.14			

* Significant at .05 level
** Significant at .01 level

Table 4.18 shows that mean ranks for the less stressful girls is 229.61 and mean ranks for moderately stressful girls is 182.77. Mean rank for the less stressful girls is higher than that for the moderately stressful girls (Z = –2.8151, P < 01). This means that less stressful girls attach more importance to forgiveness than the moderately stressful girls. Mean rank for the less stressful girls is 58.07 while mean rank for highly stressful girls is 50.00. Mean rank for the less stressful girls is not significantly different from that for highly stressful girls (Z = –1.4048, P > .05). This means that no significant difference exists between the group on forgiveness value. mean rank for the moderately stressful girls is 193.23. Mean rank for highly stressful girls is 207.98. They do not differ significantly (Z = –.9573, P > .05). This indicates that the two groups do not vary from each other on forgiveness value.

Table 4.18: Mean ranks, U-values and Z-values showing differences among girls experiencing less/moderate/high stress in society on 'forgiveness' value

S. No.	Level of stress	N	Mean rank	U-value	Z-value	P
1.	LSG	46	229.61	5699.0	–2.8151	.0049**
	MSG	330	182.77			
2.	LSG	46	58.07	1170.0	–1.4048	.1601
	HSG	60	50.00			
3.	MSG	330	193.23	9151.0	–.9573	.3384
	HSG	60	207.98			

*Significant at .05 level
** Significant at .01 level

Table 4.19 shows that mean rank for girls experiencing low stress is 229.84. Mean rank for girls experiencing

Table 4.19: Mean ranks, U-values and Z-values showing differences among girls experiencing less/moderate and high stress in society on 'helpful' value

S. No.	Level of stress	N	Mean rank	U-value	Z-value	P
1.	LSG	46	229.84	5688.5	–2.8627	.0042**
	MSG	330	182.74			
2.	LSG	46	61.55	991.5	–2.6222	.0087**
	HSG	60	47.03			
3.	MSG	330	197.36	9285.0	–.7917	.4285
	HSG	60	185.25			

*Significant at .05 level
** Significant at .01 level

moderate stress is 182.74. Mean rank for less stressful girls is greater than that for moderately stressful girls ($Z = -2.8627$, $P < .01$). This means that girls find the value named helpful more important than girls experiencing high level of stress in society. Mean rank for less stressed girls is 61.55. Mean rank for highly stressful girls is 47.03. Mean rank for less stressful girls is higher than the mean rank for highly stressful girls ($Z = -2.6222$. $P < .01$). This allows to infer that highly stressful girls give less importance to "helpful" value than the girls who experience low stress. Mean rank for moderately stressful girls is 197.36. Mean rank for highly stressed girls is 185.25. They are not significantly different ($Z = -.7917$, $P > .05$). This means that girls experiencing moderate and high stress in society give equal importance to value named helpful.

It was hypothesized that "Girls experiencing low, moderate and high level of stress in school do not differ significantly from one another on values".

Table 4.20 presents results of Kruskal Wallis one way ANOVA amongst girls experiencing different levels of stress in school. Observations of chi-square values shows that out of 40 values only four are significant. Two values are significant at .05 level and two values are significant at .01 level. This allows the acceptance of the null hypothesis with respect to 36 values. This mean girls experiencing low, moderate and high level of stress in school do not differ from one another on 36 values namely: a comfortable life, a sense of accomplishment, a world of peace, a world of beauty, equality, family, security, freedom, happiness, inner harmony. National security, pleasure, salvation, self-respect, social recognition, true friendship, wisdom, equity, power, social justice, ambitious, cheerful, clean, courageous, forging, helpful, honesty, imagination, independent, intellectual, logical, loving, obedient, polite, responsible, self-control and self-determinantion.

Significant values of chi-squares were found for four values namely, an exciting life, mature love, broadminded and capable. These allows partial rejection of the null hypothesis. It can be inferred that girls experiencing low, moderate and high level stress in school, differ from one another with respect to four values. Further analysis was done by using Mann-Whitney 'U' test. Result are shown in table 4.21 to 4.24.

Table 4.21 shows that mean rank for less stressful girls is 222.49 and mean rank for moderately stressful girls is 178.85. Mean rank for less stressful girls is greater than that for moderately stressful girls ($Z = -2.7768$, $P < .01$). This indicates that less stressed girls prefer an exciting life more than the highly stressed girls. Mean rank for low stressful girls is 62.17 while mean rank for the girls experiencing high level of stress in school is 58.31. They are not significantly different ($Z = -.6185$, $P > .05$). This means that less stressful and highly stressful girls do not differ from one another on value named an exciting life. Mean

Table 4.20: Means ranks and chi-square values showing difference on various values among girls experiencing low/moderate/high stress in school

Sl. No.	Values	Level of Stress			Chi-Sq.	Sign.
		Low[1]	Moderate[2]	High[3]		
1	2	3	4	5	6	7
1.	A comfortable life	209.04	214.46	244.95	4.9321	.0849
2.	An exciting life	258.16	207.80	238.35	9.3869	.0092**
3.	A sense of accomplishment	230.32	216.95	216.65	.5601	.7557
4.	A world of peace	220.05	221.56	202.84	1.6590	.4363
5.	A world of beauty	232.90	217.72	211.01	1.0817	.5822
6.	Equality	233.32	216.84	214.87	.9245	.6299
7.	Family security	229.05	213.33	234.78	2.2397	.3263
8.	Freedom	216.14	212.51	248.68	5.0356	.0806
9.	Happiness	244.58	218.96	196.10	4.7421	.0934
10.	Inner harmony	234.94	210.67	242.77	4.7860	.0914
11.	Mature love	169.30	225.42	223.95	9.4582	.0088**
12.	National security	241.64	214.43	219.80	2.4689	.2910
13.	Pleasure	236.28	215.83	217.33	1.2763	.5283

(Table Contd...)

(Table 4.20: Contd...)

1	2	3	4	5	6	7
14.	Salvation	215.87	217.29	226.29	.3234	.8507
15.	Self-respect	229.09	215.73	223.38	.7167	.6988
16.	Social recognition	230.33	215.81	222.04	.7446	.6891
17.	True friendship	215.14	217.96	223.68	.2218	.8950
18.	Wisdom	238.38	218.51	203.02	2.6879	.2608
19.	Equity	249.61	212.40	223.21	.3866	.1116
20.	Power	242.55	210.81	236.21	4.6279	.0989
21.	Social justice	250.52	213.63	216.67	4.5016	.1053
22.	Ambitious	223.48	212.74	241.87	3.3026	.1918
23.	Broadminded	253.16	208.64	238.27	7.9592	.0187*
24.	Capable	258.67	214.83	204.67	6.7866	.0336*
25.	Cheerful	189.61	220.85	229.78	3.6886	.1581
26.	Clean	211.30	218.48	224.17	.4517	.7978
27.	Courageous	240.41	212.94	227.80	2.7956	.2471
28.	Forgiving	225.52	211.83	244.60	4.1559	.1252
29.	Helpful	229.80	217.51	214.42	.5479	.7604

(Table Contd...)

(Table 4.20: Contd...)

1	2	3	4	5	6	7
30.	Honesty	231.75	213.04	234.04	2.7931	.2474
31.	Imagination	209.97	219.56	220.11	.2841	.8676
32.	Independent	216.36	217.99	222.60	.0981	.9521
33.	Intellectual	225.95	222.64	193.13	3.4248	.1804
34.	Logical	217.67	218.36	219.78	.0099	.9951
35.	Loving	238.50	217.12	209.51	1.8328	.4000
36.	Obedient	225.70	219.14	209.87	.5773	.7493
37.	Polite	225.75	221.34	199.44	2.0323	.3620
38.	Responsible	239.94	215.21	217.43	1.8877	.3891
39.	Self-control	238.55	213.51	226.56	2.2041	.3322
40.	Self-determinantion	210.72	220.10	216.98	.3023	.8597

1 N = 52
2 N = 317
3 N = 67
* Significant at .05 level
** Significant at .01 level

rank for moderately stressed girls is 187.95. Mean rank for girls experiencing high level of stress is 214.04. They are not significantly different from one another (Z = –1.7749, P > .05. This indicates that the moderately and highly stressful girls do not vary significantly from one another on value named an exciting life.

Table 4.21: Mean ranks, U-values and Z-value showing differences among girls experiencing low, moderate and high level of stress in school on 'an exciting life' value

S. No.	Level of stress	N	Mean rank	U-value	Z-value	P
1.	LSG	52	222.49	6292.5	–2.7768	.055**
	MSG	317	178.85			
2.	LSG	52	62.17	1629.0	–.6185	.5363
	HSG	67	58.31			
3.	MSG	317	187.95	9176.5	–1.7749	.0759
	HSG	67	214.04			

* Significant at .05 level
** Significant at .01 level

Table 4.22 shows that mean rank for the girls who are experiencing less stress is 143.13 and mean rank for moderately stressful girls is 191.87. Mean rank of less stressed girls is lower than that for the moderately stressed girls (Z = –3.1325, P < .01). This indicates that less stressful girls give less importance to value named mature love than the girls experiencing moderate stress in school. Mean rank for less stressful girls is 52.67. Mean rank for highly stressful girls is 65.69. The former is significantly lower than the mean rank for the highly stressful girls (Z = –2.1144, P < .05). This indicates that as compared to girls experiencing high stress in school, girls experiencing low stress attach less importance to value named mature love. Mean rank of moderately stressful girls is 192.55. Mean rank for highly stressful girl is 192.26. Mean rank of the two groups do not differ significantly (Z = –.0198, P > .05). This indicates that moderately and highly stressful girls assign equal importance to value named mature love.

Table 4.22: Mean ranks, U-values and Z-values showing differences among girls experiencing low, moderate and high level of stress in school on value named 'mature love'

Sl. No.	Level of stress	N	Mean rank	U-value	Z-value	P
1.	LSG	52	143.13	6064.5	–3.1325	.0017**
	MSG	317	191.87			
2.	LSG	52	52.67	1361.0	–2.1144	.0345*
	HSG	67	65.69			
3.	MSG	317	192.55	10603.5	–.0198	.9849
	HSG	67	192.26			

* Significant at .05 level
** Significant at .01 level

Table 4.23 shows that mean rank for less stressful girls is 217.85 while mean rank for moderately stressful girls is 179.61. The former is significantly greater than the latter (Z = –2.4575, P > .01). This implies that less stressful girl give more preference to broadminded value than the girls experiencing moderate stress in school. Mean rank for the less stressful girls is 61.82. Mean rank for highly stressful girls is 58.59. They are not significantly different (Z = –.5333, P > .05). This means that both less and moderately stressful girls do not vary from each other on broadminded value. Mean rank for moderately stressful girls is 188.02 while mean rank for highly stressful girls is 213.68. They do not differ significantly from one another (Z = –1.7643, P > .05). So, it can be inferred that moderately stressful girls do not differ from highly stressful girls on braodminded value.

Table 4.23: Mean ranks, U-values and Z-values showing differences among girls experiencing less/moderate/high level of stress in school on 'broadminded' value

Sl. No.	Level of stress	N	Mean rank	U-value	Z-value	P
1.	LSG	52	217.85	6534.0	–2.4575	.0140**
	MSG	317	179.61			
2.	LSG	52.	61.82	1647.5	–.5333	.5938
	HSG	67	58.59			
3.	MSG	317	188.02	9200.5	–1.7643	.0777
	HSG	67	213.68			

* Significant at .05 level
** Significant at .01 level

Table 4.24 shows mean rank for less stressed girls is 217.29. Mean rank for moderately stressful girls is 179.70. Mean rank of less stressful girls is greater than that for highly stressful girls (Z = –2.4349, P < .05). This allows to infer that less stressful girls give more importance to value named capable than the high stressful girls. Mean rank for less stressful girls is 67.88 while mean rank for highly stressful girls is 53.88. Mean rank for less stressed girls is greater than that for highly stressed girls (Z = –2.2880, P < .05). It indicates that girls experiencing less stress in school attach more importance to value named capable than the girls who are highly stressed. Mean rank for moderately stressed girls is 194.13 while mean rank for highly stressed girls is 184.79. They do not differ significantly from one another (Z = –.6447, P > .05). This indicates that girls experiencing moderate and high stress in school give equal importance to the value named capable.

Table 4.24: Mean ranks, U-values and Z-values showing differences among girls experiencing less/moderate/high level of stress in school on 'capable' value

Sl. No.	Level of stress	N	Mean rank	U-value	Z-value	P
1.	LSG	52	217.29	6563.0	–2.4349	.0149*
	MSG	317	179.70			
2.	LSG	52	67.88	1332.0	–2.2880	.0221*
	HSG	67	53.88			
3.	MSG	317	194.13	10103.0	–.6447	.5191
	HSG	67	184.79			

* Significant at .05 level
** Significant at .01 level

It was hypothesized that "Girls experiencing low, moderate and high level of stress in self do not differ from one another in values".

Table 4.25 presents results of Kruskal Wallis one way ANOVA for values among girls experiencing different level of stress in self observation of chi-square values shows that out of 40 values only three are significant. One is significant at .05 level while two values are significant at .01 level. This allows acceptance of the null hypothesis with respect to 37 values. This means that girls experiencing low, moderate and high level of stress related to self do not differ from one another on 37 values namely: a comfortable life, an exciting

Table 4.25: Means ranks and chi-square values showing differences on various values among girls experiencing low/moderate/high level of stress in self

Sl. No.	Value	Level of Stress			Chi-Sq.	Sign.
		Low[1]	Moderate[2]	High[3]		
1	2	3	4	5	6	7
1.	A comfortable life	214.75	220.76	213.04	.4145	.8128
2.	An exciting life	188.47	223.72	221.75	4.0924	.1292
3.	A sense of accomplishment	242.34	211.99	224.54	3.3647	.1859
4.	A world of peace	230.29	212.38	232.04	2.9100	.2334
5.	A world of beauty	214.12	213.37	240.43	3.5133	.1726
6.	Equality	232.44	214.47	222.84	2.2608	.5324
7.	Family security	202.06	225.63	204.72	3.2592	.1960
8.	Freedom	201.06	217.15	236.33	3.0848	.2139
9.	Happiness	244.30	220.09	193.60	6.2451	.0440*
10.	Inner harmony	201.86	220.69	222.83	1.2834	.5264
11.	Mature love	166.39	224.86	233.93	12.8358	.0016**
12.	National security	204.96	220.59	220.90	.9486	.6223
13.	Pleasure	231.37	213.62	226.76	1.5283	.4657

(Table Contd...)

(Table 4.25: Contd...)

1	2	3	4	5	6	7
14.	Salvation	223.43	216.26	223.00	.3025	.8596
15.	Self-respect	216.13	222.66	205.11	1.4516	.4839
16.	Social recognition	225.02	215.99	222.80	.4222	.8097
17.	True friendship	216.80	214.88	232.93	1.8719	.3922
18.	Wisdom	233.70	215.75	217.25	1.1913	.5512
19.	Equity	220.45	215.81	226.85	.5528	.7585
20.	Power	220.16	214.61	231.46	1.2089	.5464
21.	Social justice	218.31	212.41	240.81	3.7789	.1512
22.	Ambitious	171.98	225.14	228.77	10.3396	.0057**
23.	Broadminded	212.68	215.88	232.34	1.3030	.5213
24.	Capable	217.86	217.65	222.07	.0852	.9583
25.	Cheerful	207.06	222.00	214.23	.8893	.6411
26.	Clean	216.23	217.66	223.24	.2176	.8969
27.	Courageous	200.64	223.54	213.39	1.9802	.3715
28.	Forgiving	226.10	217.80	215.41	.2923	.8640
29.	Helpful	216.71	218.55	219.64	.0202	.9899

(Table Contd...)

(Table 4.25: Contd...)

1	2	3	4	5	6	7
30.	Honesty	227.79	214.51	226.15	1.1750	.5557
31.	Imagination	198.95	224.00	212.95	2.2631	.3225
32.	Independent	202.88	223.79	210.80	1.8786	.3909
33.	Intellectual	214.14	219.09	219.57	.0890	.9565
34.	Logical	197.68	221.85	221.72	1.9715	.3732
35.	Loving	233.93	218.15	208.36	1.5473	.4613
36.	Obedient	213.42	221.42	211.65	.5800	.7483
37.	Polite	203.56	223.94	209.76	1.9420	.3787
38.	Responsible	228.14	223.19	194.28	4.1025	.1286
39.	Self-Control	218.90	218.78	217.19	.0115	.9943
40.	Self-determination	221.62	214.44	238.40	2.9246	.2317

1 N = 60
2 N = 295
3 N = 81
* Significant at .05 level
** Significant at .01 level

life, sense of accomplishment, a world of peace, a world of beauty, equality, family security, freedom, inner harmony, national security, pleasure, salvation, self-respect, social recognition, true friendship, wisdom, equity, power, social justice, broadminded, capable, cheerful, clean, courageous, forgiving, helpful, honesty, imagination, independent, intellectual, logical, loving, obedient, polite, responsible, self-control and self-determinantion.

Significant values of chi-squares were found for three values namely: happiness, mature love and ambitious. These values allow partial rejection of the null hypothesis. This allows us to infer that girls experiencing low, moderate and high level of stress in home differ from one another with respect to three values.

Further analysis was done by using Mann-Whitney 'U' test. Results are shown in the following table 4.26 to 4.28.

Table 4.26 shows mean rank for less stressful girls is 194.29. Mean rank for moderately stressed girls is 174.69.

Table 4.26: Mean ranks, U-values and Z-values showing differences among girls experiencing low, moderate and high stress in self on value 'happiness'

Sl. No.	Level of stress	N	Mean rank	U-value	Z-value	P
1.	LSG	60	194.29	7872.5	–1.4155	.1569
	MSG	295	174.69			
2.	LSG	60	80.51	1859.5	–2.4794	.0132**
	HSG	81	63.96			
3.	MSG	295	193.40	10501.0	–1.7388	.0821
	HSG	81	170.64			

* Significant at .05 level
** Significant at .01 level

They do not differ significantly (Z = –1.4155, P > .05). This indicates that no significant difference exists between the groups on value happiness. Mean rank for less stressful girls is 80.51 while mean rank for highly stressful girls is 63.96 mean rank for less stressful girls is greater than that for highly stressful girls (Z = –2.4794, P < .01). This allows us to infer that girls experiencing less self stress give more importance to value named happiness than the girls experiencing high self stress. Mean rank for moderately and highly stressful girls are 193.40 and 170.64 respectively. They do not differ significantly from one another (Z = –1.7388, P > .05). This allows to infer that moderately stressed girls do not differ from highly stressed girls on value named happiness.

Table 4.27 shows mean rank for less stressful girls is 138.02. Mean rank for moderately stressful girls is 186.13. Mean rank for less stressful girls is lower than for moderately stressful girls (Z = –3.3984, P < .01). This indicates that girls experiencing low self stress give least

Table 4.27: Mean ranks, U-values and Z-values showing differences among girls experiencing low/moderate/high level of stress in self on 'mature love' value

Sl. No.	Level of stress	N	Mean rank	U-value	Z-value	P
.1.	LSG	60	138.02	6451.5	–3.3984	.0007**
	MSG	295	186.13			
2.	LSG	60	58.87	1702.0	–3.983	.0019**
	HSG	81	79.90			
3.	MSG	295	186.73	11426.0	–.6167	.5374
	HSG	81	194.94			

* Significant at .05 level
** Significant at .01 level

importance to value named mature love than the girls experiencing moderate self stress. Mean rank for less stressful girls is 58.87 and mean rank for the highly stressful girls is 79.99. Latter is greater than the former (Z = –3.0983, P < 01). This allows to infer that highly stressed girls give more importance to value named mature love than the girls experiencing less self stress.

Mean rank for moderately stressful girls is 186.73 while mean rank for highly stressful girls is 194.94. They do not differ significantly from one another (Z = .6167, P > .05). This means that both moderately and highly stressed girls give equal importance to mature love.

The table 4.28 shows that mean rank for the less stressful girls is 141.41. Mean rank for the moderately stressful girls is 185.44. The mean rank of moderately stressful girls is greater than that for less stressful girls (Z = –3.1427, P < .01). This means that as compared to girls experiencing less self stress, girls experiencing moderate

Table 4.28: Mean ranks, U-values and Z-values showing differences among girls experiencing low/moderate/high levels of self stress on 'ambitious' value

Sl. No.	Level of stress	N	Mean rank	U-value	Z-value	P
1.	LSG	60	141.41	6654.5	–3.1427	.0017**
	MSG	295	185.44			
2.	LSG	60	61.07	1834.0	–2.5796	.0099**
	HSG	81	78.36			
3.	MSG	295	187.70	11711.5	–.2854	.7754
	HSG	81	191.41			

* Significant at .05 level
** Significant at .01 level

self stressed give more importance to the value named ambitious. Mean rank for low stress girls is 61.07 while mean rank for highly stressful girls is 78.36. The former is significantly lower than the latter (Z = 2.5796, P < .01). This allows to infer that highly stressed girls give more importance to ambitious value than the less stressed girls. Mean rank for the moderately stressed girls is 187.70 while mean rank for the highly stressed girls is 191.41. They do not differ significantly from one another (Z = –.2854, P > .05). This means that moderately and highly stressed girls do not differ on value named ambitious.

It was hypothesized that "Girls experiencing low moderate and high overall stress do not differ from each other in values."

Table 4.29 presents result of Kruskal-Wallis one way ANOVA used for comparing values among girls experiencing different level of all stress. Observations of the chi-square values shows that out of 40 values, only three values are significant. One value is significant at .05 level while two values are significant at .01 level. This allows acceptance of the hypothesis with respect to 37 values. This means that girls experiencing low, moderate and high overall stress do not differ from one another on 37 values, namely: A comfortable life, an exciting life, a sense of accomplishment, a world of peace, a world of beauty, equality, family security, freedom, national security, pleasure, salvation, self-respect, social recognition, true friendship, wisdom, power, social justice, ambitious, broadminded, capable, cheerful, clean, courageous forgiving, helpful, honesty, imagination, independent, intellectual, logical, loving, obedient, polite, responsible, self-control, self-determinantion.

Significant values of chi-square were found for three values namely: Happiness, mature love and equity. These vales allow partial rejection of the null hypothesis. This leads us to infer that girls experiencing low, moderate and high level of overall stress differ from one another with respect three values.

Table 4.29: Mean ranks and chi-square values showing differences on various values among girls experiencing different levels of overall stress

Sl. No.	Values	Level of Stress			Chi-Sq.	Sign.
		Low[1]	Moderate[2]	High[3]		
1	2	3	4	5	6	7
1.	A comfortable life	211.10	214.14	246.51	5.1577	.0759
2.	An exciting life	235.25	216.40	214.20	1.1878	.5522
3.	A sense of accomplishment	245.18	214.13	216.73	3.1293	.2092
4.	A world of peace	224.27	219.63	207.88	.8062	.6682
5.	A world of beauty	230.78	216.80	216.15	.7122	.7004
6.	Equality	242.73	215.57	211.74	2.7016	.2590
7.	Family security	207.42	214.96	245.69	4.0686	.1308
8.	Freedom	212.86	215.79	236.80	1.7680	.4131
9.	Happiness	268.47	218.28	175.88	17.5933	.0002**
10.	Inner harmony	224.12	211.29	249.16	5.1413	.0765
11.	Mature love	172.52	224.25	230.32	9.1118	.0105**
12.	National security	219.20	218.44	218.34	.0013	.9993
13.	Pleasure	230.68	213.39	233.08	2.0488	.3590

(Table Contd...)

(Table 4.29: Contd...)

1	2	3	4	5	6	7
14.	Salvation	209.96	217.80	229.44	.7857	.6751
15.	Self-respect	228.22	213.81	233.17	1.8939	.3879
16.	Social recognition	230.29	215.91	220.98	.7376	.6915
17.	True friendship	229.78	216.87	216.70	.7318	.6936
18.	Wisdom	238.68	219.70	194.94	4.3183	.1154
19.	Equity	256.64	209.93	227.45	7.5765	.0226*
20.	Power	231.16	215.43	222.59	.8634	.6494
21.	Social justice	240.47	213.64	223.25	2.6500	.2658
22.	Ambitious	204.57	219.16	227.41	1.0979	.5775
23.	Broadminded	229.00	210.62	248.23	5.4874	.0643
24.	Capable	251.09	214.39	210.30	4.6453	.0980
25.	Cheerful	203.28	221.43	217.35	1.0836	.5817
26.	Clean	200.43	220.91	222.44	1.9650	.3744
27.	Courageous	236.05	211.65	236.98	3.7178	.1558
28.	Forgiving	237.51	212.26	232.66	3.0243	.2204
29.	Helpful	236.53	219.17	199.41	2.8311	.2428

(Table Contd...)

(Table 4.29: Contd...)

1	2	3	4	5	6	7
30.	Honesty	239.91	214.00	221.97	2.6377	.2674
31.	Imagination	190.70	224.46	213.38	3.7029	.1570
32.	Independent	216.42	218.15	222.05	.0736	.9639
33.	Intellectual	230.63	215.24	223.98	.9011	.6373
34.	Logical	215.22	221.96	204.30	1.1296	.5685
35.	Loving	234.20	220.3	195.63	3.3035	.1917
36.	Obedient	241.96	217.49	202.98	3.4371	.1793
37.	Polite	222.88	218.57	214.34	.1497	.9279
38.	Responsible	235.58	217.18	210.09	1.4743	.4785
39.	Self-control	236.45	214.64	221.85	1.5598	.4585
40.	Self-determination	221.18	217.47	229.13	.7206	.6975

1 N = 56
2 N = 316
3 N = 64
* Significant at .05 level
** Significant at .01 level

Further analysis was done by using Mann-Whitney 'U' test. Results are shown in the following tables 4.30 to 4.32.

Table 4.30 shows that mean rank for girls experiencing low overall stress is 223.74. Mean rank for the moderately stressful girls is 179.90. The former is greater than the latter (Z = –2.9493, P <.01). This allows us to infer that girls experiencing low overall stress give more importance to happiness value that the moderately stressful girls. Mean rank for the less stressful girls is 73.23 while mean rank for highly stressful girls is 49.36. The former is greater than the latter (Z = –3.9561, P <.01). This indicates that less stressful girls give more importance to value named happiness than the girls experiencing high stress. Mean rank for moderately stressful girls is 196.88 while mean rank for highly stressed girls is 159.02. Mean rank of moderately stressed girls is greater than the mean rank for

Table 4.30: Mean ranks, U-values and Z-values showing differences among girls experiencing low, moderate and high level of overall stress on 'happiness' value

Sl. No.	Level of stress	N	Mean rank	U-value	Z-value	P
1.	LSG	56	223.74	6762.5	–2.9493	.0032**
	MSG	316	179.90			
2.	LSG	56	73.23	1079.0	–3.9561	.0001**
	HSG	64	49.36			
3.	MSG	316	196.88	8097.5	–2.6110	.0090**
	HSG	64	159.02			

* Significant at .05 level
** Significant at .01 level

highly stressed girls (Z = –2.6110, P < .01). This lead us to infer that more preference is given to happiness by the moderately stressed girls than highly stressed girls.

Table 4.31 shows that the mean rank for the less stressful girls is 147.99 and that for moderately stressful girls is 193.32. Mean rank for the less stressful girls is smaller than that for the girls experiencing moderate stress (Z = –2.9885, P < .01). This indicates that girls experiencing less stress give less importance to value named mature love than the girls experiencing moderate stress. Mean rank

Table 4.31: Mean ranks, U-values and Z-values showing differences among girls experiencing low moderate and high level of overall stress on 'matre love' value

Sl. No.	Level of stress	N	Mean rank	U-value	Z-value	P
1.	LSG	56	147.99	6691.5	–2.9885	.0028**
	MSG	316	193.32			
2.	LSG	56	53.03	1373.5	–2.2539	.0242*
	HSG	64	67.04			
3.	MSC	316	189.43	9774.0	–.4314	.6662
	HSG	64	195.78			

* Significant at .05 level
** Significant at .01 level

for the less stressful girls is 53.03 while mean rank for the highly stressful girls is 67.04. The former is smaller than the latter (Z = –2.2539, P < .05). This indicates that highly stressed girls give more importance to mature love than the girls experiencing less stress. Mean rank for moderately stressed girls is 189.43 and mean rank for highly stressed girls is 195.78. They do not differ significantly (Z = –.4314,

P > .05). This indicates that no significant difference exist between the groups on mature love.

Table 4.32 shows that mean rank for less stressful girls is 220.52. Mean rank for moderately stressful girls is 180.47. Mean rank for less stressful girls is higher than the mean rank for moderately stressful girls (Z = –2.6851, P < .01). This allows us to infer that less stressful girls consider value named equity as more important than the moderately stressful girls. Mean rank for less stressful girls is 64.63 while mean rank for highly stressful girls is 56.89. They do not differ significantly from one another (Z = 1.3096, P > .05). This means that they give equal importance to equity. Mean rank for moderately stressful girls is 187.96 and mean rank for highly stressful girls is 203.06. Mean ranks for both the group do not differ significantly from one another (Z = –1.0448, P > .05). This means that moderately and highly stressful girls give equal importance to equity value.

Table 4.32: Mean ranks, U-values and Z-values showing differences among girls experiencing low, moderate and high level of overall stress on 'equity' values

Sl. No.	Level of stress	N	Mean rank	U-value	Z-value	P
1.	LSG	56	220.52	6943.0	–2.6851	.0073**
	MSG	316	180.47			
2.	LSG	56	64.63	1561.0	–1.3096	.1903
	HSG	64	56.89			
3.	MSG	316	187.96	9308.0	–1.0448	.2961
	HSG	64	203.06			

* Significant at .05 level
** Significant at .01 level

Discussion

Our efforts to study effect of stress on values revealed that high, moderate and low stressed girls differ from one another on fifteen values. Out of these fifteen values namely: A world of beauty, happiness, pleasure, wisdom, helpful, imagination, equality, true friendship, forgiving, an exciting life, mature love, broadminded, capable, ambitious and equity, only mature love and ambitious are provided more importance by the highly stressed girls.

In comparison to girls experiencing low stress, girls experiencing moderate and high level of stress overall as well as that related to school and self place more emphasis on mature love value. Rokech, (1973) claimed that values are cognitive transformation of needs. According to this view when one tells about his value, he is surely telling about his needs. High value placed on mature love by moderate and highly stressful girls suggests about their high n-affiliation. It seems that as the stress increases more importance is assigned to mature love study by Schachter (1959) predicted that affilative behaviour appears in response to social anxiety. Zimbardo and Formica (1963) showed that with the induction of anxiety, subjects low in self esteem exhibited a greater affiliative tendency than those with high self esteem. Vogal et. al., (1959) has shown that individual high in affiliation motive feel more stress when affiliation motive is endangered.

As compared to girls experiencing less stress, moderately and highly stress in self prefer 'ambitious' value. It can be inferred that moderately and highly stressed girls are more achievement oriented. They seem to have high need achievement. This draws support from the findings of Ansari, Udupa and Agrawal (1979) who showed that patient with stress disorders had a high level of anxiety as well as stronger achievement motive than controls. Vogel et. al., (1959) demonstrated that stress is minimal when the stimulus conditions occur in the presence of a weak motive and greater when a powerful motive is engaged. He found that the group high in achievement motive showed greatest reaction when achievement motive was threatened. Burnam, et. al., (1973) provided experimented evidence to show that those having competitive achievement striving are more prone to stress than those who are low in need for achievement. Hamiltaon (1979) thinks that measure potential sources of stress resides in each person's systems of needs. Considerable strain can be experienced in satisfying achievement motivation. Individual have two types of orientation to satisfy this need: to seek or approach success and to avoid failure. Stressor may be assumed to be potentially present in both orientations, where, however, there is a fear of failure anxiety tends to be high and number of goal and/or the level of goal achievement is reduced, whereas success seeking is characterized by low level of anxiety, determination to overcome obstacles and optimistic attitude towards outcome (Atkinson and Feather, 1966). So, it can be said that girls experiencing less stress might not be having strong need for achievement and this may be responsible for the low importance they give to 'ambitious' value.

In comparison to less stressed, moderately stress girls give more importance to 'imagination' value. Girls experiencing high stress in home do not differ from girls experiencing low or moderate stress. Girls experiencing less as well as high level of stress are comparatively lower with respect to the emphasis on 'imagination' value. It reveals the inimical influence of high stress. It is obvious that girls experiencing high level of stress will spend more time in coping with their stress and they will tend to postpone imagination. Low stress may not help in developing the need for creative thinking. Paramesh (1970) observed that the creative individual is neither extraverted nor introverted and is neither high nor low in anxiety. Ariel's findings (1988) show that stress adversely affects creativity in science. These views indicate that high and low stress do not facilitate development of creative thinking and moderate level of stress may help enhancing motivation to use imagination. This lends support to over finding.

In comparison to low stress girls, girls experiencing high stress show less preference to values like happiness, wisdom, helpful, a world of beauty, pleasure, equality, true friendship and capable values. Most sensitive value affected by stress is happiness. Girls experiencing moderate and high level of stress overall as well as related to home, school and self put less emphasis on happiness values. Happiness value stands for contentedness and satisfaction but stress may arise when there is dissatisfaction. So, it is quite reasonable to infer that girls experiencing moderate or high level of stress may not feel happy. Various negative life events are reported before the onset of the diseases like coronary heart disease (Hinkle, 1974, Bhargava, Sharma and Agrawal, 1982), ulcerative colitis (Chakravorty, Shah and Parikh, 1983, Khurana 1983), breast cancer (Christoper, 1979), carcinoma in various part of the body (Udupa, 1980), pulmonary tuberculosis (Gupta and Srivastava, 1983) and psychiatric disorders (Saxena, Dubey, Sundaram and Chawla, 1983). There diseases or even one's views about the likehood of their occurrence may make one unhappy. Dissatisfaction of needs is bound to lead to unhappiness and stress.

'Wisdom' value stand for mature understanding of life. Girls experiencing high stress in home and society give less importance to wisdom value than less stressful girls. Our daily experiences show that under stressful conditions persons are not likely to exhibit a mature understanding of life. With the passage of time highly stressed girls can learn to give low priority to wisdom value. This reflected in the result of this study.

'True friendship' value is rated low by highly stressed girls than it is by girls experiencing less stress in society. This draw support from the findings of Buunk and Hooren, Byrne, et. al., Teichman, Buunk and Schaufeli. Buunk and Hooren (1992) concluded on the basis of research on inter personal attraction that stress, in the form of negative effect may make others look less attractive. Research by Byrne (1971) has shown that people in whom the negative mood was induced perceive others less positively than people in whom appositive mood is induced. Teichmann (1973) found that stressful circumstances at work may decrease actual affiliation with others due to fear of looking incompetent. Buunk and Schaufeli have shown that although individuals with a high degree of occupational stress had a relatively high need for affiliation, a desire to talk with others about problems at works, they tended at the same time to avoid the company of their colleagues. These studies show that girls experiencing high stress in society may give less importance to true friendship value. Coyne, (1976) has provided evidence to show that interacting with depressed individual is seen to be aversive. Literature on social comparison shows that individual under stress are often avoided by others, a process through which people who are under high stress may end up isolated (Rabbie, 1963) and therefore they may not be in contact of reality and are not having friends who can constantly share and support their worries and anxieties. Because of their own perceived stress, the high stressed girls may consider that true friendship is not possible in reality, hence, it is less important though the highly stress girls may long for it. Girls experiencing high and moderate stress in home and society show less preference for 'helpful' value than those who are less stressed. It seems that girls under high stress do not seem to maintain reciprocity in their interpersonal relationship. Gottllieb (1985) suggests that psychiatric patient tend to maintain asymmetrical helping relationships, failing to reciprocate the support they receive from others. This lends support to the above finding.

'A world of beauty' value finds less importance place among highly stressed girls than those who are experiencing less stress in home. It seems as if the stress has destroyed the young adolescent's initial appreciation of beauty in world.

'Pleasure' value finds less importance place among girls who are experiencing moderate are high stress in home. It may be that due to stress in home highly stress girls might not be experiencing pleasure in life. It is also possible that girls might be feeling stressed as they tried to adopt stereotype image of a student, who, according to our Indian tradition, should not give an important place to pleasure. They might by perceiving some degree of role-conflict also.

Girls experiencing high stress in society find 'equality' value less important than girls under low stress. Girls experiencing moderate and high stress are equal on equality value. Equality is a social value girls under stress might be perceiving inequality in the social system. Perhaps their appreciation for equality value have not been reinforced positively by different social institutions.

'Capable' value is given less importance by highly and moderately stressful girls whereas girls experiencing low stress in school put more emphasis on capable value. Sells (1970) emphasized the critical role of cognitive system in controlling stress reactions. Onset of stress is largely determined by individual's ability to make an effective response and his assessment of the consequences of failure. This shows that the less stressful girls will give more importance to capability. Values like equity, forgiving, an exiting life, broadminded, differentiated less and moderately stressed girls in overall society and school respectively whereas girls experiencing high stress are equal to less stressful as well as moderately stressful girls.

Girls experiencing low overall stress show more preference for equity value. Studies have shown the importance of a global perception of equity for satisfaction in personal relationships (Hatfielt, Traupmann, Sprecher, Utne and Hay, 1984; Van Yperen & Buunk, 1990). Roberto and Scott (1986) found less distress among older adults who perceived their relationship with their best friends as equitable. In equity theory, the most influential social exchange theory, inter personal relationships are viewed as consisting of an exchange of benefits governed by a norm of equity. It is predicted that any disturbance of this expected reciprocity, either in the form of not being able to return benefits or not receiving benefits in return from other, will leave to negative affective reactions (Walster, Walster & Berscheid, 1978). It indicates that girls perceiving moderate stress may not be perceiving equitable relationship and this may be the reason for providing less importance to equity value.

Girls experiencing high or low stress in school and society have been found to give equal importance to 'broadminded' and 'forgiving' values respectively. Moderately stressed girls gave comparatively low importance to these values than less stressed girls. Low stressed girls in school in comparison to moderately stressed girls, give more importance to an exiting life.

Values which have not been found to be affected by stress-overall as well as that in the four areas of home, school, society and self are a comfortable life, a sense of accomplishment, a world of peace, family security, freedom, inner harmony, national security, salvation, self respect, social recognition, power, social justice, cheerful, clean, courageous, honesty, independent, intellectual, logical, loving, obedient, polite, responsible, self control, and self determinantion. It may be that development of these value is not vulnerable to the effects of stress.

Effects of Stress on Moral Judgement

Results

Results of analysis done for finding out weather girls experiencing different levels of stress—overall as well as stress in home, school, society and self, differ with respect to overall moral judgement and moral reasoning as shown for the different items of the Moral Judgement Questionnaire.

It was hypothesized that "Girls experiencing different levels of stress do not differ significantly on moral judgement". Kruskal Wallis one way ANOVA was used to test this hypothesis. Results have been shown in the Table 4.33.

Observations of table 4.33 shows that value of chi-squares for home society, school and self areas are .2130, .2675, .1197, and .2066 respectively. They are not significant at .05 level. So, it can be inferred that girls experiencing low, moderate and high stress in home/school/society/self areas do not differ from one another on moral judgement.

Table 4.33: Comparison of overall moral judgement among girls experiencing different level of stress in home, society, school and self

Sl. No.	Independent variable	Level of stress	N	Mean rank	Chi-squire	P
1.	Stress in home	Low	57	229.77		
		Moderate	310	221.69	3.0933	.2130
		High	69	194.86		
2.	Stress in society	Low	46	234.37		
		Moderate	330	220.29	2.6370	.2675
		High	60	196.48		
3.	Stress in school	Low	52	247.74		
		Moderate	317	217.57	4.2448	.1197
		High	67	200.20		
4.	Stress in self	Low	60	229.20		
		Moderate	295	222.33	3.1542	.2066
		High	81	196.64		

* Significant at .05 level
** Significant at .01 level

It may be that girls experiencing different levels of stress may differ in moral judgement exhibited for various items of MJQ*. So, data pertaining to moral judgement for

* MJQ: Refers to Moral Judgement Questionnaire

various items of MJQ for girls experiencing different levels of stress, in different areas was analysed. Results has been shown in table 4.34 to 4.42.

It was hypothesized that "Girls experiencing less, moderate and high stress in home do not differ from one another on moral judgement as measured by various items of MJQ".

Table 4.34 presents results of Kruskal Wallis on one way ANOVA for various items of MJQ among girls experiencing different level of stress in home. Observation of chi-square values shows that out of twelve, only one is significant at .05 level. This allows acceptance of the hypothesis with respect to eleven items of M.J.Q. It means girls experiencing less, moderate and high stress in home do not differ from one another on moral reasoning exhibited in case of eleven items of MJQ. Significant value of chi-square was found for ninth item of MJQ. This difference allows rejection of null hypothesis with regard to this item. This leads us to infer that girls experiencing low, moderate and high level of stress in home differ from one another with respect to moral judgement as measured by the item ninth of M.J.Q. on demand of death by a beautiful girl.

Further analysis was done by using Mann-Whitney 'U' test. Result is shown in the table 4.35.

Table 4.35 shows mean ranks for less stress girls is 202.41. Mean rank for moderately stressed girls is 180.61. Mean ranks for both groups do not differ from one another ($Z = -1.4723$, $P > .05$). This implies that both less and moderately stressed girls do not differ from one another on moral judgement as measured by the ninth item of MJQ. Mean ranks for less and highly stressed girls are 72.03 and 56.46 respectively. Mean rank for less stressed girls is significantly greater than that for highly stressed girls ($Z = -2.4803$, $P < .01$). This indicates that less stressful girls excel highly stressful girls on moral judgement as measured by the ninth item of MJQ. Mean rank for girls experiencing

Table 4.34: Difference among girls experiencing less, moderate and high stress in home on various items of Moral Judgement Questionnaire

S. No.	Item Title	Level of Stress			Chi-Sq.	Sign.
		Low[1]	Moderate[2]	High[3]		
	Items of M.J.Q.					
1.	Half cost ticket	217.42	216.91	226.52	.3900	.8228
2.	Lost examination question paper	235.52	216.18	214.85	1.3845	.5004
3.	Mischievous student's group	221.68	220.30	207.78	.8177	.6644
4.	Dilemma of friendship	215.25	216.10	231.99	1.1183	.5717
5.	Obtaining fruits without payment	224.41	221.96	198.05	2.4572	.2927
6.	Broken chair for the teacher	241.10	216.57	208.49	2.7514	.2527
7.	Act of a ball	221.61	222.25	199.08	2.1399	.3430
8.	Unclaimed money	216.59	222.08	203.98	1.6042	.4484
9.	Demand for killing by a beautiful girl	245.44	219.25	192.88	5.8607	.0534*
10.	Dishonestful honesty	226.61	219.50	207.33	.9347	.6267
11.	Sympathy of a thief friend	229.20	221.45	196.43	3.1346	.2086
12.	Improper action and friendship	225.94	222.42	194.76	4.0288	.1334

1 N = 56
2 N = 310
3 N = 69
* Significant at .05 level
** Significant at .01 level

Table 4.35: Difference among less, moderately and highly stressful girls in home on ninth items of MJQ

Sl. No.	Level of stress	N	Mean rank	U-value	Z-value	P
1.	Low	57	202.41	7785.5	–1.4723	.1409
	Moderate	310	180.61			
2.	Low	57	72.03	1480.5	–2.4803	.0131**
	High	69	56.46			
3.	Moderate	310	194.13	9413.5	–1.6141	.1065
	High	69	171.43			

* Significant at .05 level
** Significant at .01 level

moderate and high stress are 194.13 and 171.43 respectively. Former is not different from latter (Z = –1.6141, P > .05). It leads us to infer that moderately and highly stressed girls are equal on moral judgement as measured by ninth items of M.J.Q.

It was hypothesized that "girls experiencing less, moderate and high stress in society do not differ from one another on moral judgement as measured by various items of MJQ".

Table 4.36 presents results of Kruskal Wallis one way ANOVA for various items of MJQ for girls experiencing less, moderate and high level of stress in society. Observation of chi-square values shows that out of twelve items of MJQ only one is significant at .05 level. This allows acceptance of null hypothesis with respect to moral judgement as measured by eleven items of MJQ. Significant value of chi-square is found for sixth item of MJQ, broken chair for the teacher. It is significant .05 level. This allows rejection of null hypothesis with respect to moral judgement as measured by the sixth item. This means that girls

Table 4.36: Difference on various items of MJQ among girls experiencing less, moderate and high stress in society

S. No.	Item Title	Level of Stress Low[1]	Moderate[2]	High[3]	Chi-Sq.	Sign.
	Items of M.J.Q.					
1.	Half cost ticket	212.65	220.10	214.19	.2604	.8779
2.	Lost examination question paper	242.22	216.44	211.65	2.1825	.3358
3.	Mischievous students group	250.58	215.56	210.07	4.6823	.0962
4.	Dilemma of friendship	227.77	217.04	219.43	.3527	.8383
5.	Obtaining fruits without payment	223.61	218.12	216.67	.1030	.9498
6.	Broken chair for the teacher	250.60	218.58	193.45	6.2945	.0430*
7.	Act of a ball	233.39	219.24	203.00	1.7153	.4242
8.	Unclaimed money	231.15	216.34	220.67	.7859	.6751
9.	Demand for killing by a beautiful girl	247.29	218.84	194.55	4.9005	.0863
10.	Dishonestful honesty	203.18	221.43	214.11	1.0910	.5796
11.	Sympathy of a thief friend	214.39	222.45	199.91	1.9519	.3768
12.	Improper action and friendship	222.46	221.19	200.65	1.9142	.3840

1 N = 46
2 N = 330
3 N = 60
* Significant at .05 level
** Significant at .01 level

experiencing less, moderate and high level of stress in society differ from one another on moral judgement as measured by the sixth item of MJQ.

Further analysis was done by using Mann Whitney U test. Result is shown in table 4.37.

Table 4.37: Differences among girls experiencing different levels of stress in society on sixth item of Moral Judgement Questionnaire

Sl. No.	Level of stress	N	Mean rank	U-value	Z-value	P
1.	Low	46	212.59	6482.0	–1.7437	.0812
	Moderate	330	185.14			
2.	Low	46	61.51	1011.5	–2.5531	.0107**
	High	60	47.36			
3.	Moderate	330				
	High	60				

* Significant at .05 level
** Significant at .01 level

Table 4.37 shows that mean rank for less stressed girls is 212.59. Mean rank for moderately stressed girls is 185.14. Difference between the mean ranks is not statistically significant ($Z = -1.7437, P > .05$). It implies that less stressful girls do not differ from moderately stressful girls on moral judgement as measured by the sixth item of the MJQ. Mean ranks for less stressed and highly stressed girls are 61.51 and 47.36 respectively. Mean rank for less stressful girls is greater than that for highly stressful girls ($Z = 2.551$, $P < .01$). It means that less stressful girls excel highly stressful girls on moral judgement as measured by sixth item of MJQ.

It was hypothesized that "Girls experiencing less, moderate and high level of stress in school do not differ

Table 4.38: Differences on various items of MJQ among girls experiencing less, moderate and high level of stress in school

Sl. No.	Item Title	Level of Stress			Chi-Sq.	Sign.
		Low[1]	Moderate[2]	High[3]		
	Items of M.J.Q.					
1.	Half cost ticket	236.34	213.33	229.11	2.4013	.3010
2.	Lost examination question paper	243.87	216.97	206.07	3.2316	.1987
3.	Mischievous student's group	227.09	219.10	209.01	.8588	.6509
4.	Dilemma of friendship	216.07	216.32	230.71	.8834	.6430
5.	Obtaining fruits without payment	245.07	215.66	211.34	3.0357	.2192
6.	Broken chair for the teacher	234.17	222.05	189.52	5.4058	.0670
7.	Act of a ball	243.27	218.88	197.47	4.2596	.1189
8.	Unclaimed money	213.96	219.01	219.62	.1059	.9484
9.	Demand for killing by a beautiful girl	260.71	214.71	203.69	7.5547	.0229*
10.	Dishonestful honesty	235.31	217.43	210.50	1.4269	.4900
11.	Sympathy of a thief friend	234.47	219.93	199.32	2.8219	.2439
12.	Improper action and friendship	224.23	220.77	203.30	1.6211	.4446

1 N = 52
2 N = 317
3 N = 67
* Significant at .05 level
** Significant at .01 level

significantly from one another on moral judgement as measured by Moral Judgement Questionnaire."

Table 4.38 presents results of Kruskal Wallis one way ANOVA for various items of moral judgement among girls experiencing less, moderate and high level of stress in school. Observation of chi-square values show that out of twelve only one is significant at 0.5 level. This shows acceptance of the hypothesis with respect to eleven items of MJQ. It means girls experiencing less, moderate and high level of stress in school do not differ from one another on moral judgement as measured by eleven items of MJQ. significant chi-squre value was found for ninth item of the MJQ. It is significant at .05 level. This allows rejection of the null hypothesis with respect to ninth item of MJQ. This leads us to infer that girls experiencing different levels of stress in school differ from one another with respect to ninth item of MJQ.

Further analysis was done by using Mann Whitney U test. Result in shown in the table 4.39.

Table 4.39: Differences among girls experiencing different levels of stress in school on ninth item of MJQ

Sl. No.	Level of stress	N	Mean rank	U-value	Z-value	P
1.	Low	52	218.53	6498.5	–2.5286	.0115**
	Moderate	317	179.50			
2.	Low	52	68.68	1290.5	–2.4956	.0126**
	High	67	53.26			
3.	Moderate	317	194.21	10079.0	–.6799	.4966
	High	67	184.43			

* Significant at .05 level

** Significant at .01 level

Table 4.39 shows that mean rank for less stressful girls is 218.53 and mean rank for moderately stressed girls is 179.50. Mean rank for less stressful girls is greater than that of moderately stress girls (Z = –2.5286, P < .01). This indicates that less stressed girls excel moderately stressed girls on moral judgement as measured by ninth item of MJQ. Mean rank for less and highly stressful girls are 68.68 and 53.26 respectively. Mean rank for less stressed girls is greater than that for highly stressed girls (Z = –2.4956, P < . 01). So, it can be inferred that less stressful girls excel girls who are experiencing high level of stress in school, on moral judgement as measured by ninth item of MJQ. Mean rank for moderately stressful girls is 194.21 and mean rank for highly stressful girls is 184.43. Difference between mean rank of moderately and highly stressed girls is not significant (Z = –.6799, P > .05). This allows us to infer that girls experiencing moderate and high level of stress do not differ from one another on moral judgement as measured by the ninth item of MJQ.

It was hypothesized that "Girls experiencing low moderate and high level of self-stress do not differ from one another on various items of moral judgement." Table 4.40 presents results of Kruskal Wallis one way ANOVA for various items of MJQ for girls experiencing less, moderate and high level of self-stress. Observation of chi-square values reveals that out of twelve item of MJQ only two are significant. These values are significant at .05 level. This allows expectance of the null hypothesis that with respect to ten items of MJQ. It implies that girls experiencing less, moderate and high level of self-stress do not differ from one another on ten items of MJQ. Significant chi-square values are found for sixth and seventh items of MJQ. These values allow partial rejection of null hypothesis with respect to sixth and seventh items of MJQ. It leads us to infer that girls experiencing less, moderate and high level of self-stress differ from one another with respect to moral judgement has measured by sixth and seventh items of MJQ.

Table 4.40: Differences on various items of MJQ among girls experiencing different level of stress related to self

Sl. No.	Item Title	Level of Stress Low[1]	Moderate[2]	High[3]	Chi-Sq.	Sign.
	Items of M.J.Q.					
1.	Half cost ticket	213.84	225.31	197.14	3.8308	.1473
2.	Lost examination question paper	224.53	223.21	196.86	3.3837	.1842
3.	Mischievous student's group	211.55	221.62	212.30	.7631	.6828
4.	Dilemma of friendship	228.73	215.55	221.65	.7224	.6969
5.	Obtaining fruits without payment	216.48	223.62	201.36	2.2584	.3233
6.	Broken chair for the teacher	247.17	220.12	191.36	8.1234	.0172*
7.	Act of a ball	231.33	223.92	189.25	6.0757	.0479*
8.	Unclaimed money	227.32	220.21	205.76	1.5981	.4498
9.	Demand for killing by a beautiful girl	222.18	216.20	224.14	.3342	.8461
10.	Dishonestful honesty	229.68	221.36	199.81	2.8178	.2444
11.	Sympathy of a thief friend	230.44	215.82	219.40	.7856	.6752
12.	Improper action and friendship	204.98	224.67	206.06	2.9895	.2243

1 N = 60
2 N = 295
3 N = 81
* Significant at .05 level
** Significant at .01 level

Further analysis was done by using Mann Whitney U test. Results are shown in the table 4.41 and 4.42.

Table 4.41: Differences among girls experiencing different levels of stress related to self on sixth item of MJQ

Sl. No.	Level of stress	N	Mean rank	U-value	Z-value	P
1.	Low	60	196.39	7746.5	–1.6541	.0981
	Moderate	295	174.26			
2.	Low	60	81.28	1813.5	–2.7794	.0054**
	High	81	63.39			
3.	Moderate	295	193.86	10365.5	–1.9805	.0477*
	High	81	168.97			

* Significant at .05 level
** Significant at .01 level

Table 4.41 shows that mean rank for less stressful girls is 196.39 and mean rank for moderately stressful girls is 174.26. Mean rank for less stressful girls is not significantly different from that for moderately stressful girls ($Z = -1.6541$, $P > .05$). This means that both less and moderately stressful girls do not differ from one another on moral judgement as measured by the sixth item of MJQ. Mean ranks for less and highly stressful girls are 81.28 and 63.39 respectively. Mean rank for less stressful girls is greater than for highly stressful girls ($Z = -2.7794$, $P < .01$). This indicates that less stressful girls excel highly stressful girls on moral judgement as measured by the sixth item of MJQ.

Mean rank for moderately stressed girls 193.86 while mean rank for highly stressed girls is 168.97. The former is greater than the letter. ($Z = -1.9805$, $P < .05$). It implies that girls experiencing moderate level of self-stress excel highly stressed girls on moral judgement as measured by the sixth item of MJQ.

It was hypothesized that "Girls experiencing low, moderate and high level of overall stress do not differ from one another on moral judgement as measured by different items of MJQ".

Table 4.42 shows mean rank for less stressed girls is 183.53 and mean rank for moderately stressed girls is 176.87. They do not differ significantly (Z = –.4801, P > .05). This allows us to infer that both less and moderately stressful girls do not differ from one another on moral judgement as measured by the seventh item of MJQ. Mean rank for less stressed girls is 78.30 and mean rank for highly stressed girls is 65.59. The differences between the two groups is not significant (Z = –1.0915, P > .05). It means less stressful girls do not differ from highly stressful girls on of moral judgement as measured by seventh item of MJQ. Mean ranks for moderately and highly stressful girls are 195.05 and 164.66 respectively. Mean rank for moderately stressful girls is greater than that for less stressed girls (Z = –2.3432, P < .05). It allows us to infer that moderately stressed girls excel highly stressed girls on moral judgement as measured by the seventh item of MJQ.

Table 4.42: Differences among girls experiencing different level of stress related to self on seventh item of moral judgement

Sl. No.	Level of stress	N	Mean rank	U-value	Z-value	P
1.	Low	60	183.53	8518.0	–.4801	.6311
	Moderate	295	176.87			
2.	Low	60	78.30	1992.0	–1.9015	.0572
	High	81	65.59			
3.	Moderate	295	195.05	10016.5	–2.3432	.0191*
	High	81	164.66			

* Significant at .05 level

** Significant at .01 level

It was hypothesized that "Girls experiencing low, moderate and high level of overall stress do not differ from one another on moral judgement as measured by different items of MJQ'.

Table 4.43 present results of Kruskal Wallis one way ANOVA for various items of MJQ among girls experiencing different levels of overall stress. Observation of chi-square values shows that out of twelve, only two are significant. They are significant at .05 level. This allows acceptance of the hypothesis with respect to ten items of MJQ. Significant values of chi-square are found for sixth and ninth items of MJQ. This difference allows rejection of null hypothesis with regard to sixth and ninth items of MJQ. This allows to infer that girls experiencing low, moderate and high level of overall stress differ from one another with respect to moral judgement as measured by sixth and ninth items of MJQ, titled as broken chair for the teacher and demand of killing by a beautiful girl.

DISCUSSION

Results pertaining to comparison of moral judgement among girls experiencing different level of stress in home, society, school and self indicate that stress has no effect on moral judgement. It seems that home environment might have moderated the effects of stress. It is also possible that the level of stress has not reached threshold level in order to produced adverse effect on moral judgement as measured by most of the items of the Moral Judgement Questionnaire. It becomes obvious when we ponder over the fact that Indians have shown high level morality even under very stressful situations. These significant differences may be attributed to the content of moral dilemmas and the sensitivity of stressful girls towards them. This draws support from the study of Sigman & Erdynast, (1988) which revealed that stressors may not be related to social and moral understanding.

Table 4.43: Differences among girls experiencing different levels of overall stress on various items of MJQ

Sl. No.	Item Title	Level of Stress Low[1]	Moderate[2]	High[3]	Chi-Sq.	Sign.
	Items of M.J.Q.					
1.	Half cost ticket	216.18	218.08	222.62	.1064	.9482
2.	Lost examination question paper	238.04	219.15	198.20	3.4747	.1760
3.	Mischievous student's group	226.06	219.00	209.39	.7392	.6910
4.	Dilemma of friendship	215.27	215.29	237.19	1.9605	.3752
5.	Obtaining fruits without payment	241.07	219.75	192.59	5.1163	.0774
6.	Broken chair for the teacher	215.38	218.53	189.61	8.4333	.0147*
7.	Act of a ball	245.29	218.97	192.73	5.7231	.0572
8.	Unclaimed money	215.52	221.77	204.98	1.3318	.5138
9.	Demand for killing by a beautiful girl	241.53	220.62	187.88	6.1505	.0462*
10.	Dishonestful honesty	232.08	221.05	194.01	3.7468	.1536
11.	Sympathy of a thief friend	216.96	225.08	187.38	5.5476	.0624
12.	Improper action and friendship	217.30	222.93	197.66	2.9335	.2307

1 N = 56

2 N = 316

3 N = 64

* Significant at .05 level

** Significant at .01 level

Moral judgement as measured by ninth, sixth and seventh items of MJQ has been found to be adversely affected by stress. Girls experiencing high stress in overall, home and school show relatively lower level of moral reasoning as exhibited on ninth item of MJQ than those who are less stressed. Less stressed girls excel moderately stressed girls on moral judgement as measured by ninth item of MJQ. It seems that, due to their perceived stress they are more sensitive to this item titled as 'demand of killing by a beautiful girl'. Girls experiencing high overall stress and stress in society and self are lower on moral judgement as measured by sixth item of MJQ than those who are experiencing less stress. Girls experiencing moderate or low level of stress exhibit similar moral reasoning.

In comparison to girls experiencing high level of stress in self, girls experiencing moderate level of stress excel on moral judgement as measured by seventh item of the MJQ. Girls experiencing less or moderate and girls experiencing less or high stress exhibit similar type of moral reasoning on seventh item of MJQ.

Effect of Home Environment on Values

Three criterion groups were formed for each dimensions of home environment on the basis of mean ±1 S.D. Then Kruskal-Wallis one way ANOVA was used for comparing girls perceiving less moderate and high level in each of ten dimensions of home environment on various values. Result have been described in this section.

RESULTS

It was hypothesized that "Girls perceiving less, moderate and high level of control in home environment do not differ from one another in values".

Table 4.44 presents result of Kruskal-Wallis one way ANOVA for values among girls perceiving low, moderate and high control in Home environment. Observation of chi-square values show that out of 40 values, 37 values are

Table 4.44: Mean rank and chi-square value showing differences on various values among girls perceiving low, moderate and high level of control in home environment

Sl. No.	Values	Level of Stress			Chi-Sq.	Sign.
		Low[1]	Moderate[2]	High[3]		
1	2	3	4	5	6	7
1.	A comfortable life	211.41	216.41	234.73	1.9652	.3743
2.	An exciting life	206.25	217.29	235.93	2.0239	.3635
3.	A sense of accomplishment	233.88	212.95	227.90	2.1134	.3476
4.	A world of peace	217.11	216.14	230.30	.9586	.6192
5.	A world of beauty	224.89	222.67	193.74	3.6452	.1616
6.	Equality	234.12	214.47	220.97	1.5196	.4678
7.	Family security	213.51	213.40	245.99	4.2609	.1188
8.	Freedom	228.96	218.60	207.75	1.0526	.5908
9.	Happiness	221.69	213.09	239.31	2.6747	.2625
10.	Inner Harmony	196.73	221.99	224.51	2.4847	.2887
11.	Mature love	226.04	216.04	221.94	.4249	.8086
12.	National Security	235.24	209.24	243.01	6.3521	.0417*
13.	Pleasure	236.32	214.50	218.65	1.7727	.4122

(Table Contd...)

(Table 4.44: Contd...)

1	2	3	4	5	6	7
14.	Salvation	217.20	212.17	247.80	4.6616	.0972
15.	Self-respect	218.27	213.06	242.79	3.5669	.1681
16.	Social recognition	196.49	221.54	226.72	2.8513	.2403
17.	True friendship	224.44	221.12	203.02	1.7369	.4196
18.	Wisdom	194.16	223.36	220.98	3.4670	.1767
19.	Equity	196.31	217.97	242.71	5.0313	.0808
20.	Power	212.33	215.03	239.94	2.4815	.2892
21.	Social justice	234.74	215.62	215.23	1.5402	.4630
22.	Ambitious	202.58	220.41	225.72	1.4763	.4780
23.	Broadminded	211.31	216.15	235.96	1.7218	.4228
24.	Capable	204.01	217.67	236.47	2.4353	.2959
25.	Cheerful	203.44	225.88	200.68	3.6514	.1611
26.	Clean	211.79	217.67	228.80	.9720	.6151
27.	Courageous	194.69	217.60	245.92	6.1570	.0460*
28.	Forgiving	221.35	221.49	202.47	1.3806	.5014
29.	Helpful	222.41	217.14	220.65	.1285	.9378

(Table Contd...)

(Table 4.44: Contd...)

1	2	3	4	5	6	7
30.	Honesty	214.74	220.27	214.37	.2453	.8846
31.	Imagination	211.14	217.48	230.28	.8814	.6436
32.	Independent	200.90	221.93	220.65	1.6689	.4341
33.	Intellectual	209.66	215.49	240.55	2.7326	.2550
34.	Logical	223.74	213.87	233.82	1.5833	.4531
35.	Loving	226.65	222.12	194.43	3.2653	.1954
36.	Obedient	196.93	227.59	199.51	5.9477	.0511*
37.	Polite	228.13	217.70	212.55	.6042	.7393
38.	Responsible	225.67	216.80	218.94	.2978	.8617
39.	Self-control	197.60	218.04	241.13	4.2648	.1186
40.	Self-determinantion	233.13	211.15	236.61	3.8888	.1431

1 N = 67
2 N = 301
3 N = 68
* Significant at .05 level
** Significant at .01 level

not significant at .05 level. They allow acceptance of the hypothesis with respect to 37 values. This means that girls perceiving low, moderate and high control in home environment do not differ from one another on 37 values namely: a comfortable life, an exciting life, a sense of accomplishment, a word of peace, a word of beauty, equality, family security, freedom, happiness, inner harmony, mature love, pleasure, salvation, self-respect, social recognition, true friendship, wisdom, equity, power, social justice, ambitious, broadminded, capable, cheerful, clean, forgiving, helpful, honesty, imagination, independent, intellectual logical, loving, polite, responsible, self-control and self-determinantion.

Significant values of chi-square were found three values namely: National security, courageous and obedient. This allows partial rejection of null hypothesis with respect to these values. It means that girls perceiving low, moderate and high level of control in home environment differ from one another with respect to three values.

Further analysis was done by using Mann-Whitney 'U' test. Results are shown in the following table 4.45 to 4.47.

Table 4.45 shows that mean rank for girls perceiving less control is 202.39 and mean rank for girls perceiving moderate control is 180.52. Mean ranks for the two groups are not significantly different ($Z = -1.6430$, $P > .05$). Mean rank for girls perceiving less control is 66.85. Mean rank for girls perceiving high control is 69.13. Mean rank for the girls perceiving less control is not significantly different from those perceiving high control ($Z = -.3821$, $P > .05$). So both groups give equal importance to the 'national security' value. Mean rank for girls perceiving moderate control is 179.72 and mean rank for the girls perceiving high control is 208.38. Mean rank for girls perceiving high control is greater than that for the girls perceiving moderate control ($Z = -2.1634$, $P < .05$). This indicates that girls

Table 4.45: Mean ranks, U-values and Z-values showing differences among girls perceiving less, moderate and high level of control in home environment on 'national security'

Sl. No.	Level of Control	N	Mean rank	U-value	Z-value	P
1.	Low	67	202.39	8885.0	–1.6430	.1004
	Moderate	301	180.52			
2.	Low	67	66.85	2201.0	–.3821	.7024
	High	68	69.13			
3.	Moderate	301	179.72	8644.0	–2.1634	.0305*
	High	68	208.38			

* Significant at .05 level
** Significant at .01 level

perceiving high control place more importance to national security value than girls perceiving moderate control.

Table 4.46 shows mean rank for the girls perceiving less control is 168.67. Mean rank for the girls perceiving moderate control is 188.02. Mean ranks for both groups do not differ significantly ($Z = -1.4022, P > .05$). This means that girls perceiving less and moderate control give equal importance to value named courageous. Mean rank for the girls perceiving less control is 60.02 while mean rank for the girls perceiving high control is 75.86. Mean rank for girls perceiving high control is greater than that for girls perceiving less control ($Z = -2.4636, P < .01$). This leads us to infer that girls perceiving high control give more preference to value named courageous than those perceiving less control. Mean rank for girls perceiving moderate and high control are 180.58 and 204.56 respectively. Difference is not significant ($Z = -1.7598, P > .05$). This leads us to infer that girls perceiving high control do not differ from girls perceiving moderate control on courageous value.

Table 4.46: Mean ranks, U-values and Z-values showing differences among girls perceiving low, moderate and high control in home environment on value named 'courageous'

Sl. No.	Level of Control	N	Mean rank	U-value	Z-value	P
1.	Low	67	168.67	9023.0	–1.4022	.1609
	Moderate	301	188.02			
2.	Low	67	60.02	1743.5	–2.4636	.0138**
	High	68	75.86			
3.	Moderate	301	180.58	8904.0	–1.7598	.0784
	High	68	204.56			

* Significant at .05 level
** Significant at .01 level

Table 4.47 shows mean ranks for girls perceiving less and moderate level of control are 163.18 and 189.25 respectively. Mean rank for the latter is greater than the former (Z = –1.9743, P < .05). It can be inferred that girls perceiving less control in home give less importance to obedient value than those who perceive moderate level of control in home environment. Mean ranks for girls perceiving less and high level of control are 67.75 and 68.25 respectively. Difference between the mean ranks for both groups are not significant (Z = –.0788, P > .05) . It implies that girls perceiving less control do not differ from girls perceiving high control in home environment on obedient value. Mean ranks for girls perceiving moderate and high control in home environment are 189.35 and 165.76 respectively. Mean ranks for both groups do not vary from one another (Z =–1.7968, P > .05). It can be inferred that girls perceiving moderate control and girls perceiving high control, give equal importance to obedient value.

Table 4.47: Mean ranks, U-values and Z-values showing differences among girls perceiving less, moderate and high control in home environment on 'obedient' value

Sl. No.	Level of Control	N	Mean rank	U-value	Z-value	P
1.	Low	67	163.18	8655.0	–1.9743	.0484*
	Moderate	301	189.25			
2.	Low	67	67.75	2261.0	–.0788	.9372
	High	68	68.25			
3.	Moderate	301	189.35	8925.5	–1.7968	.0724
	High	68	165.76			

* Significant at .05 level
** Significant at .01 level

It was that hypothesized that "Girls perceiving less, moderate and high level of protectiveness in home environment do not differ from each other in values". Table 4.48 presents result of Kruskal-Wallis one way ANOVA for values among girls perceiving less, moderate and high level of protectiveness in home environment. Observations of the chi-square values show that out of 40 values 16 are significant. Nine values are significant at .05 level while seven values are significant at .01 level. The non-significant chi-square values allows acceptance of the null hypothesis with respect to 24 values. This means that girl perceiving less, moderate and high level of protectiveness in home environment do not differ from one another on 24 values namely: A comfortable life, an exciting life, a sense of accomplishment, equality, freedom, inner harmony, mature love, national security, pleasure, salvation, self-respect, true friendship, wisdom, social justice, clean, courageous, forgiving, helpful, honesty, imagination, independent, loving, polite and responsible.

Table 4.48: Mean ranks and chi-square values showing differences among girls perceiving less, moderate and high level of 'protectiveness' in home environment on various values

Sl. No.	Values	Level of Protectivenes			Chi-Sq.	Sign.
		Low[1]	Moderate[2]	High[3]		
1	2	3	4	5	6	7
1.	A comfortable life	204.71	221.17	220.59	1.3341	.5132
2.	An exciting life	214.94	213.67	239.89	2.7849	.2485
3.	A sense of accomplishment	222.07	214.61	230.05	1.0548	.5901
4.	A world of peace	210.65	212.95	246.51	6.2652	.0436*
5.	A world of beauty	210.09	211.11	253.84	8.5761	.0137**
6.	Equality	209.38	214.98	239.86	3.1152	.2106
7.	Family security	175.90	221.49	244.83	12.5498	.0019**
8.	Freedom	189.51	223.97	223.42	4.6901	.4958
9.	Happiness	189.27	216.24	252.85	10.3342	.0057**
10.	Inner harmony	204.67	216.65	237.71	2.7831	.2487
11.	Mature love	216.63	219.35	216.95	.0419	.9793
12.	National security	205.65	218.95	228.23	1.3793	.5017
13.	Pleasure	195.65	219.34	235.49	3.9354	.1398

(Table Contd...)

(Table 4.48: Contd...)

1	2	3	4	5	6	7
14.	Salvation	210.99	213.41	244.36	4.1521	.1254
15.	Self-respect	198.12	222.84	225.41	4.1084	.1282
16.	Social recogniton	198.25	211.66	262.22	13.4981	.0012**
17.	True friendship	210.92	214.63	239.82	3.8737	.1442
18.	Wisdom	211.43	215.65	235.51	2.0591	.3572
19.	Equity	205.51	213.23	249.90	6.5858	.0371*
20.	Power	196.24	216.42	246.01	6.1791	.0455*
21.	Social justice	212.08	215.36	236.05	2.1682	.3382
22.	Ambitious	185.83	217.69	250.40	10.3167	.0058**
23.	Broadminded	176.40	219.31	252.63	14.0139	.0009**
24.	Capable	213.29	210.08	254.92	8.3743	.0152*
25.	Cheerful	174.55	222.66	241.57	12.1833	.0023**
26.	Clean	214.51	213.77	239.88	3.9808	.1366
27.	Courageous	205.75	215.71	240.29	3.4362	.1794
28.	Forgiving	202.37	219.67	228.34	1.7036	.4266
29.	Helpful	226.50	213.24	231.32	1.7024	.4269

(Table Contd...)

(Table 4.48: Contd...)

1	2	3	4	5	6	7
30.	Honesty	227.01	215.26	223.23	.7789	.6774
31.	Imagination	204.92	218.32	231.16	1.6394	.4406
32.	Independent	238.04	211.58	227.42	3.1192	.1202
33.	Intellectual	217.69	209.89	251.77	7.1154	.0285*
34.	Logical	209.26	211.29	253.92	7.6811	.0215*
35.	Loving	231.26	214.07	223.97	1.3046	.5209
36.	Obedient	190.80	217.03	248.51	9.0118	.0110**
37.	Polite	194.43	218.74	238.87	4.8960	.0865
38.	Responsible	210.93	214.04	242.03	3.6021	.1651
39.	Self-control	188.29	219.24	242.40	7.0620	.0293*
40.	Self-determinantion	202.21	214.73	247.13	6.2723	.0434*

1 N = 68
2 N = 291
3 N = 77
* Significant at .05 level
** Significant at .01 level

Significant values of chi-squre were found for 16 values namely, a world at peace: A world of beauty, family security, happiness, social recognition, equity, power, ambitious, broadminded, capable, cheerful, intellectual, logical, obedient, self-control, self-determinantion. This allows partial rejection of the hypothesis. This leads us to infer that girls perceiving less, moderate and high level of protectiveness in home environment differ from one another with respect to 16 values. Further analysis was done by using Mann-Whitney 'U' test. Results are shown in table 4.49 to 4.64.

Table 4.49 shows that mean rank for the girls perceiving less protection is 178.74. Mean rank for the moderately protected girls is 180.29. Mean rank for the girls perceiving less protection is not significantly different from the girls perceiving moderate protection (Z = –.1265,

Table 4.49: Mean ranks, U-values and Z-values showing differences among girls perceiving less, moderate and high level of protectiveness in home environment on value 'a world at peace'

Sl. No.	Level of protectiveness	N	Mean rank	U-value	Z-value	P
1.	Low	68	178.74	9808.5	–.1265	.8993
	Moderate	291	180.29			
2.	Low	68	66.40	2169.5	–2.1419	.0322*
	High	77	78.82			
3.	Moderate	291	178.63	9495.0	–2.4086	.0160*
	High	77	206.69			

* Significant at .05 level

** Significant at .01 level

P > .05). This means that girls perceiving less and moderate protection do not differ from one another on a word at peace value. Mean rank for the girls perceiving less protection in home environment is 66.40 and mean rank for the girls perceiving high protection is 78.82. Mean rank for the girls perceiving high protection is higher than mean rank for the girls perceiving less protection (Z = –2.1419, P < .05). This indicates that girls perceiving high protection give more importance to value named a world at peace than those perceiving less protection. Mean rank for the girls perceiving moderate protection in home is 178.63 while mean rank for the girls perceiving high protection is 206.69. Mean rank for the girls perceiving high protection is greater than that for girls perceiving moderate protection (Z = –2.4086, P < .05). This indicates that girls perceiving high protection give more preference to value named a world at peace than the girls who perceived moderate protection.

Table 4.50 shows that the mean rank for the girls perceiving less protection is 179.00 and mean rank for girls perceiving moderate protection is 180.23. Mean ranks for both the groups are not significantly different (Z = –.0943, P > .05). This indicates that both girls perceiving less protection and girls perceiving moderate protection do not differ from one another on value named a word of beauty. Mean rank for the girls perceiving less protection is 79.55. Mean ranks for highly protected girls is greater than that for less protected girls (Z = –2.2200, P < .05). This means that highly protected girls give more importance to a world of beauty value than those who perceive less protection in homes. Mean rank for moderately protected girls is 176.88 and mean rank for highly protected girls is 213.30. Mean rank for highly protected girls is greater than that for moderately protected girls (Z = –2.8867, P < .01). This indicates that girls perceiving high protection give more preference to a word of beauty value than those who are moderately protected.

Table 4.50: Mean ranks, U-values and Z-values showing differences among girls perceiving less, moderate and high protectivness on 'a world of beauty' value

Sl. No.	Level of protectiveness	N	Mean rank	U-value	Z-value	P
1.	Low	68	179.00	9826.0	–.0943	.9249
	Moderate	291	180.23			
2.	Low	68	65.59	2114.0	–2.2200	.0264*
	High	77	79.55			
3.	Moderate	291	176.88	8986.0	–2.8867	.0039**
	High	77	213.30			

* Significant at .05 level
** Significant at .01 level

Table 4.51 shows that mean rank for the girls perceiving less protection at home is 149.36 and mean rank for girls perceiving moderate protection is 187.16. Mean rank for the moderately protected girls is higher than that for less protected girls (Z = –2.8377, P < .01). This allows us to infer that value family security finds more important place among girls perceiving moderate protection than among those who are less protected. Mean rank for the less protected girls is 61.04 while mean rank for highly protected girls is 83.56. Mean rank for highly protected girls is greater than that for less protected girls (Z = –3.3815, P < .01). This allows us to infer that family security finds more important place among girls who are highly protected than among less protected girls. Mean rank for moderately protected girls is 180.33 while mean rank for girls perceiving high protection is 200.27. Mean rank for highly protected girls is not significantly different from that for moderately protected girls (Z = –1.5532, P < .05). This permit us to infer that moderately and highly protected girls do not differ from each other on family security value.

Table 4.51: Mean ranks, U-values and Z-values showing differences among girls experiencing less, moderate and high protectiveness in home environment on 'family security' value

Sl. No.	Level of protectiveness	N	Mean rank	U-value	Z-value	P
1.	Low	68	149.36	7810.5	–2.8377	.0045**
	Moderate	291	187.16			
2.	Low	68	61.04	1805.0	–3.3815	.0007**
	High	77	83.56			
3.	Moderate	291	180.33	9989.0	–1.5532	.1204*
	High	77	200.27			

* Significant at .05 level
** Significant at .01 level

Observation of table 4.52 shows mean ranks for less protected girls is 161.63 and mean rank for moderately protected girls is 184.29. Mean rank for both the groups are not significantly different [Z = –1.6839, P > .05). This allows us to infer that girls perceiving less protection do not differ significantly from girls perceiving moderate protection on happiness value. Mean rank for less protected girls is 62.14 while mean rank for highly protected girls is 82.59. Mean rank for highly protected girls is significantly greater than that for less protected girls [Z = –3.0705, P < .01). This allows us to infer that value happiness is preferred by highly protected girls than the less protected girls. Mean rank for moderately protected girls is 177.95. Mean rank for highly

Table 4.52: Mean ranks, U values and Z-values showing difference among girls perceiving less, moderate and high protectiveness at home on 'happiness' value

Sl. No.	Level of control	N	Mean rank	U-value	Z-value	P
1.	Low	68	161.63	8645.0	–1.6839	.0922
	Moderate	291	184.29			
2.	Low	68	62.14	1879.5	–3.0705	.0021**
	High	77	82.59			
3.	Moderate	291	177.95	9297.5	–2.4104	.0159*
	High	77	209.26			

* Significant at .05 level
** Significant at .01 level

protected girls is 209.26. Mean rank for highly protected girls is significantly higher than that for moderately protected girls (Z = –2.5104, P < .05). This indicates that girls perceiving high protection give more importance to value happiness than girls perceiving moderate protection.

Table 4.53 shows mean rank for less protected girls is 171.07 and mean rank for the girls perceiving moderate protection in home is 182.09. Mean ranks for both the groups are not significantly different from one another (Z = –.8287, P > .05). This allows us to infer that girls perceiving less protection do not differ from girls perceiving moderate protection on social recognition value. Mean rank for less protected girls is 61.88 while mean rank for highly protected girls is 83.00. Mean rank for highly protected girls is greater than that for less protected girls (Z = –3.3326, P < .01). This allows us to infer that girls perceiving high protection give more importance to value named social recognition than less protected girls. Mean rank for moderately protected girls is 175.58 and mean rank for highly protected girls is 218.22. Mean rank for moderately protected girls is significantly lower than that for highly protected girls (Z = –3.3546, P < .01). This indicates that moderately protected girls consider value named social recognition as less important than the highly protected girls.

Table 4.53: Mean ranks, U-values and Z-values showing differences among girls perceiving less, moderate and high protectiveness in home 'social recognition' value

Sl. No.	Level of protectiveness	N	Mean rank	U-value	Z-value	P
1.	Low	68	171.07	9287.0	–.8287	.4073*
	Moderate	291	182.09			
2.	Low	68	61.68	1848.0	–3.3326	.0009**
	High	77	83.00			
3.	Moderate	291	175.58	8607.0	–3.3546	.0008**
	High	77	218.22			

* Significant at .05 level
** Significant at .01 level

Table 4.54 shows mean rank for less protected girls is 175.12. Mean rank for moderately protected girls is 181.14. Mean rank for less protected girls is not significantly different from that for moderately protected girls (Z = –.4487, P > .05). It indicates that there exists no significant difference between less and moderately protected girls on value named equity. Mean rank for less protected girls is 64.89 while mean rank for girls perceiving high protection is 80.16. Mean rank for highly protected girls is higher than that for less protected girls (Z = –2.3018, P < .05). So, it can be

Table 4.54: Mean ranks, U-values and Z-values showing differences among girls perceiving less, moderate and high protectiveness in home on value 'equity'

Sl. No.	Level of protectiveness	N	Mean rank	U-value	Z-value	P
1.	Low	68	175.12	9562.0	–.4487	.6536
	Moderate	291	181.14			
2.	Low	68	64.89	2066.5	–2.3018	.0213*
	High	77	80.16			
3.	Moderate	291	178.09	9337.5	–2.3610	.0182*
	High	77	208.73			

* Significant at .05 level
** Significant at .01 level

inferred that highly protected girls give more preference to equity value than the less protected girls. Mean rank for girls perceiving moderate protection is 178.09. Mean rank for highly protected girls is 208.73. Mean rank for highly protected girls is greater than mean rank for less protected girls (Z = –2.3610, P < .05). This allows us to infer that highly protected girls give more importance to value named equity than moderately protected girls.

Table 4.55 shows mean rank for girls perceiving less protection is 166.22 and mean rank for girls perceiving less moderate protection is 183.22. Mean rank for girls perceiving protection is not significantly different from that for girls perceiving moderate protection (Z = –1.2491, P > .05). This allows us to infer that girls perceiving less protection are not different from girls perceiving moderate protection on Power value. Mean rank for girls perceiving less protection is 64.51 while mean rank for girls perceiving

Table 4.55: Mean ranks, U-values and Z-values showing differences among girls perceiving less, moderate and high protectiveness at home on value 'power'

Sl. No.	Level of protectiveness	N	Mean rank	U-value	Z-value	P
1.	Low	68	166.22	8957.0	–1.2491	.2116
	Moderate	291	183.22			
2.	Low	68	64.51	2041.0	–2.3464	.0190*
	High	77	80.49			
3.	Moderate	291	179.20	9662.5	–1.9028	.0571
	High	77	204.51			

* Significant at .05 level
** Significant at .01 level

high protection is 80.49. Mean rank for girls perceiving high protection is greater than that for less protected girls ($Z = -2.3464$, $P < .05$). This leads us to infer that value named power finds an important place among girls perceiving high protection than among girls perceiving less protection. Mean rank for girls perceiving moderate protection is 179.20. Mean rank for girls perceiving high protection is 204.51. Mean rank for girls perceiving high protection is not different from that for moderately protected girls ($Z = -1.9028$, $P > .05$). This indicates that girls perceiving high protection do not differ from girls perceiving moderate protection on power value.

Table 4.56 shows that mean rank for less protected girls is 158.74 and mean rank for moderately protected girls is 184.97. Mean rank for less protected girls is less than that for moderately protected girls ($Z = -1.9459$, $P < .05$). This allows us to infer that girls perceiving less protection

Table 4.56: Mean ranks, U-values and Z-values showing differences among girls perceiving less, moderate and high protectiveness in home on 'ambitious', value

Sl. No.	Level of protectiveness	N	Mean rank	U-value	Z-value	P
1.	Low	68	158.74	8448.0	–1.9459	.0517*
	Moderate	291	184.97			
2.	Low	68	61.60	1842.5	–3.1976	.0014*
	High	77	83.07			
3.	Moderate	291	178.73	9523.0	–2.1182	.0342*
	High	77	206.32			

* Significant at .05 level
** Significant at .01 level

give less importance to value named ambitious than those who perceive moderate protection. Mean rank for less protected girls is 61.60 while mean rank for highly protected girls is 83.07. Mean rank for highly protected girls is greater than that for less protected girls ($Z = -3.1976$, $P < .01$). This leads us to infer that value named ambitious finds an important place among girls perceiving high protection in home than among the girls perceiving less protection. Mean rank for moderately protected girls is 178.73 and mean rank for highly protected girls is 206.32. Mean rank for highly protected girls is greater than that for moderately protected girls ($Z = -2.1182$, $P < .05$). This leads us to infer that highly protected girls give more importance to value named ambitious than moderately protected girls.

Table 4.57 shows that mean rank for less protected girls is 150.99 and mean rank for moderately protected girls is 186.78. Mean rank for moderately protected girls is greater

Table 4.57: Mean ranks, U-values and Z-values showing differences among girls perceiving less, moderate and high protectiveness in home on 'broad-minded' value

Sl. No.	Level of protectiveness	N	Mean rank	U-value	Z-value	P
1.	Low	68	150.99	7921.5	–2.6301	.0085**
	Moderate	291	186.78			
2.	Low	68	59.90	1727.5	–3.6330	.0003**
	High	77	84.56			
3.	Moderate	291	178.53	9466.0	–2.1557	.0311*
	High	77	207.06			

* Significant at .05 level
** Significant at .01 level

than that for less protected girls (Z = –2.6301, P > .01). Moderately protected girls regard value named broadminded as more important than the girls who perceive less protection at home. Mean rank for girls perceiving less and moderate protection are 59.90 and 84.56 respectively. Mean rank for the girls perceiving high protection is greater than that for less protected girls (Z = –3.6330, P < .01). It indicates that value named broadminded is regarded as more important by highly protected girls than by those who are less protected. Mean rank for moderately protected girls is 178.53 while mean rank for the girls perceiving high protection in home is 207.06. Mean rank for highly protected girls is greater than that for moderately protected girls (Z = –2.1557, P < .05). This indicates that highly protected girls consider broadminded value more important than the girls perceiving moderate protection in home.

Table 4.58 shows that mean ranks for less protected and moderately protected girls are 182.26 and 179.47

Table 4.58: Mean ranks, U-values and Z-values showing differences among girls perceiving less, moderate and high protectiveness in home on 'capable' value

Sl. No.	Level of protectiveness	N	Mean rank	U-value	Z-value	P
1.	Low	68	182.26	9740.0	–.2057	.8370
	Moderate	291	179.47			
2.	Low	68	65.53	2110.0	–2.0988	.0358*
	High	77	79.60			
3.	Moderate	291	176.61	8907.0	–2.8596	.0042*
	High	77	214.32			

* Significant at .05 level
** Significant at .01 level

respectively. Mean rank for both groups to not differ significantly from one another (Z = –2057, P > .05). This indicates that no significant difference exists between less and moderately protected girls on value named capable. Mean rank for less protected girls is 65.53 and for highly protected girls it is 79.60. mean rank for highly protected girls is greater than that for less protected girls (Z = –2.0988, P < .05). This allows us to infer that girls perceiving high protection give more importance to value named capable than those who perceive less protection. Mean ranks for girls perceiving moderate and high protection are 176.61 and 214.32 respectively. Mean rank for girls perceiving high protection is greater than that for girls perceiving moderate protection (Z = –2.8596 P < .01). This permits us to infer that girls perceiving high protection regard value named capable as more important than those who perceive moderate protection.

Table 4.59 shows that mean rank for less protected girls is 148.06 and mean rank for moderately protected girls

Table 4.59: Mean ranks, U-values and Z-values showing differences among girls perceiving less, moderate and high protectiveness on 'cheerful' value

Sl. No.	Level of protectiveness	N	Mean rank	U-value	Z-value	P
1.	Low	68	148.06	7722.0	–2.9368	.0033**
	Moderate	291	187.46			
2.	Low	68	60.99	1801.5	–3.3499	.008**
	High	77	83.60			
3.	Moderate	291	181.20	10243.5	–1.2174	.2235
	High	77	196.97			

* Significant at .05 level
** Significant at .01 level

is 187.46. Mean rank for moderately protected girls is greater than that for less protected girls (Z = –2.9368, P < .01). This leads us to infer that value cheerful finds more important place among moderately protected girls than among those who perceive less protection in home. Mean ranks for less protected and highly protected girls are 60.99 and 83.60 respectively. Mean rank for highly protected girls is greater than that for less protected girls (Z –3.3499, P < .01). This indicates that value cheerful is regarded as more important by the girls who perceive high protection in home than by those who perceive less protection. Mean rank for moderately protected girls is 181.20. While mean rank for highly protected girls is 196.97. Mean ranks for both the group do not differ significantly from one another (Z = –1.2174, P > .05). This indicates that moderately and highly protected girls give equal importance to cheerful value.

Table 4.60 shows that mean ranks for girls perceiving less and moderate protection are 185.20 and 178.79 respectively. Mean ranks for both the groups are not

Table 4.60: Mean ranks, U-values and Z-values showing differences among girls perceiving less, moderate and high protectiveness in home on 'intellectual' value

Sl. No.	Level of protectiveness	N	Mean rank	U-value	Z-value	P
1.	Low	68	185.20	9540.5	–.4702	.6382
	Moderate	291	178.79			
2.	Low	68	66.99	2209.5	–1.6833	.0923
	High	77	78.31			
3.	Moderate	291	177.10	9050.5	–2.6683	.0076**
	High	77	212.46			

* Significant at .05 level
** Significant at .01 level

significantly different from one another (Z =–4702, P > .05). This indicates that no significant difference exists between less and moderately protected girls on value named intellectual. Mean rank for less protected girls is 66.99 while mean rank for highly protected girls is 78.31. Mean rank for highly protected girls is not significantly different (Z = –1.6833, P > .05). This allows us to infer that highly and less protected girls give equal importance to value named intellectual. Mean rank for moderately protected girls is 177.10 while mean rank for highly protected girls is 212.46. Mean rank for highly protected girls is greater than that for less protected girls (Z =–2.6683, P < . 01). This allows us to infer that highly protected girls regard value named intellectual as more important than moderately protected girls.

Table 4.61 shows that mean rank for less protected girls is 178.38 and mean rank for moderately protected girls is 180.38. Mean rank for both the groups are not significantly

Table 4.61: Mean ranks, U-values and Z-values showing differences among girls perceiving less, moderate and high protectiveness in home on value 'logical'

Sl. No.	Level of protectiveness	N	Mean rank	U-value	Z-value	P
1.	Low	68	178.38	9783.5	–.1462	.8838
	Moderate	291	180.38			
2.	Low	68	65.39	2100.5	–2.0984	.0359*
	High	77	79.72			
3.	Moderate	291	176.91	8993.5	–2.7091	.0067**
	High	77	213.20			

* Significant at .05 level
** Significant at .01 level

different from one another (Z = –.1462, P > .05). This leads us to infer that less and moderately protected girls give equal importance to logical value, and rank for less protected girls is 65.39 while mean rank for high protected girls is 79.72. Mean rank for highly protected girls is greater than that for less protected girls (Z = –2.0984, P < .05). This indicates that highly protected girls give more preference to logical value than less protected girls. Mean ranks for girls perceiving moderate and high protection are 176.91 and 213.20 respectively. Mean rank for highly protected girls is greater than that for moderately protected girls (Z = –2.7091, P < .01). This allows us to infer that highly protected girls consider value named logical as more important than those perceiving moderate protection.

Table 4.62 shows that mean rank for girls perceiving less protection is 162.23 and mean rank for girls perceiving moderate protection is 184.15. Mean ranks for both the groups are not significantly different (Z = –1.6807, P > .05).

Table 4.62: Mean ranks, U-values and Z-values showing differences among girls perceiving less, moderate and high protectiveness in home on value 'obedient'

Sl. No.	Level of protectiveness	N	Mean rank	U-value	Z-value	P
1.	Low	68	162.23	8685.5	–1.6807	.0928
	Moderate	291	184.15			
2.	Low	68	63.07	1943.0	–2.9337	.0033**
	High	77	81.77			
3.	Moderate	291	178.88	9568.0	–2.1470	.0318*
	High	77	205.74			

* Significant at .05 level
** Significant at .01 level

This allows us to infer that less protected girls and moderately protected girls do not vary from each other or value named obedient. Mean rank for less protected girl is 63.07 while mean rank for highly protected girls is 81.77. Mean rank for highly protected girls is greater than that for less protected girls (Z = –2.9337, P < .01). This allows us to infer that highly protected girls give more importance to obedient value than less protected girls. Mean rank for moderately and highly protected girls are 178.88 and 205.74 respectively. Mean rank for highly protected girls is greater than that for less protected girl (Z = –2.1470, P < .05). This indicates that value named obedient finds more important place among highly protected girls than among less protected girls.

Table 4.63 shows that mean rank for girls perceiving less and moderate protection are 159.68 and 184.75 respectively. Mean rank for both the group do not vary significantly from one another (Z =–1.8406, P > .05). This

Table 4.63: Mean ranks, U-values and Z-values showing differences among girls perceiving less, moderate and high level of protectiveness on 'self-control' value

Sl. No.	Level of protectiveness	N	Mean rank	U-value	Z-value	P
1.	Low	68	159.68	8512.0	–1.8406	.0657
	Moderate	291	184.75			
2.	Low	68	63.11	1945.5	–2.7356	.0062**
	High	77	81.73			
3.	Moderate	291	180.49	10035.5	–1.4489	.1474
	High	77	199.67			

* Significant at .05 level
** Significant at .01 level

indicates that less and moderately protected girls give equal importance to self-control value. Mean rank for less protected girls is 63.11 while mean rank for highly protected girls is 81.73. Mean rank for highly protected girls is greater than that for less protected girls (Z = –2.7356, P < .01). This allows us to infer that highly protected girls give more importance to self-control value than the girls perceiving less protection at home. Mean ranks for moderately and highly protected girls are 180.49 and 199.67 respectively. Mean ranks for both the groups are not significantly different from each other (Z = –1.4489, P > .05). This leads us to infer that moderately protected girl do not differ from highly protected girls on self control value.

Table 4.64 shows mean rank for girls perceiving less and moderate protection are 171.73 and 181.93 respectively. Mean rank for less protected girls do not vary significantly from that for moderately protected girls (Z = –.7807, P > .05). This allows us to infer that less protected girls do

Table 4.64: Mean ranks, U-values and Z-values showing differences among girls perceiving less, moderate and high protectiveness in home on 'self-determination' value

Sl. No.	Level of protectiveness	N	Mean rank	U-value	Z-value	P
1.	Low	68	171.73	9331.5	–.7807	.4350
	Moderate	291	181.93			
2.	Low	68	64.98	2072.5	–2.3652	.0180*
	High	77	80.08			
3.	Moderate	291	178.80	9544.5	–2.1739	.0297*
	High	77	206.05			

* Significant at .05 level
** Significant at .01 level

not differ from moderately protected girls on value named self-determination. Mean rank for less protected girls is 64.98 while mean rank for highly protected girls is 80.08. Mean rank for highly protected girls is greater than that for less protected girls ($Z = -2.3652$, $P < .05$). This indicates that girls perceiving high protection in home give more importance to value named self-determination than the girls who perceive less protection. Mean rank for moderately protected girls is 178.80 and mean rank for highly protected girls is 206.05. Mean rank for highly protected girls is greater than that for moderately protected girls ($Z = -2.1739$, $P < .05$). This allows us to infer that highly protected girls give more importance to value named self-determination than moderately protected girls.

It was hypothesized that "Girls perceiving less, moderate and high punishment do not differ from one another in values". Table 4.45 presents results of Kruskal-Wallis one way ANOVA for values among girls perceiving less, moderate and high level of punishment. Observation of chi-square values shows that out of 40 values, 39 are not significant at .05 level. This allows acceptance of the hypothesis with respect to 39 values. It means that girls perceiving less, moderate and high level of punishment do not differ from one another on 39 values namely: A comfortable life, an exciting life, a sense of accomplishment, a world of beauty, equality, family security, freedom, happiness, inner harmony, mature love, national security, pleasure, salvation, self-respect, social recognition, true friendship, equity, power, social justice, ambitious, broadminded, capable, cheerful, clean, courageous, forgiving, helpful, honesty, imagination, independent, intellectual, logical, loving obedient, polite, responsible, self-control and self-determination.

Observation of the table 4.65 reveal that one chi-square value is significant at .05 level. It is wisdom value. This allows rejection of the null hypothesis with regard to wisdom value. It mean that girls perceiving less, moderate and high level of punishment in home differ from one another with respect to wisdom value. Further analysis was done by using Mann-Whitney 'U' test. Result is shown in the table 4.66.

Observation of the table 4.66 reveals that mean ranks for girls perceiving less and moderate punishment are 155.10 and 188.12 respectively. The former is significantly lower than the latter ($Z = -2.4141$, $P < .05$). This implies that girls perceiving moderate punishment give more importance to value named wisdom than the less punished girls. Mean rank for girls perceiving less punishment in home is 57.97 while mean rank for girls perceiving high punishment is 75.11. Mean rank for highly punished girls is greater than that for less punished ($Z = -2.8071$, $P < .01$). It means that girl perceiving high punishment in home give more importance to value named wisdom than girls perceiving less punishment. Mean ranks for girls perceiving moderate and high punishment are 184.82 and 198.73 respectively. Mean ranks for moderately and highly punished girls do

Table 4.65: Mean ranks and Chi-square values showing differences among girls perceiving less, moderate and high 'punishment' in home

Sl. No.	Values	Level of Punishment Low[1]	Moderate[2]	High[3]	Chi-Sq.	Sign.
1	2	3	4	5	6	7
1.	A comfortable life	194.90	222.73	211.06	3.5156	.1724
2.	An exciting life	222.99	217.26	219.82	.1194	.9420
3.	A sense of accomplishment	219.35	218.51	217.74	.0059	.9971
4.	A world of peace	222.68	213.18	237.23	2.9676	.2268
5.	A world of beauty	224.72	213.09	235.83	2.4098	.2997
6.	Equality	216.94	215.83	231.03	.9539	.6207
7.	Family security	215.65	217.62	224.65	.2425	.8858
8.	Freedom	219.69	218.73	216.49	.0273	.9864
9.	Happiness	233.90	218.74	204.23	2.0190	.3644
10.	Inner Harmony	197.65	220.72	227.14	2.2183	.3298
11.	Mature love	231.85	214.74	222.80	1.1012	.5766
12.	National Security	218.24	214.18	236.86	2.2240	.3289
13.	Pleasure	239.65	215.94	211.03	2.2922	.3197

(Table Contd...)

(Table 4.65: Contd...)

1	2	3	4	5	6	7
14.	Salvation	222.96	210.47	242.30	4.5175	.1045
15.	Self-respect	219.00	216.24	227.57	.5446	.7617
16.	Social recogniton	210.27	218.46	225.77	.5731	.7509
17.	True	226.47	215.93	222.43	.6311	.7294
18.	Wisdom	181.57	221.45	237.94	8.4013	.0150*
19.	Equity	189.43	221.99	228.90	4.4057	.1105
20.	Power	240.05	212.67	224.40	2.7552	.2522
21.	Social justice	209.67	220.82	216.38	.5000	.7788
22.	Ambitious	209.55	219.72	221.09	.4029	.8175
23.	Broadminded	204.53	218.77	229.38	1.3749	.5029
24.	Capable	202.71	217.69	235.49	2.4492	.2939
25.	Cheerful	210.67	222.68	207.72	1.1975	.5495
26.	Clean	220.83	217.93	218.88	.0414	.9795
27.	Courageous	217.13	218.35	219.55	.0135	.9933
28.	Forgiving	210.35	218.51	225.49	.5097	.7750
29.	Helpful	207.38	220.48	219.77	.6093	.7374

(Table Contd...)

(Table 4.65: Contd...)

1	2	3	4	5	6	7
30.	Honesty	211.41	221.41	212.41	.6699	.7154
31.	Imagination	238.58	212.83	225.01	2.4885	.2882
32.	Independence	232.48	213.05	229.30	1.9975	.3683
33.	Intellectual	196.12	225.99	206.38	3.8996	.1423
34.	Logical	190.01	221.51	230.39	4.1328	.1266
35.	Loving	208.75	220.61	218.03	.4961	.7803
36.	Obedient	240.85	212.29	225.29	3.3904	.1836
37.	Polite	218.65	220.09	211.71	.2801	.8693
38.	Responsible	219.90	217.61	221.02	.0562	.9723
39.	Self-control	198.20	218.54	235.79	3.1296	.2091
40.	Self-determination	193.09	222.32	224.37	3.4499	.1782

1 N = 62
2 N = 302
3 N = 72
* Significant at .05 level
** Significant at .01 level

Table 4.66: Mean ranks, U-values and Z-values showing differences among girls perceiving less, moderate and high level of punishment on value 'wisdom'

Sl. No.	Level of punishment	N	Mean rank	U-value	Z-value	P
1.	Low	62	155.10	7663.5	–2.4141	.0158*
	Moderate	302	188.12			
2.	Low	62	57.97	1641.0	–2.8071	.0050**
	High	72	75.71			
3.	Moderate	302	184.82	1063.5	–1.0746	.2826
	High	72	198.73			

* Significant at .05 level
** Significant at .01 level

not differ from one another (Z = –1.0746, P > .05). This implies that girls perceiving moderate punishment in home do not differ significantly from those who perceive high punishment, on value named wisdom.

It was hypothesized that "Girls perceiving less, moderate and high level of conformity in home environment do not differ from one another on values". Table 4.67 presents results of Kurskal-Wallis one way ANOVA for comparing values of girls perceiving less moderate and high level of conformity in home environment. Observation of the chi-squre values shows that out of 40 values, thirty five are not significant. This allow acceptance of null hypothesis with respect to 35 values. It means that girls perceiving less, moderate and high level of conformity in home do not differ from one another with respect to importance given to values namely: A comfortable life, an exciting life, a sense of accomplishment, a world of peace, a world of beauty, equality, freedom, inner harmony, mature love, pleasure, salvation, self-respect, social

Table 4.67: Mean ranks and chi-square values showing differences among the girls perceiving less, moderate and high level of conformity in home environment, on various values

Sl. No.	Values	Level of Conformity			Chi-Sq.	Sign.
		Low[1]	Moderate[2]	High[3]		
1	2	3	4	5	6	7
1.	A comfortable life	193.50	221.31	229.86	4.8583	.0881
2.	An exciting life	206.55	222.89	213.17	1.1482	.5632
3.	A sense of accomplishment	205.88	219.36	226.21	1.0878	.5805
4.	A world of peace	216.44	211.87	243.66	5.4546	.0654
5.	A world of beauty	208.05	213.07	246.59	5.8609	.0545
6.	Equality	210.20	221.08	216.46	.4910	.7823
7.	Family security	192.04	214.43	225.41	11.4338	.0033**
8.	Freedom	208.96	220.91	218.10	.5509	.7592
9.	Happiness	184.25	221.33	237.67	7.7611	.0206*
10.	Inner harmony	207.75	217.20	232.69	1.6758	.4326
11.	Mature love	229.74	214.61	222.66	.9551	.6203
12.	National security	216.07	217.38	224.52	.2749	.8716
13.	Pleasure	219.83	211.41	242.41	4.1300	.1268

(Table Contd...)

(Table 4.67: Contd...)

1	2	3	4	5	6	7
14.	Salvation	196.96	220.37	230.23	2.9168	.2326
15.	Self-respect	204.83	221.30	220.25	1.1200	.5712
16.	Social recogniton	193.24	220.10	234.38	4.6640	.0971
17.	True friendship	233.16	210.58	233.99	4.6775	.0964
18.	Wisdom	197.01	219.92	231.79	1.4330	.1779
19.	Equity	183.49	220.56	241.04	8.7570	.0125**
20.	Power	201.45	220.08	227.46	1.8075	.4050
21.	Social justice	205.15	219.90	224.91	1.1939	.5505
22.	Ambitious	190.21	220.34	236.09	5.5473	.0624
23.	Broadminded	190.27	221.78	230.96	4.7056	.0951
24.	Capable	205.57	221.97	217.91	.9852	.6110
25.	Cheerful	196.19	219.21	234.99	3.8828	.1435
26.	Clean	200.68	215.96	242.64	6.6033	.0368*
27.	Courageous	190.33	218.06	244.07	7.4281	.0244*
28.	Forgiving	201.34	221.00	224.29	1.6552	.4371
29.	Helpful	214.83	219.55	217.91	.0864	.9577

(Table Contd...)

(Table 4.67: Contd...)

1	2	3	4	5	6	7
30.	Honesty	194.06	225.65	214.08	4.6131	.0996
31.	Imagination	217.60	213.22	237.91	2.5389	.2810
32.	Independent	215.32	213.80	237.82	2.5254	.2829
33.	Intellectual	206.36	220.66	221.22	.8065	.6681
34.	Logical	199.54	218.67	234.06	2.9022	.2343
35.	Loving	215.73	217.90	222.97	.1537	.9260
36.	Obedient	216.38	213.88	236.62	2.4352	.2959
37.	Polite	208.12	218.72	226.57	.8722	.6465
38.	Responsible	206.50	216.19	236.88	2.6722	.2629
39.	Self-control	203.03	218.90	230.25	1.8449	.3975
40.	Self-determination	193.04	219.84	235.47	5.0425	.0804

1 N = 69
2 N = 286
3 N = 81
* Significant at .05 level
** Significant at .01 level

recognition, true friendship, wisdom, power, social justice, ambitious, broadminded, capable, cheerful, forgiving, helpful, honesty, imagination, independent, intellectual, logical, loving, obedient, polite, responsible, self-control and self-determination.

Significant chi-square value were found for five values. This allows partial rejection of null hypothesis. It mean that girls perceiving less, moderate and high level of conformity in home environment differ from one another with respect to five values namely: Family security, happiness, equity, clean and courageous. Further analysis was done by using Mann-Whitney 'U' test. Results are shown in the table 4.69 to 4.73.

Table 4.68 shows that mean rank for girls perceiving less conformity in home is 163.50 and mean rank for girls perceiving moderate conformity are 181.55. Difference between the mean ranks for less and moderately conformed girls is not significant (Z = –1.3861, P > .05). It means that

Table 4.68: Mean ranks, U-values and Z-values showing differences among girls perceiving less, moderate and high level of conformity in home environment on 'family security' value

Sl. No.	Level of conformity	N	Mean rank	U-value	Z-value	P
1.	Low	69	163.50	8852.5	–1.3861	.1657
	Moderate	286	181.55			
2.	Low	69	63.75	1983.5	–3.2519	.0011**
	High	81	85.51			
3.	Moderate	286	176.38	9404.0	–2.7425	.0061**
	High	81	210.90			

* Significant at .05 level
** Significant at .01 level

girls perceiving less conformity in home to do not differ from moderately conforming girls on family security value. Mean ranks for girls perceiving less and high conformity are 63.75 and 85.51 respectively. Mean rank for highly conformed girls is greater than that for less conformed girls (Z = –3.2519, P < .01). It mean that girls perceiving high conformity in home give more importance to family security than those perceiving less conformity. Mean rank for girls perceiving moderate and high level conformity in home are 176.38 and 210.90 respectively. The latter is greater than the former (Z = –2.7425, P < .01). It allows us to infer that as compared to girls perceiving moderate conformity, those perceiving high conformity give more priority to family security value.

Table 4.69 shows that mean ranks for girls perceiving less and moderate level of conformity are 153.88 and 181.56 respectively. Difference between the mean ranks is significant (Z = –2.2622, P < .05). This allows us to infer

Table 4.69: Mean ranks, U-values and Z-values showing differences among girls perceiving less, moderate and high level of conformity in home environment on 'happiness' value

Sl. No.	Level of conformity	N	Mean rank	U-value	Z-value	P
1.	Low	69	153.88	8203.0	–2.2622	.0237*
	Moderate	286	183.82			
2.	Low	69	65.37	2095.5	–2.7460	.0060**
	High	81	84.13			
3.	Moderate	286	181.02	10729.5	–1.0644	.2871
	High	81	194.54			

* Significant at .05 level
** Significant at .01 level

that girls perceiving moderate conformity give more importance to happiness than those who perceive less conformity. Mean ranks for girls perceiving less and high level of conformity are 65.37 and 84.13 respectively. The latter is greater than the former (Z =–2.7460, P < .01). It implies that happiness is considered more important by girls perceiving high conformity than those who perceive less conformity in home. Mean ranks for girls perceiving moderate and high conformity are 181.02 and 194.54 respectively. They do not differ significantly from each other (Z =–1.0644, P > .05). It indicates that girls perceiving moderate and high conformity give equal importance to happiness value.

Table 4.70 shows that mean ranks for girls perceiving less and moderate conformity in homes are 153.59 and 183.89 respectively. The latter is greater than former (Z =–2.2908, P < .05). It means that girls perceiving moderate conformity give more importance to equity than girls

Table 4.70: Mean ranks, U-values and Z-values showing differences among girls perceiving less, moderate and high level of conformity in home environment on 'equity' value

Sl. No.	Level of conformity	N	Mean rank	U-value	Z-value	P
1.	Low	69	153.59	8182.5	–2.2908	.0220*
	Moderate	286	183.89			
2.	Low	69	64.91	2063.5	–2.8744	.0040**
	High	81	84.52			
3.	Moderate	286	180.17	10488.0	–1.3708	.1704
	High	81	197.52			

* Significant at .05 level

** Significant at .01 level

perceiving less conformity. Mean ranks for girls perceiving less and high conformity are 64.91 and 84.52 respectively. The latter is greater than the former (Z = –2.8744, P < .01). It means that equity finds an important place among girls perceiving high conformity than among those perceiving less conformity. Further look at the table also shows that mean ranks for girls perceiving high level of conformity are 180.17 and 197.52 respectively. Difference between the two mean ranks is not significant (Z = –1.3708, P < .05). It indicates that no significant difference exists between girls perceiving moderate and high level of conformity on equity value.

Table 4.71 shows that mean ranks for girls perceiving less and moderate conformity in home are 168.20 and 180.37 respectively. They do not differ significantly (Z = –1.05502, P < .05). It implies that girls perceiving less and moderate conformity give equal importance to clean value. Mean ranks

Table 4.71: Mean ranks, U-values and Z-values showing differences among girls perceiving less, moderate and high level of conformity in home environment on 'clean' value

Sl. No.	Level of conformity	N	Mean rank	U-value	Z-value	P
1.	Low	69	168.20	9190.5	–1.0502	.2936
	Moderate	286	180.37			
2.	Low	69	67.49	2241.5	–2.5810	.0098**
	High	81	82.33			
3.	Moderate	286	179.10	10181.0	–2.0583	.0396*
	High	81	201.31			

* Significant at .05 level
** Significant at .01 level

for girls perceiving less and high conformity are 67.49 and 82.33 respectively. The latter is greater than the former (Z = –2.5810, P < .01). It leads us to infer that clean value finds more important place among the girls who perceive high level of conformity in home than among those who perceive less conformity. Mean ranks for girls perceiving moderate and high conformity are 179.10 and 201.31 respectively. The latter is greater than the former (Z =–2.0583, P < .05). It indicates that clean value is regarded as more important by girls perceiving high conformity than by those perceiving moderate conformity.

Table 4.72 shows that mean rank for girls perceiving less and moderate conformity are 159.69 and 182.42 respectively. They do not differ significantly from each other (Z = –1.7183, P > .05). So, it can be inferred that girls perceiving less and moderate level conformity in their homes give equal importance to the value named courageous. Mean ranks for girls perceiving less and high conformity are 65.64

Table 4.72: Mean ranks, U-values and Z-values showing differences among girls perceiving less, moderate and high level of conformity in home on value 'courageous'

Sl. No.	Level of conformity	N	Mean rank	U-value	Z-value	P
1.	Low	69	159.69	8603.5	–1.7183	.0857
	Moderate	286	182.42			
2.	Low	69	65.64	2114.0	–2.6891	.0072**
	High	81	83.90			
3.	Moderate	286	179.14	10192.5	–1.7346	.0828*
	High	81	201.17			

* Significant at .05 level
** Significant at .01 level

and 83.90 respectively. The latter is greater than the former ($Z = -2.689$, $P < .01$). It indicates that girls perceiving high conformity give more importance to courageous value than those perceiving less conformity. Mean rank for girls perceiving moderate and high conformity are 179.14 and 201.17 respectively. They do not differ significantly from each other ($Z = -1.7346$, $P > .05$). This allows us to infer that the girls perceiving high and moderate conformity give equal importance to courageous value.

It was hypothesized that "Girls perceiving less, moderate and high level of social isolation in home do not differ from one another in values". Table 4.73 presents results of Kruskal-Wallis one way ANOVA for values among girls perceiving different level of social isolation. Observation of chi-square values shows that out of 40 values, only thirty seven are not significant at .05 level. One value is significant at .01 level and two values are significant at .05 level. Non significant chi-square values allow acceptance of the null hypothesis with respect to 37 values. It means that girls perceiving less moderate and high level of social isolation in home environment do not differ from one another with respect to 37 values namely: An exciting life, a sense of accomplishment, a world of peace. A world of beauty, family security, freedom, inner harmony, mature love, national security, pleasure, salvation, self-respect, social recognition, true friendship, wisdom, equity, power, social justice, ambitious, broadminded, capable, cheerful, clean, courageous, forgiving, helpful, honesty, imagination, independent logical, loving, obedient, polite, responsible, self-control and self-determination.

Significant chi-square values allow partial rejection of null hypothesis. It means that girls perceiving different level of isolation less, moderate and high differ from one another with respect to three values namely: A comfortable life, equality and happiness. Further analysis was done by

Table 4.73: Mean ranks and chi-square values showing differences among girls perceiving less, moderate and high level of social isolation in home on various values

Sl. No.	Values	Level of Social Isolation			Chi-Sq.	Sign.
		Low[1]	Moderate[2]	High[3]		
1	2	3	4	5	6	7
1.	A comfortable life	224.31	226.88	178.63	11.7703	.0028**
2.	An exciting life	227.76	218.95	205.13	1.3237	.5159
3.	A sense of accomplishment	220.89	220.27	208.61	.5655	.7537
4.	A world of peace	234.17	216.26	207.57	2.6974	.2596
5.	A world of beauty	237.91	213.51	213.57	3.0914	.2132
6.	Equality	251.06	210.69	208.06	8.3452	.0154*
7.	Family security	215.82	220.47	214.18	.2126	.8992
8.	Freedom	243.68	215.01	200.49	5.7362	.0568
9.	Happiness	236.13	222.36	181.40	8.8952	.0117**
10.	Inner Harmony	232.08	219.40	197.96	3.0585	.2167
11.	Mature love	227.03	216.96	213.80	.5758	.7498
12.	National security	216.97	220.58	212.34	.3046	.8587
13.	Pleasure	234.15	220.37	191.63	5.0265	.0810

(Table Contd...)

(Table 4.73: Contd...)

1	2	3	4	5	6	7
14.	Salvation	219.52	219.16	214.67	.0828	.9594
15.	Self-respect	239.85	216.04	201.31	4.6002	.1003
16.	Social recogniton	220.62	221.81	202.96	1.4712	.4792
17.	True friendship	216.26	217.21	226.31	.4687	.7911
18.	Wisdom	211.15	221.39	216.48	.5443	.7617
19.	Equity	208.48	222.57	215.24	.9833	.6116
20.	Power	235.51	215.08	210.48	2.2228	.3291
21.	Social justice	225.99	213.64	228.01	1.3242	.5158
22.	Ambitious	219.01	219.46	214.13	.1117	.9457
23.	Broadminded	204.63	223.70	215.68	1.6750	.4328
24.	Capable	219.44	222.34	202.38	1.5190	.4679
25.	Cheerful	239.92	216.99	197.53	4.9934	.0824
26.	Clean	213.62	216.47	232.53	1.6045	.4483
27.	Courageous	216.97	221.07	210.44	.4574	.7956

(Table Contd...)

(Table 4.73: Contd...)

1	2	3	4	5	6	7
28.	Forgiving	205.46	222.10	220.87	1.2747	.5287
29.	Helpful	213.33	218.71	224.15	.3170	.8534
30.	Honesty	200.39	220.85	232.05	3.5143	.1725
31.	Imagination	207.98	222.82	214.89	1.0490	.5918
32.	Independent	229.72	241.28	220.85	1.1204	.5711
33.	Intellectual	220.18	219.30	213.30	.1565	.9248
34.	Logical	208.44	223.11	213.18	1.1035	.5759
35.	Loving	208.64	219.13	227.70	1.0141	.6023
36.	Obedient	207.38	220.14	226.06	1.1667	.5580
37.	Polite	230.33	212.84	225.65	1.7095	.4254
38.	Responsible	228.47	213.40	225.82	1.3648	.5054
39.	Self-control	201.26	219.85	234.87	3.0565	.2169
40.	Self-determination	241.38	213.23	210.31	4.3387	.1143

1 N = 89
2 N = 276
3 N = 71
* Significant at .05 level
** Significant at .01 level

using Mann-Whitney 'U' test. results are shown in the table 4.74 to 4.76.

Table 4.74 shows that mean rank for girls perceiving less and moderate social isolation in home are 181.78 and 183.39 respectively. Difference between the two mean ranks is not significant (Z = –.1491, P > .05). This allows us to infer that girls perceiving less social isolation in home do not differ from girls perceiving moderate social isolation, on value named a comfortable life. Mean ranks for the girls perceiving less and high level social isolation in home are 87.53 and 71.68 respectively mean rank for less socially isolated girls is greater than that for highly isolated girls (Z = –2.4863, P < .01). This allows us to infer that girls experiencing less social isolation in home give more importance to value named a comfortable life than highly socially isolated girls. Mean rank for the girls perceiving moderate and high level of social isolation are 181.99 and 142.94. Mean for moderately socially isolated girls is greater

Table 4.74: Mean ranks, U-values and Z-values showing differences among girls perceiving less, moderate and high level of social isolation on 'a comfortable life' values

Sl. No.	Level of social isolation	N	Mean rank	U-value	Z-value	P
1.	Low	89	181.78	12173.0	–.1491	.8815
	Moderate	276	183.39			
2.	Low	89	87.53	2533.5	–2.4863	.0129**
	High	71	71.68			
3.	Moderate	276	181.99	7593.0	–3.4431	.0096**
	High	71	142.94			

* Significant at .05 level
** Significant at .01 level

than those perceiving high social isolation (Z = –3.4431, P < .01). This indicates that moderately socially isolated girls give more importance to a comfortable life than the girls perceiving high level of social isolation in home.

Table 4.75 shows mean ranks for girls perceiving less and moderate level of social isolation in home are 208.56 and 174.76 respectively. Mean rank for less socially isolated girls is greater than that for moderately socially isolated girls (Z = –.2.7803, P < .01). It indicates that equality finds more important place among the girls perceiving less social isolation than among those who perceive moderate social isolation in home environment. Mean ranks for the girls experiencing less, and high level of social isolation in home are 87.51 and 71.72 respectively. The former is greater than the latter (Z = –2.3118, P < .05). It mans that equality is regarded as more important by girls perceiving less social isolation than those who perceive high social isolation. Mean ranks for girls perceiving moderate and high social isolation

Table 4.75: Mean ranks, U-values and Z-values showing differences among girls perceiving less, moderate and high level of social isolation on value 'equality'

Sl. No.	Level of social isolation	N	Mean rank	U-value	Z-value	P
1.	Low	89	208.56	10007.5	–2.7803	.0054**
	Moderate	276	174.76			
2.	Low	89	87.51	2536.0	–2.3118	.0208*
	High	71	71.72			
3.	Moderate	276	174.43	9680.0	–1.635	.8701
	High	71	172.34			

* Significant at .05 level
** Significant at .01 level

are 174.43 and 172.34 respectively. They do not differ significantly from each other (Z = –.1635, P > .05). This allows us to infer that girls perceiving high and moderate social isolation in home give equal importance to equality value.

Table 4.76 shows that mean ranks for girls perceiving less and moderate level of social isolation in home are 191.75 and 180.18 respectively. They do not differ significantly from each other (Z = .9456, P > 0.5). It means that girls perceiving less and moderate social isolation in home give equal importance to happiness value. Mean rank for girls perceiving less and high social isolation are 89.38 and 69.37 respectively. The former is greater than the latter (Z = –2.8260 P < .01). It means that girls perceiving less social isolation in home give more importance to happiness value than those who perceive high level social isolation. Mean ranks for girls perceiving moderate and high social

Table 4.76: Mean ranks, U-values and Z-values showing differences among girls perceiving less, moderate and high level of social isolation in home on value 'happiness'

Sl. No.	Level of social isolation	N	Mean rank	U-value	Z-value	P
1.	Low	89	191.75	11503.0	–.9456	.3444
	Moderate	276	180.18			
2.	Low	89	89.38	2369.5	–2.8260	.0047**
	High	71	69.37			
3.	Moderate	276	180.78	7954.0	–2.5445	.0109**
	High	71	148.03			

* Significant at .05 level
** Significant at .01 level

isolation are 180.68 and 148.03 respectively. The former is greater than the latter (Z = –2.5445, P < .01). This allows us to infer that happiness is regarded as more important by the girls who perceive moderate social isolation in home than the girls perceiving high level of social isolation.

It was hypothesized that "Girls perceiving different levels of reward in home do not differ from one another on values. Table 4.77 presents results of Kruskal-Waills one way ANOVA for values among girls perceiving less, moderate and high level of reward. Observation of chi-square values show that out of 40 values only eight are significant. Four values are significant at .05 level. Three values are significant at .01 level. The non-significant values allow acceptance of the null hypothesis with respect to 32 values. This means that girls perceiving less, moderate and high level of reward do not differ from on another one values namely: A comfortable life, an exciting life, a sense of accomplishment, a world of peace, a world of beauty, equality, family security, freedom, happiness, mature love, national security, pleasure, salvation, self-respect, true friendship, equity, social justice, capable, cheerful, clean, forgiving, helpful, honesty, imagination, independent, intellectual, logical, loving, obedient, polite responsible, self-determination.

Significant chi-square values are found for eight values. They allow partial rejection of the null hypothesis. This allows us to infer that girls perceiving different levels of reward in home environment do differ from one another with respect to eight values namely: Inner harmony, social-recognition, wisdom, power, ambitious, broadminded, courageous and self-control. Further analysis was done by using Mann-Whitney "U" test. Results are shown in tables 4.78 to 4.84.

Table 4.78 shows that mean rank for girls perceiving less reward is 196.08 and mean rank for girls perceiving moderate reward is 188.16. Mean rank for less rewarded

Table 4.77: Mean ranks and chi-square values showing differences among girls perceiving different level of 'reward' on various values

Sl. No.	Values	Level of Reward			Chi-Sq.	Sign.
		Low[1]	Moderate[2]	High[3]		
1	2	3	4	5	6	7
1.	A comfortable life	207.47	219.50	225.28	.9369	.6260
2.	An exciting life	202.84	223.28	209.91	1.7635	.4141
3.	A sense of accomplishment	223.59	216.23	225.16	.3968	.8201
4.	A world of peace	217.25	215.41	236.63	1.8853	.3896
5.	A world of beauty	200.45	216.65	248.45	5.4256	.0663
6.	Equality	205.57	222.03	213.66	1.1200	.5712
7.	Family security	192.23	219.56	241.75	5.3077	.0704
8.	Freedom	212.98	216.85	233.50	1.0979	.5776
9.	Happiness	200.59	218.58	237.84	2.8995	.2346
10.	Inner harmony	220.49	211.36	254.95	6.1226	.0468*
11.	Mature love	225.14	219.06	208.14	.6049	.7390
12.	National security	201.07	219.22	233.85	2.4730	.2904
13.	Pleasure	219.99	215.90	230.91	.7597	.6840

(Table Contd...)

(Table 4.77: Contd...)

1	2	3	4	5	6	7
14.	Salvation	220.05	219.79	209.81	.3340	.8462
15.	Self-respect	220.47	213.25	244.76	3.5571	.1689
16.	Social recognition	197.84	215.96	255.05	7.6438	.0219*
17.	True friendship	222.89	215.55	229.64	.9999	.6066
18.	Wisdom	179.84	220.72	249.16	11.1422	.0038**
19.	Equity	202.27	219.82	229.28	1.6665	.4346
20.	Power	178.87	224.00	232.47	8.0431	.0179*
21.	Social justice	194.68	219.75	238.04	4.3476	.1137
22.	Ambitious	174.69	221.80	248.98	12.3009	.0021**
23.	Broadminded	189.91	215.61	265.68	12.2577	.0022**
24.	Capable	206.77	215.97	245.12	3.4881	.1748
25.	Cheerful	195.20	221.08	230.24	3.0786	.2145
26.	Clean	223.67	217.21	219.78	.2168	.8973
27.	Courageous	181.16	220.48	248.97	9.9466	.0069**

(Table Contd...)

(Table 4.77: Contd...)

1	2	3	4	5	6	7
28.	Forgiving	204.62	218.48	233.91	1.7416	.4186
29.	Helpful	216.59	218.92	218.34	.0198	.9901
30.	Honesty	196.37	224.53	210.28	3.7502	.1533
31.	Imagination	206.50	217.70	236.08	1.8011	.4063
32.	Independent	222.73	216.37	225.35	.3588	.8358
33.	Intellectual	206.57	214.76	251.91	5.2091	.0739
34.	Logical	212.80	218.77	223.31	.2252	.8935
35.	Loving	213.59	220.93	210.77	.4693	.7909
36.	Obedient	197.70	219.80	234.41	3.1672	.2052
37.	Polite	218.05	214.65	239.85	2.1346	.3439
38.	Responsible	187.02	223.91	223.97	5.1190	.0773
39.	Self-control	194.94	217.52	249.81	6.1625	.0459*
40.	Self-determination	212.87	216.85	233.67	1.1943	.5504

1 N = 64
2 N = 314
3 N = 58
* Significant at .05 level
** Significant at .01 level

Table 4.78: Mean ranks, U-values and Z-values showing differences among the girls perceiving different level of reward in home environment on 'inner harmony' value

Sl. No.	Level of reward	N	Mean rank	U-value	Z-value	P
1.	Low	64	196.08	9627.0	–.5395	.5895
	Moderate	314	188.16			
2.	Low	64	56.91	1562.5	–1.5338	.1251
	High	58	66.56			
3.	Moderate	314	180.70	7285.5	–2.4718	.0134**
	High	58	217.89			

* Significant at .05 level
** Significant at .01 level

girls is not significantly different from that for moderately rewarded girls (Z= .5395, P >.05). This indicates that girls perceiving less reward do not differ from girls perceiving moderate reward on inner harmony value. Mean rank for less and highly rewarded girls are 56.91 and 66.56 respectively. Mean rank for less rewarded girls is not significantly different from that for highly rewarded girls (Z= –1.5338, P > .05). It indicates that girls perceiving less reward do not differ significantly from highly rewarded girls on value named inner harmony. Mean ranks for girls perceiving moderate and high reward are 180.70 and 217.89 respectively. Mean rank for highly rewarded girls is greater than that for moderately rewarded girls (Z= –2.4718, P < .01). It allows us to infer that girls perceiving high reward give more importance to inner harmony than girls perceiving moderate reward.

Table 4.79 shows that mean rank for less rewarded girls is 176.27 and mean rank for moderately rewarded girls is 192.20. Difference between the mean ranks for both groups is not significant (Z= –1.1228, P > .05). It means that girls perceiving less reward do not differ from those perceiving moderate reward on social recognition value. Mean ranks for less and highly rewarded girls are 54.06 and 69.71 respectively. Mean rank for highly rewarded girls is greater than that for less rewarded (Z= –2.6427, P < .05). It allows us to infer that highly rewarded girls regard social recognition as more important than the less rewarded girls. Mean rank for girls perceiving moderate reward is 181.26 while mean rank for girls perceiving high reward is 214.84. Latter is greater than the former (Z=–2.3403, P < .05). It allows to infer that girls perceiving high reward give more importance to social recognition value than those perceiving less reward.

Table 4.79: Mean ranks, U-values and Z-values showing differences among girls perceiving less, moderate and high level of reward in home on 'social recognition' value

Sl. No.	Level of reward	N	Mean rank	U-value	Z-value	P
1.	Low	64	176.27	9201.5	–1.1228	.2615
	Moderate	314	192.20			
2.	Low	64	54.06	1380.0	–2.6427	.0082**
	High	58	69.71			
3.	Moderate	314	181.26	7462.0	–2.3403	.0193*
	High	58	214.84			

* Significant at .05 level
** Significant at .01 level

Table 4.80 shows mean ranks for girls perceiving less and moderate reward in home are 160.09 and 195.50 respectively. Mean ranks for the former is less than the latter (Z = –2.5334. P <.01). It can be inferred that girls perceiving moderate reward in home give more importance to wisdom value than those who perceive less reward. Mean ranks for girls perceiving less and high reward are 52.26 and 71.70 respectively. Mean ranks for former is less than latter (Z= –3.244, P < .01). It means girls perceiving less reward in home find value wisdom less important than those who perceive high reward. Mean ranks for girls perceiving moderate and high level of reward are 182.72 and 206.96 respectively. Mean ranks for both groups do not vary from one another (Z= –1.7231, P <.05). It indicates that girls perceiving moderate and high reward in home environments give equal importance to wisdom value.

Table 4.80: Mean ranks, U-values and Z-values showing differences among girls perceiving less moderate and high level of reward in home on 'wisdom' value

Sl. No.	Level of reward	N	Mean rank	U-value	Z-value	P
1.	Low	64	160.09	8165.5	–2.5334	.0113**
	Moderate	314	195.50			
2.	Low	64	52.26	1264.5	–3.2444	.0012**
	High	58	71.70			
3.	Moderate	314	182.72	7919.5	–1.7231	.0849
	High	58	206.96			

* Significant at .05 level
** Significant at .01 level

Table 4.81 shows that mean ranks for less and moderately rewarded girls are 156.89 and 196.15 respectively. Mean rank for moderately rewarded girls is greater than that for less rewarded girls (Z= –2.6892, P < .01). This allows us to infer that moderately rewarded girls regard wisdom value as more important than less rewarded girls. Mean ranks for less and highly rewarded girls are 54.48 and 69.25 respectively. Mean rank for highly rewarded girls (Z= –2.3599, P < .05). Inference can be drawn that highly rewarded girls give more importance to power value than girls perceiving high reward. Mean ranks for girls perceiving moderate and high reward are 185.35 and 192.72 respectively. Mean rank for moderately rewarded girls is not different from that for highly rewarded girls (Z= –.4923, P > .05). This means that importance of power value is not affected by the level of reward perceived by girls in their home environment.

Table 4.81: Mean ranks, U-values and Z-values showing differences among girls perceiving less, moderate and high level of reward in home on 'power' value

Sl. No.	Level of reward	N	Mean rank	U-value	Z-value	P
1.	Low	64	156.89	7961.0	–2.6892	.0072**
	Moderate	314	196.15			
2.	Low	64	54.48	1406.5	–2.3599	.0183*
	High	58	69.25			
3.	Moderate	314	185.35	8745.0	–.4923	.6225
	High	58	192.72			

* Significant at .05 level
** Significant at .01 level

Table 4.82 shows that mean rank for girls perceiving less reward is 155.70. Mean rank for girls perceiving moderate reward is 196.39. Mean rank for moderately rewarded girls is greater than that for less rewarded girls (Z= –2.8187. P < .01). This implies that moderately rewarded girls give more importance to ambitious value than the girls perceiving less reward. Mean rank for girls perceiving less and high reward are 51.49 and 72.54 respectively. Mean rank for highly rewarded girls is greater than that for less rewarded girls (Z= –3.3868, P < .01). It allows us to infer that girls perceiving high reward assign more importance to ambitious value than those who perceive less reward in home. Mean rank for girls perceiving moderate reward is 182.91. Mean rank for girls perceiving high reward is 205.94. Mean rank for highly rewarded girls is greater than that for moderately rewarded girls (Z= –1.5726, P > .05). It leads us to infer that girls perceiving moderate reward do not differ from highly rewarded girls on 'ambitious' value.

Table 4.82: Mean ranks, U-values and Z-values showing differences among girls perceiving less, moderate and high level of reward in home on value 'ambitious'

Sl. No.	Level of reward	N	Mean rank	U-value	Z-value	P
1.	Low	64	155.70	7884.5	–2.8187	.0048**
	Moderate	314	196.39			
2.	Low	64	51.49	1215.5	–3.3868	.0007**
	High	58	72.54			
3.	Moderate	314	182.91	7978.5	–1.5726	.1158
	High	58	205.94			

* Significant at .05 level
** Significant at .01 level

Table 4.83 shows that mean rank for girls perceiving less reward is 171.67 and mean rank for the girls perceiving moderate reward in home is 193.13. Difference between the mean ranks for both groups is not significant (Z= –1.4697, P > .05). It indicates that girls perceiving moderate reward do not vary from those perceiving less reward in home on broadminded value. Mean ranks for less and highly rewarded girls are 50.73 and 73.38 respectively. Mean rank for highly rewarded girls is greater than that for less rewarded girls (Z= –3.6378, P < .01). It allows us to infer that girls perceiving high reward in home find broadminded value more important than less rewarded girls. Mean rank for moderately rewarded girls is 179.98 while mean rank for highly rewarded girls is 221.80. Mean rank for highly rewarded girls is greater than that for moderately rewarded girls (Z= –2.8088, P < .01). It leads us to infer that broadminded value is considered more important by highly rewarded girls than by those who perceive moderate reward in home.

Table 4.83: Mean ranks, U-values and Z-values showing differences among girls perceiving less, moderate and high level of reward in home on 'broadminded' value

Sl. No.	Level of reward	N	Mean rank	U-value	Z-value	P
1.	Low	64	171.67	8907.0	–1.4697	.1416
	Moderate	314	193.13			
2.	Low	64	50.73	1167.0	–3.6378	.0003**
	High	58	73.38			
3.	Moderate	314	179.98	7058.5	–2.8055	.0050**
	High	58	221.80			

* Significant at .05 level
** Significant at .01 level

Table 4.84 shows that mean rank for the girls perceiving less reward in home is 161.29 and mean rank for the girls perceiving moderate reward in home is 195.25. Mean rank for moderately rewarded girls is greater than that for less rewarded girls (Z= –2.3592, P < .05). This allows us to infer that value named courageous finds more important place among moderately rewarded girls than among those who perceive less reward in home environment. Mean ranks for girls perceiving less and high reward in home are 52.37 and 71.58 respectively. Mean rank for the girls perceiving high reward is greater than that for perceiving less reward (Z= –3.1179, P < .01). This allows us to infer that girls perceiving high reward in home give more importance to value named courageous than those who perceive less reward. Mean ranks for moderately and highly rewarded girls are 182.73 and 206.89 respectively. Mean rank of moderately rewarded girls do not differ from that for highly rewarded girls (Z= –1.6568, P > .05). This leads us to infer that girls perceiving moderate and high reward in home give equal importance to being courageous.

Table 4.84: Mean ranks, U-values and Z-values showing differences among girls perceiving less, moderate and high level of reward on 'courageous' value

Sl. No.	Level of reward	N	Mean rank	U-value	Z-value	P
1.	Low	64	161.29	8242.5	–2.3592	.0183*
	Moderate	314	195.25			
2.	Low	64	52.37	1271.5	–3.1179	.0018**
	High	58	71.58			
3.	Moderate	314	182.73	7923.5	–1.6568	.0976
	High	58	206.89			

* Significant at .05 level
** Significant at .01 level

Table 4.85 shows that mean rank for girls perceiving less reward in home is 173.13 and mean rank for girls perceiving moderate reward is 192.84. The mean ranks for both groups do not vary from each other (Z= –1.3479, P > .05). This means that girls perceiving less reward do not differ from the girls who perceive moderate reward on self-control value. Mean ranks for girls perceiving less and high reward in home are 54.31 and 69.43 respectively. Mean rank for highly rewarded girls is greater than that for less rewarded girls (Z= –2.4310, P < .05). This allows us to infer that girls perceiving high reward in home give more importance to self control value than those who perceive less reward in home. Mean ranks for girls perceiving moderate and high reward are 182.18 and 209.88 respectively. Mean rank for moderately rewarded girls do not vary from highly rewarded girls (Z= –1.8559, P > .05). This allows us to infer that girls perceiving moderate reward in home do not differ from those perceiving high reward in home on self-control value.

Table 4.85: Mean ranks, U-values and Z-values showing differences among girls perceiving less, moderate and high level of reward in home environment on value 'self-control'

Sl. No.	Level of reward	N	Mean rank	U-value	Z-value	P
1.	Low	64	173.13	9000.0	–1.3479	.1777
	Moderate	314	192.84			
2.	Low	64	54.31	1396.0	–2.4310	.0151*
	High	58	69.43			
3.	Moderate	314	182.18	7750.0	–1.8559	.0635
	High	58	209.88			

* Significant at .05 level
** Significant at .01 level

It was hypothesized that "Girls perceiving different levels of deprivation of privilege do not differ from one another in values". Table 4.86 presents results of Kruskal-wallis one way ANOVA for values among girls perceiving different level of deprivation of privilege. Observation of chi-square values shows that out of 40 values only four are significant. Three values are significant at .05 level one value is significant at .01 level. The non significant chi-square values allow acceptance of the null hypothesis with respect to 36 values. It means that girls perceiving different levels of deprivation of privilege do not differ from one another with respect to 36 values namely: A comfortable life, an exciting life, a sense of accomplishment, a world of peace, equality, family security, freedom, inner harmony, mature love, national security, pleasure, salvation, self-respect, true friendship, wisdom, equity, power, social justice ambitious, broadminded, capable, cheerful, clean, courageous, forgiving, helpful, honesty, imagination, independent, intellectual, logical, loving, obedient, responsible, self-control and self-determination.

Significant values of chi-square were found for four values, namely: A world of beauty, happiness, social recognition and polite. These values allow partial rejection of the null hypothesis. This allows us to infer that girls perceiving less, moderate and high level of deprivation of privilege in home, differ from one another with respect to four values. Further, analysis was done by using Mann-Whitney 'U' test. Results are shown in the tables 4.87 to 4.90.

Table 4.87 shows that mean ranks for girls perceiving less and moderate level of deprivation of privilege are 205.75 176.72 respectively. Mean rank for the girls perceiving less deprivation of privilege is greater than that for moderately deprived girls ($Z = -2.3499$, $P < .05$). This allows us to infer that girls perceiving less deprivation of privilege in home give more importance to a world beauty value than those who perceive moderate deprivation of privilege. Mean ranks

Table 4.86: Mean rank and chi-square value showing differences among girls perceiving different level of deprivation of privilege on various values

Sl. No.	Values	Level of Deprivation of Privilage				
		Low[1]	Moderate[2]	High[3]	Chi-Sq.	Sign.
1	2	3	4	5	6	7
1.	A comfortable life	217.12	224.33	196.57	3.8281	.1475
2.	An exciting life	217.51	221.29	208.35	.6247	.7317
3.	A sense of accomplishment	229.08	220.11	200.23	2.2591	.3232
4.	A world of peace	232.31	219.99	197.11	4.0977	.1289
5.	A world of beauty	249.51	215.26	197.06	8.1901	.0167*
6.	Equality	237.44	216.83	204.17	3.0665	.2158
7.	Family security	234.66	215.44	212.85	1.7894	.4087
8.	Freedom	238.53	212.96	218.54	2.8048	.2460
9.	Happiness	250.51	218.87	181.38	12.2848	.0021**
10.	Inner harmony	231.42	216.61	211.75	1.1456	.5639
11.	Mature love	233.19	213.44	222.52	1.6864	.4303
12.	National security	208.41	220.51	221.64	.7352	.6924
13.	Pleasure	233.01	216.61	209.97	1.5506	.4606

(Table Contd...)

(Table 4.86: Contd...)

1	2	3	4	5	6	7
14.	Salvation	218.68	218.77	217.20	.0094	.9953
15.	Self-respect	232.05	217.60	207.05	1.7492	.4170
16.	Social recognition	249.13	208.43	224.99	7.5940	.0224*
17.	True friendship	213.88	223.48	203.56	2.2057	.3319
18.	Wisdom	230.22	218.18	206.76	1.5174	.4683
19.	Equity	224.17	221.11	201.69	1.6934	.4288
20.	Power	244.74	213.38	209.94	4.4482	.1082
21.	Social justice	238.17	213.22	217.90	2.8453	.2411
22.	Ambitious	216.75	221.56	208.13	.7207	.6974
23.	Broadminded	219.84	217.17	222.38	.1146	.9443
24.	Capable	223.68	216.57	220.50	.2327	.8902
25.	Cheerful	242.80	216.61	199.08	5.1151	.0775
26.	Clean	221.72	220.22	207.99	.8856	.6422
27.	Courageous	200.30	222.69	221.89	2.2057	.3319

(Table Contd...)

(Table 4.86: Contd...)

1	2	3	4	5	6	7
28.	Forgiving	193.73	225.77	216.79	4.2522	.1193
29.	Helpful	224.70	219.58	207.26	.8380	.6577
30.	Honesty	203.41	221.55	223.02	1.7747	.4117
31.	Imagination	234.80	215.44	212.70	1.7163	.4239
32.	Independent	225.93	218.96	208.37	.7931	.6726
33.	Intellectual	222.11	215.17	227.90	.6976	.7055
34.	Logical	204.92	224.00	211.45	1.7484	.4172
35.	Loving	214.09	225.25	196.21	3.4054	.1822
36.	Obedient	203.04	225.02	209.45	2.7175	.2570
37.	Polite	249.23	211.66	211.87	6.2490	.0440*
38.	Responsible	214.84	218.75	221.57	.1201	.9417
39.	Self-control	195.85	224.37	220.06	3.3597	.1864
40.	Self-determination	224.83	213.64	231.05	1.5524	.4602

1 N= 79
2 N= 286
3 N= 71
* Significant at .05 level
**Significant at .01 level

Table 4.87: Mean ranks, U-values and Z-values showing differences among girls perceiving less, moderate and high level of deprivation of privilege on 'a world of beauty' value

Sl. No.	Level of deprivation of privilege	N	Mean rank	U-value	Z-value	P
1.	Low	79	205.75	9500.0	–2.3499	.0188*
	Moderate	286	176.72			
2.	Low	79	83.77	2151.5	–2.6979	.0070**
	High	71	66.30			
3.	Moderate	286	182.04	9284.0	–1.1927	.2330
	High	71	166.76			

* Significant at .05 level
** Significant at .01 level

for the girls perceiving less and high level of deprivation of privilege are 83.77 and 66.30 respectively. Mean rank for girls perceiving less deprivation of privilege is greater than that for girls perceiving more deprivation of privileges ($Z= -2.6979$, $P < .01$). This permits us to infer that value named a world of beauty finds more important place among girls perceiving less deprivation of privilege in home than those who perceive high deprivation of privileges. Mean rank for girls perceiving moderate level of deprivation of privileges is 182.04 while mean rank for girls perceiving high level of deprivation of privileges is 166.76. Mean ranks for both groups do not vary from one another ($Z= -1.1927$, $P > .05$). This implies that girls perceiving high and moderate level deprivation of privileges give equal importance to a world of beauty.

Table 4.88 shows that mean ranks for the girls perceiving less and moderate level of deprivation of privilege

Table 4.88: Mean ranks, U-values and Z-values showing differences among girls perceiving less, moderate and high level of deprivation of privileges in home on 'happiness' value

Sl. No.	Level of deprivation of privilege	N	Mean rank	U-value	Z-value	P
1.	Low	79	203.84	9651.0	–2.0824	.0373*
	Moderate	286	177.24			
2.	Low	79	86.68	1921.5	–3.4650	.0005**
	High	71	63.06			
3.	Moderate	286	185.13	8400.5	–2.3422	.0192*
	High	71	154.32			

* Significant at .05 level
** Significant at .01 level

in home are 203.84 and 177.24 respectively. Mean rank for girls perceiving less deprivation of privilege is greater than that for those perceiving moderate level of deprivation of privilege (Z= –2.0824, P < .05). It means that in comparison to girls perceiving moderate level of deprivation of privilege, girls perceiving less deprivation of privilege give more importance to happiness value. Mean rank for girls perceiving less and high deprivation of privileges are 86.68 and 63.06 respectively. The former is greater than the latter (Z= –3.4650, P < .01). It means that girls perceiving value less deprivation of privileges assign more importance to happiness value than those perceiving more deprivation of privileges. Mean ranks for girls perceiving moderate and high deprivation of privileges are 185.13 and 154.32 respectively. The former is greater than the latter (Z= –2.3422, P < .05). This leads us to infer that in comparison to girls perceiving high deprivation of privileges, girls perceiving moderate deprivation of privileges give more importance to happiness value.

Table 4.89 shows that mean rank for the girls perceiving less and moderate level of deprivation of privileges are 209.66 and 175.63 respectively. The former is greater than the latter (Z= –2.7003, P < .01). This leads us to infer that social recognition finds more important place among girls perceiving less deprivation of privileges in home than among those who perceive moderate level of deprivation of privileges. Mean rank for girls perceiving less and high deprivation of privileges are 79.47 and 71.08. They do not differ significantly (Z= –1.2953, P > .05). It means that girls perceiving less and high deprivation of privileges give equal importance to social recognition value. Mean rank for girls perceiving moderate and high deprivation are 176.29 and 189.91 respectively. They do

Table 4.89: Mean ranks, U-values and Z-values showing difference among girls perceiving less, moderate and high level of deprivation of privilege in home on 'social recognition' value

Sl. No.	Level of deprivation of privilege	N	Mean rank	U-value	Z-value	P
1.	Low	79	209.66	9190.5	–2.7003	.0069**
	Moderate	286	175.63			
2.	Low	79	79.47	2491.0	–1.2953	.1952
	High	71	71.08			
3.	Moderate	286	176.29	9378.5	–1.0525	.2926
	High	71	189.91			

* Significant at .05 level
** Significant at .01 level

not differ from each other (Z= –1.0525, P > .05). This leads us to infer that girls perceiving moderate and high deprivation of privileges give equal importance to social recognition, value.

Table 4.90 shows that mean rank for girls perceiving low level of deprivation of privileges is 207.61 and mean rank for the girls perceiving moderate level of deprivation of privileges is 176.20. The former is greater than latter (Z= –2.4463, P < .01). It leads us to infer that polite value finds more important place among the girls perceiving low level of deprivation of privileges in homes than among those who perceive moderate deprivation of privileges. Mean ranks for girls perceiving less and high deprivation of privileges are 81.62 and 68.69 respectively. The former is greater than the latter (Z= –1.9262, P < .05). Inference can be drawn that polite value finds more important place among the girls perceiving low level of deprivation of privileges than

Table 4.90: Mean ranks, U-values and Z-values showing differences among girls perceiving different level of deprivation of privilege on 'polite' value

Sl. No.	Level of deprivation of privilege	N	Mean rank	U-value	Z-value	P
1.	Low	79	207.61	9353.0	–2.4463	.0144**
	Moderate	286	176.20			
2.	Low	79	81.62	2321.0	–1.9262	.0541*
	High	71	68.69			
3.	Moderate	286	178.96	10140.5	–.0167	.9867
	High	71	179.18			

* Significant at .05 level
** Significant at .01 level

among those who perceive high level of deprivation of privileges. Mean rank for girls perceiving moderate and high deprivation of privileges are 178.96 and 179.18 respectively. They do not differ from each other (Z= –.0167, P > .05). This leads us to infer that the girls perceiving moderate and less deprivation of privileges give equal importance to polite value.

It was hypothesized that "Girls perceiving less, moderate and high level of nurturance in home do not differ from one another in values". Table 4.91 presents results of Kruskal-Wallis one way ANOVA for values among girls perceiving different levels of nurturance. Observation of chi-square values shows that out of 40 values thirty five are not significant at .05 level. This allows acceptance of the hypothesis with respect to 35 values. This means that girls perceiving less, moderate and high level nurturance in home environment do not differ from one another with respect to 35 values, namely: A comfortable life, an exciting life, a sense of accomplishment, a world of peace, a world of beauty, equality, family security, freedom, happiness, inner harmony, mature love, national security, pleasure, salvation, self-respect, social recognition, true friendship, wisdom, equity, power, social justice, capable, cheerful, clean, helpful, honesty, imagination, independent, intellectual, logical, loving, obedient, polite, responsible, self-determination.

Significant values of chi-square were found for five values, namely: Ambitious, broadminded, courageous, forgiving and self-control. This allows partial rejection of the null hypothesis. So, it can be inferred that girls perceiving less, moderate and high level of nurturance in home environment differ from one another with respect to five values. Further analysis was done by using Mann-Whitney 'U' test. Results have been shown in tables 4.92 to 4.96.

Table 4.92 shows that mean ranks for the girls perceiving less and moderate level of nurturance in home, are 155.79 and 191.95 respectively. The latter is greater

Table 4.91: Mean ranks and chi-square values showing differences among girls perceiving less, moderate and high level of nurturance on various values

Sl. No.	Values	Level of Nurturance			Chi-Sq.	Sign.
		Low[1]	Moderate[2]	High[3]		
1	2	3	4	5	6	7
1.	A comfortable life	210.92	221.02	214.48	.5896	.7447
2.	An exciting life	199.80	224.85	207.75	2.8011	.2465
3.	A sense of accomplishment	237.61	216.99	210.03	2.0672	.3557
4.	A world of peace	217.16	219.62	214.74	.1235	.9401
5.	A world of beauty	207.24	217.86	232.70	1.6000	.4493
6.	Equality	202.95	220.46	225.02	1.3974	.4972
7.	Family security	194.67	224.34	215.44	3.3895	.1836
8.	Freedom	212.90	219.28	220.50	.1744	.9165
9.	Happiness	213.09	212.59	251.14	5.6942	.0580
10.	Inner harmony	205.38	218.29	232.61	1.6083	.4475
11.	Mature love	235.97	215.25	216.02	1.5715	.4558
12.	National security	193,13	224.88	214.08	4.1568	.1251
13.	Pleasure	226.06	218.60	210.48	.5445	.7617

(Table Contd...)

(Table 4.91: Contd...)

1	2	3	4	5	6	7
14.	Salvation	209.83	218.15	228.77	.7894	.6739
15.	Self-respect	207.79	222.25	211.93	1.0693	.5859
16.	Social recognition	214.42	219.95	215.92	.1554	.9252
17.	True friendship	214.63	217.06	229.02	.7998	.6704
18.	Wisdom	205.27	219.99	224.86	1.0952	.5783
19.	Equity	200.02	224.53	209.19	2.7141	.2574
20.	Power	202.45	221.63	220.11	1.3355	.5129
21.	Social justice	210.17	219.58	221.84	.4180	.8114
22.	Ambitious	182.10	224.86	225.61	7.0384	.0296*
23.	Broadminded	182.29	224.97	224.93	6.7920	.0335*
24.	Capable	200.81	220.59	226.26	1.7652	.4137
25.	Cheerful	199.87	221.07	225.30	1.9207	.3828
26.	Clean	222.09	214.57	233.01	1.8093	.4047
27.	Courageous	169.40	226.82	229.27	12.9439	.0015**

(Table Contd...)

(Table 4.91: Contd...)

1	2	3	4	5	6	7
28.	Forgiving	189.94	219.00	244.75	6.6284	.0364*
29.	Helpful	196.89	224.10	214.30	2.8209	.2440
30.	Honesty	220.18	216.54	225.84	.3945	.8210
31.	Imagination	196.92	224.12	213.20	2.5947	.2733
32.	Independent	220.48	220.34	208.06	.5745	.7503
33.	Intellectual	222.28	215.01	230.79	.9728	.6148
34.	Logical	206.73	217.26	235.96	1.9429	.3785
35.	Loving	231.49	218.57	223.18	.2121	.8994
36.	Obedient	201.59	218.95	233.35	2.4707	.2907
37.	Polite	245.23	213.80	213.43	3.8136	.1486
38.	Responsible	200.99	220.72	225.77	1.7364	.4197
39.	Self-control	184.57	225.48	220.30	6.0500	.0486*
40.	Self-determination	205.30	219.54	226.89	1.2125	.5454

1 N= 66
2 N= 304
3 N = 66
* Significant at .05 level
** Significant at .01 level

Table 4.92: Mean ranks, U-values and Z-values showing differences among girls perceiving less, moderate and high level of nurturance, on 'ambitious' value

Sl. No.	Level of nurturance	N	Mean rank	U-value	Z-value	P
1.	Low	66	155.79	8071.0	–2.5901	.0096**
	Moderate	304	191.95			
2.	Low	66	59.81	1736.5	–2.0674	.0387*
	High	66	73.19			
3.	Moderate	304	185.41	10004.0	–.0373	.9703
	High	66	185.92			

* Significant at .05 level
** Significant at .01 level

than the former (Z= –2.5901, P < .01). This allows us to infer that girls perceiving moderate nurturance in home assign more importance to ambitious value than those who perceive less nurturance in homes. Mean rank for the girls perceiving less and high nurturance in home are 59.81 and 73.19. The former is greater than the latter (Z= –2.0674, P < .05). This leads us to infer that in comparison to girls perceiving less nurturance, girls perceiving high nurturance give more importance to ambitious value. Mean ranks for the girls perceiving moderate and high level of nurturance in home are 185.41 and 185.92 respectively. They do not vary from each other (Z= –.0373, P > .05). It allows us to infer that girls perceiving moderate and high nurturance in home give equal importance to ambitious value.

Table 4.93 shows that mean ranks for the girls perceiving less and moderate nurturance in home are 156.11 and 191.88 respectively. The latter is greater than the former (Z= –2.5341, P < .01). This allows us to infer that in comparison to girls perceiving less nurturance, girls

Table 4.93: Mean ranks, U-values and Z-values showing differences among girls perceiving less, moderate and high level of nurturance in home, on 'broadminded' value

Sl. No.	Level of nurturance	N	Mean rank	U-value	Z-value	P
1.	Low	66	156.11	8092.0	–2.5341	.0113**
	Moderate	304	191.88			
2.	Low	66	59.68	1728.0	–2.1040	.0354*
	High	66	73.32			
3.	Moderate	304	185.58	10006.5	–.0333	.9734
	High	66	185.11			

* Significant at .05 level
** Significant at .01 level

perceiving moderate nurturance give more importance to broadminded value. Mean ranks for girls perceiving less and high level of nurturance in home are 59.68 and 73.32 respectively. The former is lower than the latter (Z= –2.1040, P < .05). It mean that broadminded value is given importance by girls perceiving high nurturance than by those who perceive less nurturance in home. Mean ranks for girls perceiving moderate and high level of nurturance in home environment, are 185.58 and 185.11 respectively. They do not vary significantly (Z= –.0333, P > .05). It allow us to infer that no significant difference exists between the girls perceiving moderate and high level nurturance in home on broadminded value.

Table 4.94 shows that mean rank for girls perceiving less and moderate nururance are 145.64 and 194.15 respectively. The former is significantly lower than the latter (Z= –3.4894, P < .01). This allows us to infer that courageous

Table 4.94: Mean ranks, U-values and Z-values showing differences among girls perceiving less, moderate and high level of nurturance on 'courageous' value

Sl. No.	Level of nurturance	N	Mean rank	U-value	Z-value	P
1.	Low	66	145.64	7401.0	–3.4894	.0005**
	Moderate	304	194.15			
2.	Low	66	57.27	1568.5	–2.8611	.0042**
	High	66	75.73			
3.	Moderate	304	185.17	9930.5	–.1360	.8918
	High	66	187.04			

* Significant at .05 level
** Significant at .01 level

value is given more importance by girls perceiving moderate nurturance in home than by those who perceive less nurturance in home environment. Mean rank for girls perceiving less nurturance in home is 57.27. Mean rank for the girls perceiving high nurturance is 75.73. The former is significantly lower than the latter (Z= –2.8611, P < .01). It means that girls perceiving high level of nurturance in home give more importance to courageous value than those who perceive less nurturance. Mean rank for girls perceiving moderate and high level of nurturance are 185.17 and 187.04 respectively. They do not differ from each other (Z= –.1360, P < .05). It permits us to infer that girls perceiving moderate and high level of nurturance in home do not differ on courageous value.

Table 4.95 shows that mean ranks for girls perceiving less and moderate nurturance in home are 165.11 and 189.93. They do not vary significantly from each other (Z= –1.7540, P>.05). This leads us to infer that girls

Table 4.95: Mean ranks, U-values and Z-values showing differences among girls perceiving less, moderate and high level of nurturance, on 'forgiving' value

Sl. No.	Level of nurturance	N	Mean rank	U-value	Z-value	P
1.	Low	66	165.11	8686.5	–1.7540	.0794
	Moderate	304	189.93			
2.	Low	66	58.33	1638.5	–2.5296	.0114**
	High	66	74.67			
3.	Moderate	304	181.58	8839.0	–1.5624	.1182
	High	66	203.58			

* Significant at .05 level
** Significant at .01 level

perceiving less and moderate nurturance in home give equal importance to forgiving value. Mean ranks for the girls perceiving less and high level of nurturance in home are 58.33 and 74.67 respectively. The latter is greater than the former (Z= –2.5293, P < .01). This leads us to infer that girls perceiving high level of nurturance in home assign more importance to forgiving than those who perceive less nurturance in home. Mean rank for girls perceiving moderate nurturance in home is 181.58 while mean rank for those perceiving high level of nurturance in home is 203.58. Mean rank for girls perceiving moderate and high nurturance are not significantly different (Z= –1.5624, P > .05). This allows us to infer that girls perceiving moderate and high nurturance in home give equal importance to forgiving value.

Table 4.96 shows that mean ranks for girls perceiving less and moderate nurturance in home are 156.84 and 191.72 respectively. Mean rank for the girls perceiving moderate nurturance in home is greater than that for girls perceiving

Table 4.96: Mean ranks, U-values and Z-values showing differences among girls perceiving less, moderate and high level of nurturance on 'self-control' value

Sl. No.	Level of nurturance	N	Mean rank	U-value	Z-value	P
1.	Low	66	156.84	8140.5	–2.4650	.0137**
	Moderate	304	191.72			
2.	Low	66	61.23	1830.0	–1.6263	.1039
	High	66	71.77			
3.	Moderate	304	186.25	9802.5	–.3002	.7640
	High	66	182.02			

* Significant at .05 level
** Significant at .01 level

less nurturance ($Z= -2.4650$, $P < .01$). It permits to infer that in comparison to girls perceiving less nurturance in home, those perceiving moderate nurturance give more importance to self-control. Mean rank for girls perceiving less nurturance in home is 61.23. Mean rank for girls perceiving high level of nurturance in home is 71.77. They do not differ significantly ($Z = -1.6263$, $P > .05$). It means that girls perceiving less nurturance in home do not differ from girls perceiving high level of nurturance on self-control value. Mean ranks for girls perceiving moderate and high level of nurturance in home are 186.25 and 182.02 respectively. The former does not differ significantly from the latter ($Z= -.3002$, $P > .05$). It allows us to infer that girls perceiving moderate and high level of nurturance in home give equal importance to self-control value.

It was hypothesized that "Girls perceiving less, moderate and high level of rejection in home do not differ from one another in values". Table 4.97 presents results of

Table 4.97: Mean ranks and chi-square values showing differences among girls perceiving less, moderate and high level of rejection in home environment on various values

Sl. No.	Values	Level of Rejection			Chi-Sq.	Sign.
		Low[1]	Moderate[2]	High[3]		
1	2	3	4	5	6	7
1.	A comfortable life	224.37	222.90	195.89	4.0384	.1328
2.	An exciting life	230.23	221.90	198.15	3.7495	.1534
3.	A sense of accomplishment	218.11	223.87	198.18	2.6691	.2633
4.	A world of peace	256.24	216.36	190.53	13.8234	.0010**
5.	A world of beauty	241.97	221.79	183.29	9.9642	.0069**
6.	Equality	257.99	219.56	176.51	17.1763	.0002**
7.	Family security	225.47	218.06	213.49	.3803	.8268
8.	Freedom	245.21	224.20	170.91	15.9760	.0003**
9.	Happiness	256.99	215.14	194.51	10.5164	.0052**
10.	Inner harmony	261.63	212.81	199.01	11.2695	.0036**
11.	Mature love	209.81	222.84	210.12	1.0682	.5862
12.	National security	232.73	216.40	212.93	1.3511	.5089
13.	Pleasure	226.33	221.94	197.73	2.7309	.2553

(Table Contd...)

(Table 4.97: Contd...)

1	2	3	4	5	6	7
14.	Salvation	267.01	211.93	197.23	14.2566	.0008**
15.	Self-respect	256.92	214.90	195.49	10.8913	.0043**
16.	Social recognition	232.52	222.67	188.99	6.0452	.0487*
17.	True friendship	231.63	221.63	193.85	5.4458	.0657
18.	Wisdom	234.94	221.98	189.29	6.3863	.0410*
19.	Equity	252.82	216.39	193.69	9.1231	.0104**
20.	Power	235.70	220.30	195.05	4.2088	.1219
21.	Social justice	244.94	222.86	176.31	13.9654	.0009**
22.	Ambitious	227.96	225.80	181.29	8.5800	.0137**
23.	Broadminded	255.15	218.62	182.84	12.7914	.0017**
24.	Capable	255.44	215.48	194.69	9.6364	.0081**
25.	Cheerful	251.37	213.21	207.34	6.5402	.0380*
26.	Clean	234.28	218.38	203.83	3.1721	.2047
27.	Courageous	224.73	222.25	198.05	2.6343	.2679

(Table Contd...)

(Table 4.97: Contd...)

1	2	3	4	5	6	7
28.	Forgiving	236.43	222.57	185.61	7.2746	.0263*
29.	Helpful	247.23	218.27	191.82	7.6651	.0217*
30.	Honesty	224.49	218.79	211.63	.4934	.7814
31.	Imagination	227.27	218.20	211.25	.6266	.7310
32.	Independent	250.07	223.77	167.87	18.4347	.0001**
33.	Intellectual	234.02	224.14	218.88	8.4645	.0145*
34.	Logical	236.51	218.96	199.46	3.3057	.1915
35.	Loving	245.22	216.84	199.27	5.4620	.0652
36.	Obedient	227.51	222.24	195.45	3.6684	.1597
37.	Polite	243.14	221.26	184.21	7.1996	.0101**
38.	Responsible	248.74	219.13	187.04	9.6520	.0080**
39.	Self-control	231.94	217.72	208.61	1.3635	.5057
40.	Self-determination	230.90	218.99	204.72	1.8658	.3934

1 N= 72
2 N= 289
3 N= 75
* Significant at .05 level
** Significant at .01 level

Kruskal-Wallis one way ANOVA for values among girls perceiving different levels of rejection. Observation of chi-square values shows that out of 40 values, 22 are significant. Sixteen values are significant at .01 level. Six value are significant at .05 level. 18 values are not significant at .05 level and they allow acceptance of the hypothesis with respect to 18 values. It means that girls perceiving less, moderate and high level of rejection in home do not differ from one another on 18 values namely: A comfortable life, an exciting life, a sense of accomplishment, family security, mature love, national security, pleasure, true friendship, power, clean, courageous, honesty, imagination, logical, loving, obedient, self-control and self-determination.

Significant values of chi-square were found for 22 values, namely: A world of peace, a world of beauty, equality, freedom, happiness, inner harmony, salvation, self-respect, social-recognition, wisdom, equity, social justice, ambitious, broadminded, capable, cheerful, forgiving, helpful, independent, intellectual, polite, responsible. These values allow partial rejection of the null hypothesis. So, it can be inferred that girls perceiving different levels of rejection differ from one another with respect to twenty two values. Further analysis was done by using Mann-Whitney 'U' test. Results are shown in the tables 4.98 to 4.119.

Table 4.98 shows that mean ranks for girls perceiving less and moderate rejection are 207.42 and 174.42 respectively. The former is greater than the latter ($Z = -2.8541$, $P < .01$). This allows us to infer that girls perceiving less rejection in home give more importance to a world of peace value than those perceiving moderate level of rejection. Mean rank for girls perceiving less and high rejection are 85.32 and 63.13 respectively. The former is greater than the latter ($Z = -3.7254$, $P < .01$). It leads us to infer that girls perceiving less rejection give more importance to a world of peace than those perceiving high rejection in home environment. Mean ranks for girls perceiving moderate and high rejection are 186.94 and 165.39 respectively. They do not differ significantly (Z= –1.7911, P > .05). It indicates that girls perceiving moderate and high rejection give equal importance to a world of peace.

Table 4.98: Mean ranks, U-values and Z-values showing differences among girls perceiving less, moderate and high level of rejection in home on 'a world of peace' value

Sl. No.	Level of rejection	N	Mean rank	U-value	Z-value	P
1.	Low	72	207.42	8502.0	–2.8541	.0043**
	Moderate	289	174.42			
2.	Low	72	85.32	1885.0	–3.7254	.0002**
	High	75	63.13			
3.	Moderate	289	186.94	9554.5	–1.7911	.0733
	High	75	165.39			

* Significant at .05 level
** Significant at .01 level

Table 4.99 shows that means rank for girls perceiving less and moderate rejection are 194.61 and 177.61. They differ from each other significantly (Z= –1.3508, P < .05). This leads us to infer that girls perceiving moderate and less rejection do not differ from each other on value named a world of beauty. Mean ranks for girls perceiving less and high rejection in home are 83.86 and 64.53 respectively. Former is greater than the latter (Z= –2.9499, P < .01). It indicates that in comparison to girls perceiving high rejection, girls perceiving less rejection assign more importance to a world of beauty value. Mean rank for girls perceiving moderate and high rejection are 189.18 and 156.75. The former is greater than the latter (Z= –2.5476,

P < .01). This implies that girls perceiving moderate rejection give more importance to a world of beauty than those perceiving high rejection.

Table 4.99: Mean ranks, U-values and Z-values showing differences among girls perceiving less, moderate and high level of rejection in home environment on 'a world of beauty' value

Sl. No.	Level of control	N	Mean rank	U-value	Z-value	P
1.	Low	72	194.61	9424.0	–1.3508	.1768
	Moderate	289	177.61			
2.	Low	72	83.86	1990.0	–2.9499	.0032**
	High	75	64.53			
3.	Moderate	289	189.18	8906.5	–2.5476	.0108**
	High	75	156.75			

* Significant at .05 level
** Significant at .01 level

Table 4.100 shows that mean rank for girls perceiving moderate and less rejection are 174.70 and 206.28 respectively. The latter is greater than the former (Z= –2.4520, P <.01). It leads us to infer that value equality is given more importance by girls perceiving less rejection than by those who perceive moderate rejection. Mean rank for girls perceiving less and high rejection are 88.20 and 60.37 respectively. The former is greater than the latter (Z= –4.1750, P < .01). It allows to infer that girls perceiving less rejection in home regard equality as more important than those perceiving high rejection in homes. Mean ranks for girls perceiving moderate and high rejection are 189.86 and 154.14 respectively. The former is greater than the latter (Z= –2.7423, P < .01). It leads us to infer that equality is regarded as more important by girls perceiving moderate rejection than by those who perceive high rejection in home environment.

Table 4.100: Mean ranks, U-values and Z-values showing differences among girls perceiving less, moderate and high level of rejection in home on 'equality' value

Sl. No.	Level of rejection	N	Mean rank	U-value	Z-value	P
1.	Low	72	206.28	8583.5	–2.4520	.0142**
	Moderate	289	174.70			
2.	Low	72	88.20	1677.5	–4.1750	.0000**
	High	75	60.37			
3.	Moderate	289	189.86	8710.5	–2.7423	.0061**
	High	75	154.14			

* Significant at .05 level
** Significant at .01 level

Table 4.101 shows that mean rank for girls perceiving less and moderate rejection are 194.37 and 177.67 respectively. They do not differ from each other (Z= –1.2881, P > .05). It allows us to infer that girls perceiving less and moderate rejection give equal importance to freedom. Mean rank for girls perceiving less and high rejection are 87.34 and 61.19 respectively. The former is greater than the latter (Z= –3.8567, P < .01). It indicates that girls perceiving less rejection give more importance to freedom value than girls perceiving high rejection. Mean rank for girls perceiving moderate and high rejection are 191.53 and 147.71 respectively. The former is greater than the latter (Z= –3.3575, P < .01). It allows us to infer than moderately rejected girls consider freedom value as more important than those who perceive high rejection in homes.

Table 4.101: Mean ranks, U-values and Z-values showing differences among girls perceiving less, moderate and high level of rejection on 'freedom' value

Sl. No.	Level of rejection	N	Mean rank	U-value	Z-value	P
1.	Low	72	194.37	9441.5	–1.2881	.1977
	Moderate	289	177.67			
2.	Low	72	87.34	1739.5	–3.8567	.0001**
	High	75	61.19			
3.	Moderate	289	191.53	8228.5	–3.3575	.0008**
	High	75	147.71			

* Significant at .05 level
** Significant at .01 level

Table 4.102 shows that mean ranks for girls perceiving less and moderate rejection are 209.13 and 173.99 respectively. Mean rank for less rejected girls is greater than that for moderately rejected girls (Z= –2.6804, P < .01). It allows us to infer than less rejected girls give more importance to happiness value than moderately rejected girls. Mean rank for less rejected girls is 84.35 and mean rank for highly rejected girls is 64.06. Mean rank for the less rejected girls is greater than that for highly rejected (Z= –3.0334, P < .01). It allows us to infer that less rejected girls find happiness value more important than those who are highly rejected. Mean ranks for girls perceiving moderate and high rejection are 186.15 and 168.45 respectively. Mean rank of moderately and highly rejected girls do not differ (Z= –1.3493, P > .05). It indicates that girls perceiving moderate and high rejection give equal importance to happiness value.

Table 4.103 shows that mean ranks for girls perceiving less and moderate rejection are 213.03 and 173.02 respectively. Mean rank for less rejected girls is greater

Table 4.102: Mean ranks, U-values and Z-values showing differences among girls perceiving less, moderate and high level of rejection on value 'happiness'

Sl. No.	Level of rejection	N	Mean rank	U-value	Z-value	P
1.	Low	72	209.13	8378.5	–2.6804	.0074**
	Moderate	289	173.99			
2.	Low	72	84.35	1954.0	-3.0334	.0024**
	High	75	64.06			
3.	Moderate	289	186.15	9783.5	–1.3493	.1772
	High	75	168.45			

* Significant at .05 level
** Significant at .01 level

Table 4.103: Mean ranks, U-values and Z-values showing differences among girls perceiving less, moderate and high level of rejection on 'inner harmony' value.

Sl. No.	Level of rejection	N	Mean rank	U-value	Z-value	P
1.	Low	72	213.03	8097.5	–2.9678	.0030**
	Moderate	289	173.02			
2.	Low	72	85.09	1901.5	–3.1711	.0015**
	High	75	63.35			
3.	Moderate	289	184.80	10174.0	–.8344	.4041
	High	75	173.65			

* Significant at .05 level
** Significant at .01 level

than that for moderately rejected girls (Z= –2.9678, P < .01). It allows us to infer that less rejected girls consider value named inner harmony more important than moderately rejected girls. Mean rank for less rejected girls is 85.09 while mean rank for highly rejected girls is 63.35. Mean rank for less rejected girls is greater than that for highly rejected (Z= –3.1711, P < .01). It leads us to infer that less rejected girls give more importance to inner harmony than highly rejected girls. Mean ranks for girls perceiving moderate and high rejection are 184.80 and 173.65 respectively. They do not differ from each other (Z= –.8344, P > .05). It indicates that moderately rejected girls do not differ from highly rejected girls on inner harmony value.

Table 4.104 shows that mean ranks for girls perceiving less and moderate rejection are 218.08 and 271.76 respectively. Mean rank for the former is greater than that for the latter (Z= –3.4634, P < .01). It allows to infer that less rejected girls give more importance to salvation value. Mean rank for less rejected girls is 85.43 and mean rank for highly rejected girls is 63.03. Mean rank for less rejected

Table 4.104: Mean ranks, U-values and Z-values showing differences among girls perceiving low, moderate and high level of rejection in home on 'salvation' value

Sl. No.	Level of rejection	N	Mean rank	U-value	Z-valuc	P
1.	Low	72	218.08	7734.5	–3.4634	.0005**
	Moderate	289	171.76			
2.	Low	72	85.43	1877.0	–3.2512	.0011**
	High	75	63.03			
3.	Moderate	289	185.17	10065.5	–.9732	.3305
	High	75	172.21			

* Significant at .05 level

** Significant at .01 level

girls (Z= –33.2512, P < .01). It means that value salvation is more prominent among less rejected girls than among those who are highly rejected. Mean ranks for moderately and highly rejected girls are 185.17 and 172.21 respectively. Mean rank for both groups do not vary from one another (Z= –.9732, P > .05). It indicates that no significant difference exist between the two groups on salvation value.

Table 4.105 shows that mean ranks for girls perceiving less and moderate rejection are 208.93 and 174.04 respectively. Mean rank for former is greater than the latter (Z= –2.7495, P < .01). It means that less rejected girls find self-respect value more important than moderately rejected girls. Mean rank for less rejected girls is 84.49. Mean rank for highly rejected girls is 63.93. The former is greater than the latter (Z = –3.1862, P < .01). It means that highly rejected girls less importance to self-respect value than less rejected girls. Mean rank for moderately and highly rejected girls are 185.86 and 169.55 respectively. Mean ranks for both groups do not differ from each other on self-respect value.

Table 4.105: Mean ranks, U-values and Z-values showing differences among girls perceiving less, moderate and high level of rejection in home on 'self-respect' value

Sl. No.	Level of rejection	N	Mean rank	U-value	Z-value	P
1.	Low	72	208.93	8393.0	–2.7495	.0060**
	Moderate	289	174.04			
2.	Low	72	84.49	1945.0	–3.1862	.0014**
	High	75	63.93			
3.	Moderate	289	85.8	9866.5	–1.2707	.2038
	High	75	169.55			

* Significant at .05 level
** Significant at .01 level

Table 4.106 shows that mean ranks for girls perceiving less and moderate rejection are 187.92 and 179.28. Mean ranks for both groups do not vary from one another (Z= .6754, P > .05). It indicates that less rejected girls do not differ from moderately rejected girls on value social recognition. Mean ranks for less and highly rejected girls are 81.10 and 67.18 respectively. Mean rank for less rejected girls is greater than that for highly rejected girls (Z= –2.0991, P < .05). It means that girls perceiving less rejection in homes give more importance to social recognition value than those perceiving high level of rejection. Mean ranks for moderately and highly rejected girls are 188.39 and 159.81 respectively. Mean rank for moderately rejected girls is greater than that for highly rejected (Z= –2.2236, P < .05). It implies that moderately rejected girls give more importance to social recognition value than highly rejected girls.

Table 4.106: Mean ranks, U-values and Z-values showing differences among girls perceiving different level of rejection in home, on 'social-recognition' value

Sl. No.	Level of rejection	N	Mean rank	U-value	Z-value	P
1.	Low	72	187.92	9906.0	–.6754	.4994
	Moderate	289	179.28			
2.	Low	72	81.10	2188.5	–2.0991	.0358*
	High	75	67.18			
3.	Moderate	289	188.39	9135.5	–2.2236	.0262*
	High	75	159.81			

* Significant at .05 level
** Significant at .01 level

Table 4.107 shows that mean ranks for girls perceiving less and moderate rejection are 189.36 and 178.92

Table 4.107: Mean ranks, U-values and Z-values showing differences among girls perceiving less, moderate and high level of rejection in home on 'wisdom' values

Sl. No.	Level of rejection	N	Mean rank	U-value	Z-value	P
1.	Low	72	189.36	9802.0	–.8296	.4067
	Moderate	286	178.92			
2.	Low	72	82.08	2118.5	–2.3979	.0165*
	High	75	66.25			
3.	Moderate	289	188.07	9228.5	–2.1332	.0329*
	High	75	161.05			

* Significant at .05 level
** Significant at .01 level

respectively. They do not differ from one another (Z= –.8296, P < .05). It means that less rejected girls do not differ from moderately rejected girls on wisdom value. Mean rank for less rejected girls is 82.08. Mean rank for highly rejected girls is 66.25. Mean rank of former is greater than that for latter (Z= –2.3979, P < .05). It indicates that less rejected girls find wisdom value more important than highly rejected girls. Mean ranks for moderately and highly rejected girls are 188.07 and 161.05 respectively. Difference between the mean ranks for groups is not significant (Z= –2.1332, P < .05). It leads us to infer that moderately rejected girls find wisdom value more important than highly rejected girls.

Table 4.108 shows that mean ranks for girls perceiving less and moderate rejection are 205.50 and 174.90 respectively. The former is greater than the latter (Z = –2.3373, P < .05). It means that less rejected girls give more importance to equity value than the moderately rejected

Table 4.108: Mean ranks, U-values and Z-values showing differences among girls perceiving less, moderate and high rejection in home on 'equity' value

Sl. No.	Level of rejection	N	Mean rank	U-value	Z-value	P
1.	Low	72	205.50	8640.0	–2.3373	.0194*
	Moderate	289	174.90			
2.	Low	72	83.82	1993.0	–2.8853	.0039**
	High	75	64.57			
3.	Moderate	289	186.49	9684.0	–1.4798	.1389
	High	75	167.12			

* Significant at .05 level
** Significant at .01 level

girls. Mean rank for less rejected girls is 83.82. Mean rank for highly rejected girls is 64.57. Mean rank for less rejected girls is greater than that for highly rejected girls (Z = –2.8853, P < .01). It allows us to infer that less rejected girls and find equity value more important than highly rejected girls. Mean ranks for moderately and highly rejected girls are 186.49 and 167.12 respectively. Mean rank for moderately rejected girls is not significantly different from highly rejected girls (Z = –1.4798, P > .05). It indicates that no significant difference exists between moderately and highly rejected girls on equity value.

Table 4.109 shows mean ranks for less and moderately rejected girls are 195.44 and 177.40 respectively. They do not differ from each other (Z = –1.4465, P > .05). It means less rejected girls do not differ from highly rejected girls on social justice value. Mean ranks for less and highly rejected girls are 86.00 and 62.48. The former is greater than the latter (Z = –3.5650, P < .01). It leads to infer that value

Table 4.109: Mean ranks, U-values and Z-values showing differences among girls perceiving less, moderate and high rejection in home on 'social justice' value

Sl. No.	Level of rejection	N	Mean rank	U-value	Z-value	P
1.	Low	72	195.44	9364.0	–1.4465	.1480
	Moderate	289	177.40			
2.	Low	72	86.00	1836.0	–3.5650	.0004**
	High	75	62.48			
3.	Moderate	289	190.46	8537.0	–3.0411	.0024**
	High	75	151.83			

* Significant at .05 level
** Significant at .01 level

social justice finds more important place among less rejected girls than among those who are highly rejected. Mean ranks for moderately and highly rejected girls are 190.46 and 151.83 respectively. Mean rank for moderately rejected girls is greater than that for highly rejected girls ($Z = -3.0411$, $P < .01$). It means that moderately rejected girls give more importance to social justice value than highly rejected girls.

Table 4.110 shows mean ranks for less and moderately rejected girls are 182.23 and 180.69 respectively. Difference between the mean ranks for both groups is not significant ($Z = -.1169$, $P > .05$). It means less rejected girls do not differ from moderately rejected girls on ambitious value. Mean rank for less rejected girls is 82.23. Mean rank for highly rejected girls is 66.10. The former is greater than the latter ($Z = -2.3655$, $P < .05$). It means that less rejected girls regard value named ambitious as more important than highly rejected girls. Mean rank for girls perceiving moderate rejection in home, is 190.11 while mean rank for

Table 4.110: Mean ranks, U-values and Z-values showing differences among girls perceiving less, moderate and high level of rejection on value 'ambitious'

Sl. No.	Level of rejection	N	Mean rank	U-value	Z-value	P
1.	Low	72	182.23	10315.5	–.1169	.9069
	Moderate	289	180.69			
2.	Low	72	82.23	2107.5	–2.3655	.0180*
	High	75	66.10			
3.	Moderate	289	190.11	8639.5	–2.8193	.0048**
	High	75	153.11			

* Significant at .05 level
** Significant at .01 level

girls perceiving high rejection in home is 153.19. Mean rank of moderately rejected girls is greater than that for highly rejected girls (Z = –2.8193, P < .01). It allows to infer that ambitious value finds more important place among moderately rejected girls than among those who perceive high rejection in home.

Table 4.111 shows mean rank for less and moderately rejected girls are 205.36 and 174.93. The former is greater than the latter (Z = 2.2811, P < .05). It indicates that less rejected girls regard value ambitious as more important than moderately rejected girls. Mean ranks for less and highly rejected girls are 86.28 and 62.21 respectively. Mean rank for less rejected girls is greater than that for highly rejected girls (Z = –3.5170, P < .01). It allows us to infer that in comparison to highly rejected girls, less rejected girls give more importance to ambitious value. Mean ranks for moderately rejected girls is 188.69 while mean rank for highly rejected girls is 158.63. Mean rank for moderately

Table 4.111: Mean ranks, U-values and Z-values showing differences among girls perceiving less, moderate and high rejection in home on 'broadminded' value

Sl. No.	Level of rejection	N	Mean rank	U-value	Z-value	P
1.	Low	72	205.36	8650.0	–2.2811	.0225*
	Moderate	289	174.93			
2.	Low	72	86.28	1815.5	–3.5170	.0004**
	High	75	62.21			
3.	Moderate	289	188.69	9047.5	–2.2656	.0235*
	High	75	158.63			

* Significant at .05 level
** Significant at .01 level

rejected girls is greater than that for highly rejected girls (Z = –2.2656, P < .05). It allows us to infer that girls perceiving high rejection in home give less importance to ambitious value than those who perceive moderate rejection in home.

Table 4.112 shows that mean ranks for less and moderately rejected girls are 207.68 and 174.35 respectively. Mean ranks for less rejected girls is greater than that for moderately rejected girls (Z = –2.5105, P < .01). It means that girls perceiving less rejection find value capable more important than moderately rejected girls. Mean rank for less rejected girls is 84.26 while mean rank for highly rejected girls is 64.15. The former is greater than the latter (Z = –2.9930, P < .01). It allows us to infer than less rejected girls assign more importance to capable value than those who perceive high rejection in home. Mean ranks for moderately and highly rejected girls are 186.12 and 168.53

Table 4.112: Mean ranks, U-values and Z-values showing differences among girls perceiving less, moderate and high rejection in home, on 'capable' value

Sl. No.	Level of rejection	N	Mean rank	U-value	Z-value	P
1.	Low	72	207.68	8483.0	–2.5105	.0121**
	Moderate	289	174.35			
2.	Low	72	84.26	1961.5	–2.9930	.0029**
	High	75	64.15			
3.	Moderate	289	186.15	9790.0	–1.3273	.1844
	High	75	168.53			

* Significant at .05 level
** Significant at .01 level

respectively. Mean rank for moderately rejected girls is not significantly different from highly rejected girls (Z = –1.3273, P > .05). It indicates that girls perceiving moderate and high rejection give equal importance to capable value.

Table 4.113 shows that mean ranks for less and moderately rejected girls are 206.26 and 174.71 respectively. Mean rank for less rejected girls is greater than that for moderately rejected girls (Z = –2.4057, P < .05). It means that value cheerful is considered more important by less rejected girls than by moderately rejected girls. Mean rank for less and highly rejected girls are 81.60 and 66.70 respectively. The former is greater than the latter (Z = –2.2417, P < .05). It leads us to infer that value named cheerful is given more importance by less rejected girls than by those who perceive high rejection in home. Mean rank for moderately and highly rejected girls are 183.50 and 178.64 respectively. Mean ranks for both groups do not differ from each other (Z = 0.3701, P > .05). It means that

Table 4.113: Mean ranks, U-values and Z-values showing differences among girls perceiving less, moderate and high level of rejection on 'cheerful' value

Sl. No.	Level of rejection	N	Mean rank	U-value	Z-value	P
1.	Low	72	206.26	8585.0	–2.4057	.0161*
	Moderate	289	174.71			
2.	Low	72	81.60	2152.5	–2.2417	.0250*
	High	75	66.70			
3.	Moderate	289	183.50	10548.0	–.3701	.7113
	High	75	178.64			

* Significant at .05 level
** Significant at .01 level

both highly and moderately rejected girls give equal importance to cheerful value.

Table 4.114 shows that mean ranks for girls perceiving less and moderate rejection in home are 190.13 and 178.72 respectively. Mean ranks for both groups do not differ significantly from one another (Z = –.8577, P > .05). It implies that girls perceiving less rejection in home do not differ from girls perceiving moderate rejection in home on forgiving value. Mean ranks for girls perceiving less and high rejection in home are 82.80 and 65.55 respectively. Mean rank for former is greater than that for the latter (Z = –2.5134, P < .01). It means that girls perceiving less rejection in home hold forgiving value in high regard than those who perceive high level of rejection in home. Mean ranks for girls perceiving moderate and high rejection in home are 188.84 and 158.05 respectively. The former is greater than the latter (Z = –2.3203, P < .05). It indicates that forgiving is valued in high regard by the girls who perceive moderate rejection than the girls perceiving high rejection in home.

Table 4.114: Mean ranks, U-values and Z-values showing differences among girls perceiving less moderate and high level of rejection in home on 'forgiving' value

Sl. No.	Level of rejection	N	Mean rank	U-value	Z-value	P
1.	Low	72	190.13	9746.5	–.8577	.3911
	Moderate	289	178.72			
2.	Low	72	82.80	2066.5	–2.5134	.0120**
	High	75	65.55			
3.	Moderate	289	188.84	9004.0	–2.3203	.0203*
	High	75	158.05			

* Significant at .05 level
** Significant at .01 level

Table 4.115 shows that mean ranks for girls perceiving less and moderate rejection in home are 200.29 and 176.19 respectively. Mean ranks for both groups do not vary from one another (Z = –1.8277, P > .05). It means that girls perceiving less and moderate rejection in home give equal importance to helpful value. Mean ranks for girls perceiving less and high rejection are 83.44 and 64.94 respectively. The former is greater than the latter (Z = –2.7416, P < .01). It allows us to infer that girls perceiving less rejection in home give more importance to helpful value than those who perceive high rejection. Mean ranks for girls perceiving moderate and high rejection in home are 187.07 and 164.88 respectively. Mean ranks for both groups do not vary from one another (Z = –1.6481, P > .05). It can be inferred that girls perceiving moderate rejection in home do not differ from girls perceiving high rejection in home on helpful value.

Table 4.116 shows that mean ranks for girls perceiving less and moderate rejection in home are 198.86 and 176.55

Table 4.115: Mean ranks, U-values and Z-values showing differences among girls perceiving less, moderate and high level of rejection in home on 'helpful' value

Sl. No.	Level of rejection	N	Mean rank	U-value	Z-value	P
1.	Low	72	200.29	9015.0	–1.8277	.0676
	Moderate	289	176.19			
2.	Low	72	83.44	2020.5	–2.7416	.0061**
	High	75	64.94			
3.	Moderate	289	187.07	9516.0	–1.6841	.0922
	High	75	164.88			

* Significant at .05 level
** Significant at .01 level

Table 4.116: Mean ranks, U-values and Z-values showing differences among girls perceiving, moderate and high rejection in home on 'independent' value

Sl. No.	Level of rejection	N	Mean rank	U-value	Z-value	P
1.	Low	72	198.86	9118.0	–1.6973	.0896
	Moderate	289	176.55			
2.	Low	72	87.71	1713.0	–3.9553	.0001**
	High	75	60.84			
3.	Moderate	289	192.22	8027.5	–3.5714	.0004**
	High	75	145.03			

* Significant at .05 level
** Significant at .01 level

respectively mean ranks for both groups are not significantly different (Z = –1.6973, P > .05). It can be inferred that girls perceiving less rejection do not differ from girls perceiving less and high rejection in home are 87.71 and 60.84 respectively. The former is greater than the latter (Z = –3.9553, P < .01). It means that girls perceiving less rejection give more importance to independent value than those who perceive high rejection. Mean rank for girls perceiving moderate and high rejection in home are 192.22 and 145.03 respectively. Former is greater than the latter (Z = –3.5714, P < .01). It means that girls perceiving moderate rejection find independent value more important than those who are perceiving high rejection.

Table 4.117 shows that mean ranks for girls perceiving less and moderate rejection are 187.83 and 179.30 respectively. Mean ranks for both groups do not differ from each other (Z = .6402, P > .05). It means that girls perceiving less rejection are not different from highly

Table 4.117: Mean ranks, U-values and Z-values showing differences among girls perceiving less, moderate and high rejection in home on 'intellectual' value

Sl. No.	Level of rejection	N	Mean rank	U-value	Z-value	P
1.	Low	72	187.83	9912.5	–.6402	.5220
	Moderate	289	179.30			
2.	Low	72	82.69	2074.0	–2.4878	.0129**
	High	75	65.65			
3.	Moderate	289	189.84	8717.0	–2.6804	.0074**
	High	75	154.23			

* Significant at .05 level
** Significant at .01 level

rejected girls on intellectual value. Mean ranks for girls perceiving less and high level of rejection in home are 82.69 and 65.65 respectively. The former is greater than the latter (Z = –2.4878, P < .01). It indicates that girls perceiving less rejection consider intellectual values are more important than those who perceive high level rejection in home. Mean ranks for girls perceiving moderate and high level of rejection in home are 189.84 and 154.23 respectively. The former is greater than the latter (Z = –2.6804, P < .01). It can be inferred that girls perceiving moderate rejection in home give more importance to intellectual value than those perceiving high rejection.

Table 4.118 shows that mean ranks for girls perceiving less and moderate rejection are 195.32 and 177.43 respectively. Mean ranks for both groups do not differ from each other (Z = –1.3676, P > .05). It means that girls perceiving less rejection are not different from highly rejected girls on polite value. Mean ranks for girls perceiving less

Table 4.118: Mean ranks, U-values and Z-values showing differences among girls perceiving less, moderate and high rejection in home on 'polite' value

Sl. No.	Level of rejection	N	Mean rank	U-value	Z-value	P
1.	Low	72	195.32	9373.0	–1.3676	.1714
	Moderate	289	177.43			
2.	Low	72	84.32	1957.0	–2.9861	.0028**
	High	75	64.09			
3.	Moderate	289	188.83	9008.5	–2.3431	.0191*
	High	75	158.11			

* Significant at .05 level

** Significant at .01 level

and high level of rejection in home are 84.32 and 64.09 respectively. The former is greater than the latter (Z = –2.9861, P < .01). It indicates that girls perceiving less rejection consider intellectual value as more important than those who perceive high level rejection in home. Mean ranks for girls perceiving moderate and high level of rejection in home are 188.83 and 158.11 respectively. The former is greater than the latter (Z = –2.3431, P < .01). It can be inferred that girls perceiving moderate rejection in home give more importance to polite value perceive high rejection.

Table 4.119 shows that mean ranks for girls perceiving less rejection is 200.93 and mean rank for girls perceiving moderate rejection is 176.03. Difference between the mean ranks for both groups is not significant (Z = –1.9041, P > .05). It means that girls perceiving less rejection are not different from moderately rejected girls on responsible value. Mean ranks for girls perceiving less and high level of rejection in home are 84.31 and 64.10 respectively. The former is

Table 4.119: Mean ranks, U-values and Z-values showing differences among girls perceiving less, moderate and high rejection in home on 'responsible' value

Sl. No.	Level of rejection	N	Mean rank	U-value	Z-value	P
1.	Low	72	200.93	8969.0	–1.9041	.0569
	Moderate	289	176.03			
2.	Low	72	84.31	1957.5	–3.0163	.0026**
	High	75	64.10			
3.	Moderate	289	188.10	9220.5	–2.0704	.0384*
	High	75	160.94			

* Significant at .05 level

** Significant at .01 level

greater than the latter (Z = –3.0163, P < .01). It indicates that girls perceiving less rejection consider responsible values are more important than those who perceive high level rejection in home. Mean ranks for girls perceiving moderate and high level of rejection in home are 188.10 and 160.94 respectively. The former is greater than the latter (Z = –2.0704, P < .01). It leads us to infer than girls perceiving moderate rejection consider responsible value as more important than those who perceive high rejection in home.

It was hypothesized that "Girls perceiving different levels of permissiveness do not differ from one another on various values".

Table 4.120 presents results of Kruskal Wallis one way ANOVA used for comparing values among girls perceiving different level of permissiveness. Observation of chi-square values shows that out of 40 values only three values are significant at .05 level. This allows acceptance of the hypothesis with respect to 37 values. This means that girls perceiving less, moderate and high level of permissiveness, do not differ from one another on 37 values, namely a comfortable life, an exciting life, a sense of accomplishment, a world of peace, a world of beauty, equality, family security, freedom, inner harmony, mature love, national security, pleasure, salvation, self-respect, social recognition, true friendship, wisdom, equity, power, ambitious, broadminded, capable, cheerful, clean, courageous, forgiving, helpful honesty, imagination, independent, intellectual, logical, loving, obedient, responsible, self-control and self-determination. Significant values of chi-square were found for three values, namely: happiness, social justice and polite. These values allow partial rejection of the null hypothesis. This leads us to infer that girls perceiving less, moderate and high permissiveness in home differ from one another with respect to three values. Further analysis was done by using Mann Whitney 'U' test. Results are shown in the following 4.121 to 4.123 tables.

Table 4.120: Mean rank and chi-square values showing differences among girls perceiving less, moderate and high level of permissiveness in home on various values

Sl. No.	Values	Level of Permissiveness			Chi-Sq.	Sign.
		Low[1]	Moderate[2]	High[3]		
1	2	3	4	5	6	7
1.	A comfortable life	193.39	225.50	213.95	5.3429	.0692
2.	An exciting life	195.62	219.68	238.70	4.1727	.1241
3.	A sense of accomplishment	230.37	214.06	225.98	1.3335	.5134
4.	A world of peace	224.47	219.58	206.70	1.0058	.6048
5.	A world of beauty	201.72	216.58	246.36	5.2128	.0738
6.	Equality	203.82	224.33	207.69	2.3288	.3121
7.	Family security	230.08	220.78	194.79	3.3019	.1919
8.	Freedom	212.37	218.15	227.05	.5140	.7734
9.	Happiness	197.35	217.06	249.05	6.3569	.0416*
10.	Inner harmony	209.37	219.79	222.71	.5014	.7783
11.	Mature love	202.09	222.33	214.31	1.8192	.4027
12.	National security	214.29	223.67	198.98	2.5030	.2861
13.	Pleasure	212.42	218.22	226.65	.4712	.7901

(Table Contd...)

(Table 4.120: Contd...)

1	2	3	4	5	6	7
14.	Salvation	220.72	224.53	187.75	.4.7418	.0934
15.	Self-respect	207.89	217.07	237.13	2.2491	.3248
16.	Social recognition	213.51	220.19	216.19	.2143	.8984
17.	True friendship	220.22	219.37	212.51	.2449	.8847
18.	Wisdom	218.35	215.63	232.09	1.0497	.5916
19.	Equity	251.97	214.44	240.39	2.4890	.2881
20.	Power	195.14	222.12	227.81	3.2330	.1986
21.	Social justice	194.46	228.06	200.51	6.5677	.0375*
22.	Ambitious	210.82	216.65	235.84	1.6737	.4331
23.	Broadminded	202.68	220.62	226.38	1.5542	.4579
24.	Capable	217.27	214.98	236.37	1.6295	.4427
25.	Cheerful	205.56	222.74	213.20	1.3225	.5162
26.	Clean	237.25	217.96	199.96	4.4123	.1101
27.	Courageous	193.90	224.20	219.47	3.6795	.5889

(Table Contd...)

(Table 4.120: Contd...)

1	2	3	4	5	6	7
28.	Forgiving	205.61	225.75	199.02	3.4679	.1766
29.	Helpful	218.07	222.92	198.26	2.1809	.3361
30.	Honesty	221.69	220.87	203.78	1.3087	.5198
31.	Imagination	207.46	222.89	210.33	1.2414	.5376
32.	Independent	201.20	220.26	229.72	2.0688	.3554
33.	Intellectual	210.06	219.34	224.07	.4876	.7837
34.	Logical	193.32	221.91	230.82	3.8461	.1462
35.	Loving	214.42	217.74	226.68	.3866	.8242
36.	Obedient	216.87	219.89	213.82	.1603	.9230
37.	Polite	250.88	209.97	222.05	6.2779	.0346*
38.	Responsible	212.90	221.81	209.30	.7541	.6859
39.	Self-control	204.82	218.11	235.73	2.1628	.3391
40.	Self-determination	229.95	212.75	232.55	2.3524	.3085

1 N=72
2 N=300
3 N=64
* Significant at .05 level
** Significant at .01 level

Table 4.121 shows that mean ranks for girls perceiving less and moderate permissiveness are 172.58 and 189.84 respectively. Mean ranks for both groups are not different from each other (Z = –1.2724, P > .05). It means that girls perceiving less permissiveness do not differ significantly from girls perceiving, moderate permissiveness on happiness value. Mean ranks for girls perceiving less and high level of permissiveness are 61.28 and 76.63. The former is lower than the latter (Z = –2.3858, P < .05). It leads us to infer that girls perceiving less permissiveness find happiness value less important than those who perceive high level of permissiveness in home. Mean ranks for girls perceiving moderate and high level of permissiveness are 177.72 and 204.92 respectively. The former is lower than the latter (Z = –1.9655, P < .05). It can be inferred that girls perceiving moderate permissiveness in home give less importance to happiness value than those who perceive high level of permissiveness.

Table 4.121: Mean ranks, U-values and Z-values showing differences among girls perceiving less, moderate and high level of permissiveness in home on 'happiness' value

Sl. No.	Level of permissiveness	N	Mean rank	U-value	Z-value	P
1.	Low	72	172.58	9797.5	–1.2724	.2032
	Moderate	300	189.84			
2.	Low	72	61.28	1784.0	–2.3858	.0170*
	High	64	76.63			
3.	Moderate	300	177.72	8165.0	–1.9655	.0494*
	High	64	204.92			

* Significant at .05 level
** Significant at .01 level

Table 4.122 shows that mean ranks for girls perceiving less and moderate permissiveness are 163.79 and 191.95 respectively. The former is lower than latter (Z = –2.1724, P < .05). It can be inferred that girls perceiving less permissiveness give less importance to social justice value than those who perceive moderate permissiveness. Mean ranks for girls perceiving less and high level of permissiveness are 67.37 and 69.77. The former is lower than the latter (Z = –.3747, P > .05). It means that girls perceiving less permissiveness do not differ from girls perceiving high permissiveness on social justice value. Mean ranks for girls perceiving moderate and high level of permissiveness are 186.61 and 163.23. Mean ranks for both groups do not differ from each other (Z = –1.7574, P < .05). It can be inferred that girls perceiving moderate level of permissiveness do not differ from girls perceiving high ievel of permissiveness on social justice value.

Table 4.122: Mean ranks, U-values and Z-values showing differences among girls perceiving less, moderate and high level of permissiveness in home on 'social justices' value

Sl. No.	Level of permissiveness	N	Mean rank	U-value	Z-value	P
1.	Low	72	163.79	9165.0	–2.1724	.0298*
	Moderate	300	191.95			
2.	Low	72	67.37	2222.5	–.3747	.7079
	High	64	69.77			
3.	Moderate	300	186.61	8367.0	6–1.7574	.0789
	High	64	163.23			

* Significant at .05 level

** Significant at .01 level

Table 4.123 shows that mean ranks for girls perceiving less and moderate level of permissiveness are 214.59 and 179.76 respectively. The former is greater than the latter (Z = –2.5745, P < .01). It means that girls perceiving less permissiveness give more importance to polite value than those who perceive moderate permissiveness. Mean ranks for girls perceiving less and high level of permissiveness are 72.78 and 63.68 respectively. Mean ranks for both groups do not differ from each other (Z = –1.4359, P > . 05). It means that girls perceiving less permissiveness do not differ from girls perceiving high level of permissiveness, on value polite. Mean ranks for girl perceiving moderate and high level of permissiveness are 180.71 and 190.87 respectively. Mean ranks for both groups do not differ from each other (Z = –.7271, P > .05). It means that girls perceiving moderate permissiveness and girls perceiving high level of permissiveness give equal importance to polite value.

Table 4.123: Mean ranks, U-values and Z-values showing differences among girls perceiving less, moderate and high level of permissiveness in home on 'polite' value

Sl. No.	Level of permissiveness	N	Mean rank	U-value	Z-value	P
1.	Low	72	214.59	8777.5	–2.5745	.0100**
	Moderate	300	179.76			
2.	Low	72	72.78	1995.5	–1.4359	.1510
	High	64	63.68			
3.	Moderate	300	180.71	9064.5	–.7271	.4672
	High	64	190.87			

* Significant at .05 level
** Significant at .01 level

Discussion

Girls perceiving different level of control differ on values like national security, courageous and obedient. National security emerged to be preferred by girls perceiving high control in comparison to girls perceiving moderate control. It may be that this type of autocratic atmosphere may be generating a sense of insecurity among girls. This sense of insecurity would have led girls perceiving high-control to give more importance to courageous value than the girls perceiving low level of control. Girls perceiving moderate control give more importance to value obedient than the girls perceiving low level of control. It seems that moderate level of control helps in inculcating obedient value but high or low level of control does not influence this value. It is quite possible that high level of control may arouse feelings of hostility rather than respect whereas control might have led them to neglect their duties.

A world of peace and a world of beauty is given importance by girls perceiving high level of protection in home environment than girls perceiving less and moderate protectiveness. It seems that girls perceiving high protection may be free from worries as they are cared for by their parents. They may be having more time and energy to appreciate a world full of beauty. Girls perceiving high protection may be having cordial relations with their parents and this would have helped them to emphasize a world of peace. Girls perceiving high protection give more importance to family security and happiness values than those who perceive less protection. It seems that girls perceiving high protection are cared for by their parents. It is very likely for them to take care of the loved ones. This process of being taken care of and having cared for loved ones may have aroused the feeling of contentedness. This may be reason for their giving importance to happiness value. Girls perceiving high protection give more importance to equity value than those who are less protected. It seems that they perceive their relationship in the family on equitable basis. They reciprocate their parental care by taking care of the family and by being more obedient. This may be the reason that girls perceiving high and moderate protection in home environment emphasize obedient value than those who are less protected. It seems that this cohesion in the family makes these girls more light-hearted and joyful. That is why cheerful value is preferred more by highly and moderately protected girls. Girls perceiving high and moderate level of protectiveness give more importance to 'broadminded' value than girls perceiving less protection. Girls perceiving high level of protectiveness in home environment give more importance to social recognition value. They are respected and admired as well as they may be having desire to be socially recognised. Ambitious value is more emphasized by those who perceived high protection in home. They also give importance to power value. It seems that girls perceiving high protection in home have a desire to secure an important position. It may be possible that the need to secure an important position and desire to impress others may be making them more hard working and aspiring than those who perceive less protection. Girls perceiving high level of protection give more importance to capable logical and intellectual values than those who perceive less protection. It seems quite reasonable that the former will show more preference for these values as they place more emphasize on ambitious value. The emphasis on capable, logical and intellectual values show high need for achievement. Our society is also becoming more achievement oriented. In this competitive atmosphere, their need for social recognition is also satisfied if they are capable. These girls also show preference for power. It may be assumed that these girls desire to secure an important position by being capable. Here, capable is concerned with motivation to achieve by becoming competent. Self-control value finds an important place among girls perceiving high protection than those who are less protected. It seems that they control their impulsive desires as they do not want to loose parental affection. Girls perceiving high and moderate level of protectiveness give more importance to self-determination value than those who perceive less protection.

Punishment has affected wisdom value. Both moderately and highly punished girls give more importance to wisdom value. It seems that less capable students are often punished. So, they may be having inherent desire to develop their wisdom value.

Conformity aspect of home environment emerged to have effect on family security, happiness, equity, clean and courageous values. Family security is given more importance by those who perceive moderate and high level of conformity in home, than by girls perceiving less conformity. This feminine quality is very likely to be reinforced in a supportive environment. Happiness value is given more importance by girls perceiving moderate and high level of conformity, than those perceiving less conformity. They also give importance to equity value. It seems that they comply with parental demands to make them happy and the reciprocity in relationship keep the environment supportive. In such a conductive environment happiness is likely to persist. Girls perceiving high level of conformity give preference to clean value than girls perceiving moderate and less conformity in home environment. Courageous value is preferred by those perceiving high conformity in home than girls perceiving low level of conformity. Perhaps girl's behaviour to comply to parent's desire and expectation might have provided a safer and supportive home environment leading to development of courageous value.

Social isolation seems to have negative effects on the development of values like a comfortable life, equality and happiness. Girls perceiving high level of social isolation give less importance to a comfortable life than the girls perceiving less social isolation. It may be that they are frequently isolated for negative sanctions. These sanctions might have aroused feelings of discomfort in them. So, it would have been difficult for them to appreciate the equality value. High level of social isolation as perceived by girls is inimical to happiness. It is very likely that the socially isolated students will be unhappy as they are denied the company of the desired persons. This may be the reason that girls perceiving high level of social isolation give less importance to happiness value.

Reward includes material as well as symbolic rewards to strengthen or increase the probability of desired behaviour. Values like inner harmony, social recognition, wisdom, power, ambitious, broadminded, courageous and self-control have been positively affected by reward. Results related to inner harmony are not very conclusive. It differentiated only between girls perceiving moderate and high reward in home environment. Girls perceiving high level of reward give more importance to inner harmony than the girls perceiving moderate level of reward. In comparison to girls perceiving less reward girls perceiving more reward give more importance to ambitious, social recognition and power values. It seems that more reward bring more respect and praise which may result in hard working and high aspirations and higher need for an important position in groups. Thus, the values namely, ambitious, social recognition and power get reinforced. This will also motivate girls perceiving more rewards to give more importance to wisdom, courageous and broadminded values. Girls perceptions of more reward in home environment can help them to control their impulsive behaviour. As their impulsive behaviours are not reinforced, they are likely to develop self-control. This may be the reason that girls perceiving high reward in home environment give more importance to self-control value.

A world of beauty and happiness values are adversely affected by deprivation of privileges. When child's behaviour is controlled by depriving him of his right to seek love, respect and child care from the parents, is basic needs may remain dissatisfied. This may lead to inability to appreciate a world of beauty. Deprivation leads to feelings of discontent. So, it is quite reasonable for them to feel unhappy. The present study has also shown that girls perceiving more deprivation of privileges give less importance to a world of beauty and happiness values. Results related to social recognition and polite values are not conclusive though they indicate that increasing levels of deprivation of privileges has a negative effect on these values.

Nurturance indicates existence of unconditional physical and emotional attachment of parents with the child. Parents have interest in and love for the child. Nurturance seems to have positive effect on ambitious, broadminded, courageous, forgiving and self-control values. In comparison to girls perceiving less nurturance in home, girls perceiving high and moderate nurturance give priority to values like ambitious, braodminded and courageous. Both ambitious and broadminded indicate their high need achievement. Results indicate that congenial home environment helps in development of self-control too.

Rejection appeared to have adverse effect on values. Results indicate that when girls perceive rejection in their home environment they feel that they have no right to express their feelings, to be unique and become autonomous individual. Girls perceiving high level of rejection have been found to give less importance to a world of peace and a world full of beauty than those who are perceiving less rejection in home environment. It seems that they are unable to appreciate these values as their feelings of dis-satisfactions might have forced them to give less importance to peace and beauty. Girls perceiving high rejection give less importance to equality and freedom values too. It is quite obvious as they are denied of rights as a person. They fail to enjoy the rights to express their feelings. They might not give more importance to equality. Lack of good reciprocal relationship as reflected in behaviour of parents using more rejection may lead to lack of inner harmony and happiness among girls. This may be the reason for less importance assigned by girls to values like inner harmony, equity, cheerful and happiness. Girls perceiving high rejection in their home environment find that they are not recognised as a person. This adversely affects their self-esteem and their desire to seek respect and admiration. They are neither ambitious, nor broadminded. They also give less importance to capable value. It seems that perception of rejection has generated low need for achievement and less faith in competence. They also give less importance to wisdom and intellectual values. Girls perceiving high rejection give less importance to social justice. It may be due to the reason that they are denied justice. They are not forgiving and give less importance to salvation value. As they are not receiving help so they do not seem to think about being helpful. Girls perceiving moderate and high rejection give less importance to polite value than thcse who perceive less rejection. This reflects the development of tendency to oppose and react to use of rejection. Thus the results of study indicate that use of rejection is detrimental to development of value.

Permissiveness includes provisions of opportunities for child to express his views freely and act according to his desire with no interference from parents. This aspect of home environment can facilitate the development of happiness, social justice and polite values. The present study has also shown that girls perceiving high level of permissiveness give more importance to happiness, social justice and polite values.

Effect of Home Environment on Moral Judgement

Results

It was hypothesized that "Girls perceiving less, moderate and high level of control in home environment do not differ from one another in moral judgement."

Table 4.24 presents results of Kruskal Wallis one way ANOVA for over all moral judgement and various items of MJQ among girls perceiving different level of control in home environment. Observation of chi-square values shows that neither over all moral judgement nor moral judgement as measured by various items of MJQ is significant. This allows acceptance of the hypothesis. It means that girls perceiving low, moderate and high level of control do not differ from one another on moral judgement.

Table 4.124: Mean rank and chi-squre values showing differences among girls perceiving low, moderate and high level of control on moral judgement

Sl. No.	Item Title	Level of Control			Chi-Sq.	Sign.
		Low[1]	Moderate[2]	High[3]		
A.	Overall moral judgement	203.60	220.51	224.29	1.1601	.5599
B.	Various items of moral judgement					
1.	Half cost ticket	226.01	217.53	215.37	.3490	.8399
2.	Lost examination question paper	213.36	219.62	218.60	.1562	.9249
3.	Mischievous student's group	205.45	218.56	231.07	1.9065	.3855
4.	Dilemma of friendship	216.474	221.47	207.35	.8517	.6532
5.	Obtaining fruits without payment	204.96	225.70	199.96	3.6451	.1616
6.	Broken chair for the teacher	223.51	214.34	231.96	1.4214	.4913
7.	Act of a ball	192.20	223.48	222.35	3.7922	.1502
8.	Unclaimed money	225.84	220.67	201.68	2.0775	.3539
9.	Demand for killing by a beautiful girl	209.83	218.93	225.13	.5454	.7613
10.	Dishonestful honesty	206.57	217.74	233.63	1.8649	.3936
11.	Sympathy of a thief friend	218.67	219.03	216.00	.0374	.9815
12.	Improper action and friendship	214.64	221.36	209.65	.7555	.6854

1 N = 67
2 N = 301
3 N = 68
* Significant at .05 level
** Significant at .01 level

It was hypothesized that "Girls perceiving less, moderate and high level of protectiveness in home do not differ from one another on moral judgement".

Table 4.125 presents results of Kruskal Wallis one way ANOVA for overall moral judgement and moral judgement as measured by various items of MJQ for girls perceiving less, moderate and high level of protectiveness in home environment. Observation of chi-square values shows that chi-square value for overall moral judgement is not significant at .05 level. Out of twelve values given for various items of MJQ only two are significant at .05 level. This allows acceptance of the hypothesis with respect to overall moral judgement and ten items of MJQ. It means that girls perceiving less, moderate and high level of protectiveness in home environment do not differ from one another on overall moral judgement and moral reasoning as exhibited in case of ten items of MJQ. Significant values of chi-square were found for ninth and twelfth items of MJQ. It allows partial rejection of null hypothesis with respect to these items. It leads us to infer that girls perceiving less, moderate and high level of protectivness in home environment differ from one another with respect to moral judgement as measured by the items namely: demands for killing by a beautiful girl and improper action and friendship.

Further analysis was done by using Mann Whitney 'U' test. Results are shown in table 4.126 to 4.127.

Table 4.126 shows that mean ranks for "Girls perceiving less and moderate level of protectiveness in home are 158.68 and 184.98 respectively'. The former is lower than the latter ($Z = -1.9526, P < .05$). It means that girls perceiving moderate protection in home excel girls perceiving less protection in home on moral judgement as measured by ninth item of MJQ. Mean rank for girls perceiving less protection in home in 61.97 while mean rank for girls perceiving high protection

Table 4.125: Difference among girls perceiving less, moderate and high level of protectiveness in home on moral judgement

Sl. No.	Item Title	Level of Protectiveness			Chi-Sq.	Sign.
		Low[1]	Moderate[2]	High[3]		
A.	Overall moral judgement	196.33	219.07	235.92	3.5940	.1658
B.	Various items of moral judgement					
1	Half cost ticket	218.92	219.39	214.76	.0974	.9524
2.	Lost examination question paper	196.72	223.41	219.67	2.9755	.2259
3.	Mischievous student's group	218.05	215.04	231.96	1.5004	.4723
4.	Dilemma of friendship	213.76	220.83	213.69	.3562	.8369
5.	Obtaining fruits without payment	219.21	215.67	228.55	.7208	.6974
6.	Broken chair for the teacher	222.91	217.64	217.86	.1163	.9435
7.	Act of a ball	221.41	215.02	229.10	.8825	.6432
8.	Unclaimed money	208.15	219.35	224.45	.8749	.6457
9.	Demand for killing by a beautiful girl	186.15	218.58	246.76	8.9564	.0114**
10.	Dishonestful honesty	202.63	215.59	243.53	5.0069	.0818
11.	Sympathy of a thief friend	212.90	216.89	229.53	.8964	.6388
12.	Improper action and friendship	202.85	215.33	244.29	6.0952	.0475*

1 N = 68
2 N = 291
3 N = 77
* Significant at .05 level
** Significant at .01 level

Table 4.126: Mean ranks, U-values and Z-values showing differences among girls perceiving less, moderate and high protectiveness in home on ninth item of MJQ

Sl. No.	Level of permissiveness	N	Mean rank	U-value	Z-value	P
1.	Low	68	158.68	8444.0	–1.9526	.0509*
	Moderate	291	184.98			
2.	Low	68	61.97	1868.0	–3.0960	.0020**
	High	77	82.74			
3.	Moderate	291	179.60	9777.5	–1.7727	.0763
	High	77	203.02			

* Significant at .05 level
** Significant at .01 level

is 82.74. The former mean rank is lower than the latter (Z = –3.0960, P < .01). It leads us to infer that girl perceiving high protection excel the girls perceiving less protection on moral judgement. Mean ranks for girls perceiving moderate and high level of protection are 179.60 and 203.02 respectively. Mean ranks for both groups do not differ from each other (Z = –1.7729, P > . 05) . It can be inferred that girls perceiving moderate and high protection in home are equal on moral judgement as measured by ninth item of MJQ.

Table 4.127 shows that mean ranks for girls perceiving less and moderate protectiveness are 171.81 and 181.91 respectively. Mean rank for both groups do not differ from one another (Z = –.8316, P > .05). It means that girls perceiving moderate and less protectiveness are equal on moral judgement. Mean ranks for girls perceiving less and high protection in home are 65.54 and 79.58 respectively.

Table 4.127: Mean ranks, U-values and Z-values showing differences among girls perceiving less, moderate and high protectiveness is home environment on twelfth item of MJQ

Sl. No.	Level of protectiveness	N	Mean rank	U-value	Z-value	P
1.	Low	68	171.81	9337.0	–.8316	.4056
	Moderate	291	181.91			
2.	Low	68	65.54	2111.0	–2.4329	.0150*
	High	77	79.58			
3.	Moderate	291	179.42	9724.5	–2.0925	.0364*
	High	77	203.71			

* Significant at .05 level
** Significant at .01 level

The former is lower than the latter (Z = –2.4329, P < .05). It can be inferred than girls perceiving high protection excel those who perceive less protection in home on moral judgement at measured by 12th item of MJQ. Mean ranks for moderately and highly protected girls are 179.42 and 203.71 respectively. The former is lower than the latter (Z = –2.0925, P < .05). It leads us to infer that girls perceiving high protection excel girls perceiving moderate protection on moral judgement as measured by twelfth item of MJQ.

It was hypothesized that "Girls perceiving less, moderate and high punishment in home environment do not differ from one another on moral judgement."

Table 4.128 presents result of Kruskal Wallis one way ANOVA for overall moral judgement and various items of MJQ for girls perceiving different levels of punishment in home. Observation of chi-square values shows that none

Table 4.128: Differences among girls perceiving less, moderate and high level of punishment in home environment on moral judgement

Sl. No.	Item Title	Level of Punishment			Chi-Sq.	Sign.
		Low[1]	Moderate[2]	High[3]		
A.	Overall moral judgement	204.32	218.94	228.87	1.2804	.5272
B.	Various items of moral judgement					
1.	Half cost ticket	225.79	213.42	233.53	2.0185	.3645
2.	Lost examination question paper	213.77	214.33	240.05	2.9055	.2339
3.	Mischievous student's group	224.99	216.02	223.29	.5261	.7687
4.	Dilemma of friendship	218.34	219.91	212.72	.2255	.8934
5.	Obtaining fruits without payment	224.71	216.27	222.51	.3593	.8355
6.	Broken chair for the teacher	224.43	211.91	241.04	3.8401	.1466
7.	Act of a ball	211.77	216.92	230.92	1.0140	.6023
8.	Unclaimed money	188.63	224.68	218.31	5.7224	.0572
9.	Demand for killing by a beautiful girl	214.15	220.15	215.35	.1829	.9126
10.	Dishonestful honesty	201.61	222.53	216.13	1.6965	.4283
11.	Sympathy of a thief friend	205.41	220.05	223.28	.9505	.6217
12.	Improper action and friendship	212.10	217.49	228.24	.8338	.6591

1 N = 62
2 N = 302
3 N = 72
* Significant at .05 level
** Significant at .01 level

of them is significant at .05 level. This allows acceptance of the hypothesis. It means that girls perceiving different levels of punishment do not differ on overall moral judgement and moral judgement as measured by various items of MJQ.

It was hypothesized that "girls perceiving less, moderate and high level of conformity do not differ from one another on moral judgement."

Table 4.129 presents results of Kruskal Wallis one way ANOVA for overall moral judgement and various items of MJQ for girls perceiving less, moderate and high level of conformity in home. A look at the table reveals that chi-square value for overall moral judgement is not significant at .05 level. Out of twelve values given for various items of MJQ, only one is significant at .05 level. This allows acceptance of the hypothesis with respect to overall moral judgement and eleven items of MJQ. It means that girls perceiving different levels of conformity in home do not differ from one another on overall moral judgement and moral judgement as exhibited in the case of eleven items of MJQ. Significant chi-square value was found for seventh item of MJQ. It allows partial rejection of null hypothesis with respect to seventh item. It means that girls perceiving different levels of conformity in home environment differ from one another with respect to moral judgement as measured by item act of a ball. Further analysis was done by using Mann Whitney 'U' test. Result is shown in table 4.130.

Table 4.130 shows that mean ranks for girls perceiving less and moderate level of conformity in home are 152.15 and 184.24 respectively. Mean rank for the latter is greater than the former ($Z = -2.4450$, $P < .05$). It means that girls perceiving moderate level of conformity in home excel those perceiving low level of conformity, on moral judgement as measured by seventh item of MJQ. Mean ranks for girls perceiving less and high level of conformity in home are 71.93 and 78.54 respectively. Mean ranks for both groups do not differ from each other ($Z = -.9829$, $P > .05$). It shows

Table 4.129: Differences among girls perceiving less, moderate and high level of conformity in home environment on moral judgement

Sl. No.	Item Title	Level of Conformity Low[1]	Moderate[2]	High[3]	Chi-Sq.	Sign.
A.	Overall moral judgement	201.31	222.87	217.72	1.6361	.4413
B.	Various items of moral judgement					
1.	Half cost ticket	231.70	216.19	215.40	1.0557	.5899
2.	Lost examination question paper	221.19	213.48	233.93	1.9578	.3757
3.	Mischievous student's group	213.80	218.44	222.73	.2555	.8801
4.	Dilemma of friendship	206.93	222.74	213.38	1.2353	.5392
5.	Obtaining fruits without payment	203.53	224.29	210.81	2.1206	.3464
6.	Broken chair for the teacher	217.54	216.53	226.27	.4489	.7989
7.	Act of a ball	189.08	227.82	210.66	6.1933	.0452*
8.	Unclaimed money	202.66	223.94	212.80	2.4312	.2965
9.	Demand for killing by a beautiful girl	206.42	221.06	219.73	.8150	.6653
10.	Dishonestful honesty	216.97	219.32	216.90	.0414	.9795
11.	Sympathy of a thief friend	222.13	218.48	215.48	.1208	.9414
12.	Improper action and friendship	213.70	219.30	219.77	.1641	.9212

1 N = 69
2 N = 286
3 N = 81
* Significant at .05 level
** Significant at .01 level

that girls perceiving less conformity do not differ from girls perceiving high conformity on moral judgement. Mean rank for girl perceiving moderate and high level of conformity are 187.08 and 173.12 respectively. Difference between the means is not significant (Z = –1.0940, P > .05). It can be inferred that girls perceiving moderate conformity are not different from girls who perceive high level of conformity in home on moral judgement as shown in response to the seventh items of MJQ.

Table 4.130: Mean ranks U-values and Z-values showing differences among girls perceiving less, moderate and high level of confirmity in home on seventh item of MJQ

Sl. No.	Level of conformity	N	Mean rank	U-value	Z-value	P
1.	Low	69	152.15	8083.5	–2.4450	.0145*
	Moderate	286	184.24			
2.	Low	69	71.93	2548.0	–.9829	.3257
	High	81	78.54			
3.	Moderate	286	187.08	10701.5	–1.0940	.2730
	High	81	173.12			

* Significant at .05 level
** Significant at .01 level

It was hypothesized that a "Girls perceiving different levels of social isolation in home do not differ from one another on moral judgement".

Table 4.131 presents results of Kruskal Wallis one way ANOVA for overall moral judgement and various items of MJQ among girls perceiving different levels of social isolation. Observation of chi-square values shows that none of them is significant at .05 level. This allows acceptance of

Table 4.131: Differences among girls perceiving less, moderate and high level of social isolation in home environment on moral judgement

Sl. No.	Item Title	Level of Social Isolation Low[1]	Moderate[2]	High[3]	Chi-Sq.	Sign.
A.	Overall moral judgement	214.96	218.02	224.80	.2527	.8813
B.	Various items of moral judgement					
1.	Half cost ticket	219.39	221.34	206.34	.9441	.6237
2.	Lost examination question paper	204.82	223.64	215.67	1.7779	.4111
3.	Mischievous student's group	223.86	217.54	215.50	.2966	.8622
4.	Dilemma of friendship	226.79	213.06	229.25	1.6838	.4309
5.	Obtaining fruits without payment	207.99	218.70	230.91	1.4761	.4780
6.	Broken chair for the teacher	219.01	213.67	236.63	2.2059	.3319
7.	Act of a ball	209.79	220.72	220.78	.5866	.7458
8.	Unclaimed money	213.79	219.86	219.11	.2149	.8981
9.	Demand for killing by a beautiful girl	224.53	216.10	220.26	.3408	.8433
10.	Dishonestful honesty	211.74	220.41	219.55	.3800	.8270
11.	Sympathy of a thief friend	219.77	219.54	212.87	.1968	.9063
12.	Improper action and friendship	225.75	214.56	224.72	1.0081	.6041

1 N = 89
2 N = 276
3 N = 71
* Significant at .05 level
** Significant at .01 level

the null hypothesis. It means that girls perceiving different levels of social isolation do not differ from one another on overall moral judgement and moral judgement as measured by various items of MJQ.

It was hypothesized that "Girls perceiving less, moderate and high levels of reward do not differ from one another on moral judgement."

Table 4.132 presents results of Kruskal Wallis one way ANOVA for overall moral judgement and various items of MJQ among girls perceiving less, moderate and high level of reward in home environment. Observation of chi-square values reveals that none of them is significant at .05 level. This allows acceptance of the null hypothesis. It mans that girls perceiving different levels of reward in home environment do not differ from one another on moral judgement overall as well as that measured by various items of MJQ.

It was hypothesized that "Girls perceiving less, moderate and high level of depreciation of privileges in home do not differ from one another on moral judgement.

Table 4.133 present results of Kruskal Wallis one way ANOVA for overall moral judgement and various items of MJQ for girls perceiving different levels of deprivation of privileges. Observation of chi-square values reveal that none of them is significant at .05 level. This allows acceptance of the null hypothesis. It means that girls perceiving less, moderate or high levels of social isolation do not differ from one another on over all moral judgement and moral judgement as measured by items of MJQ.

It was hypothesized that "Girls perceiving less, moderate and high level of nurturance in home do not differ from one another on moral judgement."

Table 4.134 presents results of Kruskal moral judgement and various items of MJQ among girls perceiving

Table 4.132: Differences among girls perceiving less, moderate and high level of reward in home on moral judgement

Sl. No.	Item Title	Level of Reward			Chi-Sq.	Sign.
		Low[1]	Moderate[2]	High[3]		
A.	Overall moral judgement	207.70	218.66	229.53	.9176	.6320
B.	Various items of moral judgement					
1.	Half cost ticket	206.63	221.01	217.99	.8121	.6663
2.	Lost examination question paper	207.43	218.10	232.86	1.4401	.4867
3.	Mischievous student's group	207.37	218.03	233.35	1.7890	.4088
4.	Dilemma of friendship	211.13	217.83	230.24	.8688	.6776
5.	Obtaining fruits without payment	220.66	219.32	211.69	.2274	.8925
6.	Broken chair for the teacher	218.45	218.61	217.97	.0015	.9992
7.	Act of a ball	213.89	221.59	206.86	.8447	.6555
8.	Unclaimed money	217.28	213.10	249.10	5.4429	.0658
9.	Demand for killing by a beautiful girl	200.24	220.17	229.61	1.9827	.3711
10.	Dishonestful honesty	220.55	220.98	202.82	1.2145	.5448
11.	Sympathy of a thief friend	218.30	218.65	217.89	.0023	.9988
12.	Improper action and friendship	227.14	215.42	225.64	.9222	.6306

1 N = 64
2 N = 314
3 N = 58
* Significant at .05 level
** Significant at .01 level

Table 4.133: Differences among girls perceiving less, moderate and high level of deprivation of privileges in home on moral judgement

Sl. No.	Item Title	Level of Deprivation of Privileges			Chi-Sq.	Sign.
		Low[1]	Moderate[2]	High[3]		
A.	Overall moral judgement	223.61	220.04	206.59	.8099	.6677
B.	Various items of moral judgement					
1.	Half cost ticket	220.04	216.06	226.62	.4850	.7847
2.	Lost examination question paper	207.81	222.92	212.61	1.2382	.5384
3.	Mischievous student's group	219.36	219.45	213.73	.1663	.9202
4.	Dilemma of friendship	215.72	221.45	209.70	.6445	.7245
5.	Obtaining fruits without payment	202.85	228.04	197.49	5.4509	.0655
6.	Broken chair for the teacher	226.55	213.01	231.68	1.9304	.3809
7.	Act of a ball	215.41	217.01	227.95	.5349	.7653
8.	Unclaimed money	224.60	218.31	212.47	.4734	.7892
9.	Demand for killing by a beautiful girl	228.04	221.20	197.01	2.8402	.2417
10.	Dishonestful honesty	231.06	219.24	201.55	2.4367	.2957
11.	Sympathy of a thief friend	229.66	216.34	214.77	.8904	.6407
12.	Improper action and friendship	226.25	217.58	213.60	.5768	.7495

1 N = 79
2 N = 286
3 N = 71
* Significant at .05 level
** Significant at .01 level

Table 4.134: Differences among girls perceiving less, moderate and high level of nurturance in home on moral judgement

Sl. No.	Item Title	Level of Nurturance Low[1]	Moderate[2]	High[3]	Chi-Sq.	Sign.
A.	Overall moral judgement	184.24	225.50	220.53	5.8527	.0536
B.	Various items of moral judgement					
1.	Half cost ticket	190.23	224.42	219.50	4.6795	.0963
2.	Lost examination question paper	189.50	225.50	215.27	5.1555	.0759
3.	Mischievous student's group	207.53	221.61	215.17	.9983	.6070
4.	Dilemma of friendship	216.34	219.49	216.11	.0733	.9640
5.	Obtaining fruits without payment	193.70	224.51	215.61	3.7069	.5267
6.	Broken chair for the teacher	199.78	225.62	204.39	3.8282	.1475
7.	Act of a ball	182.30	226.11	219.64	7.2059	.0272*
8.	Unclaimed money	211.42	218.10	227.44	.7386	.6912
9.	Demand for killing by a beautiful girl	197.74	219.28	235.68	3.2475	.1972
10.	Dishonestful honesty	215.07	219.01	219.58	.0689	.9661
11.	Sympathy of a thief friend	218.73	224.41	211.05	2.9341	.2305
12.	Improper action and friendship	212.49	220.25	216.44	.3095	.8566

1 N = 66
2 N = 304
3 N = 66
* Significant at .05 level
** Significant at .01 level

less, moderate and high level of nuturance in home environment. Observation of chi-square value for overall moral judgement is not significant. Out of the twelve values given for the various items of MJQ only one is significant at .05 level. This allows acceptance of the hypothesis with respect to overall moral judgement and eleven items of MJQ. It means girls perceiving less, moderate, and high level of nurturance in home environment do not differ from one another on overall moral judgement and moral reasoning as exhibited in the case of eleven items of MJQ.

Significant chi-square value was found for the seventh item of MJQ. It allows partial rejection of null hypothesis with respect to this item. It can be inferred that girls perceiving less, moderate and high level of nurturance in home environment differ from one another with respect to moral judgement as measured by the item entitled act of a ball. Further analysis was done by using Mann Whitney 'U' test. Result are shown in the table 4.135.

Table 4.135 shows that mean ranks for girls perceiving less and moderate nurturance in home are 155.51 and 192.01 respectively. The former is lower than the latter ($Z = -2.6272$, $P < .01$). It leads us to infer that girls perceiving moderate nurturance in home excel girls perceiving less nurturance in home on moral judgement as exhibited in case of seventh item of MJQ. Mean ranks for girls perceiving less and high level of nurturance in home are 60.30 and 72.70 respectively. The former is lower than the latter ($Z = -1.9891$, $P < .01$). It allows us to infer that girls perceiving high level of nurturance in home excel girls perceiving less nurturance in home on moral judgement as measured by the seventh item of MJQ. Mean ranks for girls perceiving moderate and high level of nurturance are 186.60 and 180.23 respectively. Mean ranks for both groups do not differ from each other ($Z = -.4449$, $P > .05$). It means girls perceiving moderate or high level of nurturance do not differ on moral judgement as measured by seventh item of MJQ.

Table 4.135: Mean ranks, U-values and Z-values showing differences among girls perceiving less, moderate and high level of nurturance in home on seventh item of MJQ

Sl. No.	Level of nurturance	N	Mean rank	U-value	Z-value	P
1.	Low	66	155.51	8052.5	–2.6272	.0086**
	Moderate	304	192.01			
2.	Low	66	60.30	1768.5	–1.9891	.0467*
	High	66	72.70			
3.	Moderate	304	186.60	9697.5	–.4449.	.6564
	High	66	180.43			

* Significant at .05 level
** Significant at .01 level

It was hypothesized that "Girls perceiving less, moderate and high level of rejection in home do not differ from one another in moral judgement."

Table 4.136 presents result of Kruskal Wallis one way ANOVA for overall moral judgement and various items of MJQ for girls perceiving less, moderate and high level of rejection in home environment. Observation of chi-square values shows that chi-square value for overall moral judgement is significant at .01 level. Out of the twelve values given in the table for various items of MJQ three are significant at .01 level. It means that girls perceiving less, moderate and high level of rejection in home do not differ from one another on moral judgement as measured by nine items of MJQ. Significant values were found for overall moral judgement and third, ninth and. tenth items of MJQ. It allows rejection of null hypothesis with respect to overall moral judgement and moral judgement as measured by third, ninth and tenth items of MJQ. It can

Table 4.136: Differences among girls perceiving less, moderate and high level of rejection in home on moral judgement

Sl. No.	Item Title	Level of Rejection			Chi-Sq.	Sign.
		Low[1]	Moderate[2]	High[3]		
A.	Overall moral judgement	243.01	222.32	176.41	11.5562	.0031**
B.	Various items of moral judgement					
1.	Half cost ticket	244.52	216.08	202.83	5.0778	.0790
2.	Lost examination question paper	233.78	220.99	194.22	4.5559	.1025
3.	Mischievous student's group	237.91	221.99	186.43	9.2714	.0097**
4.	Dilemma of friendship	226.95	222.39	195.39	3.7093	.1565
5.	Obtaining fruits without payment	218.97	222.90	201.11	2.0111	.3658
6.	Broken chair for the teacher	216.90	223.97	202.06	1.9797	.3716
7.	Act of a ball	207.44	224.53	205.85	2.1604	.3395
8.	Unclaimed money	220.64	223.50	197.17	3.5692	.1679
9.	Demand for killing by a beautiful girl	244.65	223.58	173.83	13.9321	.0009**
10.	Dishonestful honesty	243.94	221.16	183.83	10.2388	.0060**
11.	Sympathy of a thief friend	238.67	218.62	198.67	4.3022	.1164
12.	Improper action and friendship	244.28	215.27	204.28	5.6132	.0604

1 N = 72
2 N = 289
3 N = 75
* Significant at .05 level
** Significant at .01 level

be inferred that girls perceiving less, moderate and high level of rejection differ from one another on overall moral judgement and moral judgement as measured by the items entitled as mischievous students group, demand for killing by a beautiful girl and dishonestful honesty. Further analysis was done by using Mann Whitney 'U' test. Results are shown in the table 4.137 to 4.140.

Table 4.137: Mean rank, U-values and Z-values showing differences among girls perceiving less, moderate and high rejection on overall moral judgement

Sl. No.	Level of rejection	N	Mean rank	U-value	Z-value	P
1.	Low	72	194.31	9445.5	–1.2120	.2255
	Moderate	289	177.68			
2.	Low	72	85.20	1893.5	–3.1301	.0017**
	High	75	63.25			
3.	Moderate	289	190.63	8487.0	–2.8998	.0037**
	High	75	151.16			

* Significant at .05 level
** Significant at .01 level

Table 4.137 shows that mean rank for girls perceiving less rejection in home are 194.31 and 177.68 respectively. Mean ranks for both groups do not differ from one another ($Z = -1.2120$, $P > .05$). It means that girls perceiving less rejection in home are not different from girls perceiving moderate rejection on overall moral judgement. Mean ranks for girls perceiving less rejection in home is 85.20 while mean rank for girls perceiving high rejection in home is 63.25. The former is greater than the latter ($Z = -3.1301$, $P < .01$). It means that girls perceiving less rejection exhibit superior level of moral judgement than those perceiving high level of rejection in home. Mean ranks for girls perceiving moderate and high rejection in home are 190.63 and 151.16 respectively. The former is greater than the latter (Z = –2.8998, P < .01). It leads us to infer that girls perceiving moderate rejection excel girls perceiving high rejection in home, one overall moral judgement.

Table 4.138 shows that mean ranks for girls perceiving less and moderate rejection are 191.75 and 178.32 respectively. Mean rank for both the groups do not differ from one another (Z = –1.1481, P > .05). It means girls perceiving less and moderate rejection in home exhibit similar type of moral judgement on third item of MJQ. Mean rank for girls perceiving less and moderate rejection in home are 82.66 and 65.69 respectively. The former is greater than the latter (Z = –2.7399, P < .01). So, it can be inferred that girls perceiving less rejection in home excel girls perceiving high rejection in home on moral judgement as exhibited for

Table 4.138: Mean ranks, U-values and Z-values showing differences among girls perceiving less, moderate and high level of rejection in home on third item of MJQ

Sl. No.	Level of rejection	N	Mean rank	U-value	Z-value	P
1.	Low	72	191.75	9630.0	–1.1481	.2509
	Moderate	289	178.32			
2.	Low	72	82.66	2076.5	–2.7399	.0061**
	High	75	65.69			
3.	Moderate	289	188.67	9055.5	–2.5879	.0097**
	High	75	158.74			

* Significant at .05 level
** Significant at .01 level

the third item of MJQ. Mean rank for girls perceiving moderate and high rejection in home are 188.67 and 158.74 respectively. The former is greater than the latter (Z = –2.5879, P < .01). It allows us to infer that girls perceiving moderate rejection in home excel girls perceiving high rejection in home on moral judgement as measured by third item of MJQ.

Table 4.139: Mean ranks, U-values, and Z-values showing differences among girls perceiving less, moderate and high rejection in home on ninth item of MJQ

Sl. No.	Level of rejection	N	Mean rank	U-value	Z-value	P
1.	Low	72	195.44	9364.0	–1.3568	.1748
	Moderate	289	177.40			
2.	Low	72	85.71	1857.0	–3.3863	.0007**
	High	75	62.76			
3.	Moderate	289	191.18	8330.0	–3.2052	.0013**
	High	75	149.07			

* Significant at .05 level
** Significant at .01 level

Mean ranks for girls perceiving less and moderate rejection in home are 195.44 and 177.40 respectively. Mean ranks for both groups do not differ from each other (Z = –1.3568, P > .05). It means that girls perceiving less and moderate rejection give similar types of moral judgement on the ninth item of MJQ. Mean rank for girls perceiving less rejection is 85.71 while mean rank for girls perceiving high rejection is 62.76. The former is greater than the latter (Z = –3.3863, P < .01). It leads us to infer that girls perceiving less rejection in home excel girls perceiving high rejection in home on moral judgement as measured by ninth item of MJQ. Mean rank for girls perceiving moderate and high rejection in home are 191.18 and 149.07 respectively. The former is greater than the latter (Z = –3.2052, P < .01). It can be inferred that girls perceiving moderate rejection in home excel girls perceiving high rejection in home on moral judgement measured by ninth item of MJQ.

Table 4.140 shows that mean ranks for girls perceiving less and moderate rejection in home are 196.56 and 177.12 respectively. The former is greater than the latter (Z = –2.5112, P > .05). It means that girls perceiving less rejection in home show superior moral judgement on tenth item of MJQ than those perceiving high rejection in home. Mean ranks for girls perceiving less rejection in home is 83.88 while mean rank for girls perceiving high rejection in home is 64.52. The former is greater than the latter (Z = –2.9486, P < .01). It leads us to infer that girls perceiving less rejection in home excel the girls perceiving high rejection in home, on moral judgement as measured by tenth item of MJQ. Mean ranks for girls perceiving

Table 4.140: Mean ranks, U-values and Z-values showing differences among girls perceiving less, moderate and high rejection on tenth item of MJQ

Sl. No.	Level of rejection	N	Mean rank	U-value	Z-value	P
1.	Low	72	196.56	9283.5	–1.5458	.1221
	Moderate	289	177.12			
2.	Low	72	83.88	1989.0	–2.9486	.0032**
	High	75	64.52			
3.	Moderate	289	189.04	8948.5	–2.5112	.0120**
	High	75	157.31			

* Significant at .05 level
** Significant at .01 level

moderate and high rejection are 189.04 and 157.31 respectively. Former is greater than the latter (Z = –2.512, P < .01). It allows us to infer that girls perceiving moderate rejection in home excel girls perceiving high rejection in home, on moral judgement as measured by tenth item of MJQ.

It was hypothesized that "girls perceiving less, moderate and high level of permissiveness in home do not differ from one another on moral judgement."

Table 4.141 presents results of Kruskal Wallis one way ANOVA for overall moral judgement and various items of MJQ among girls perceiving less, moderate and high level of permissiveness in home environment. A look at the table reveals that chi-square value for over all moral judgement is not significant at .05 level. Out of twelve chi-square values given for various items of MJQ only one is significant at .05 level. The non-significant values of chi-square allow acceptance of the null hypothesis with respect to overall moral judgement as measured by eleven items of MJQ. It means that girls perceiving less, moderate and high level of permissiveness in home environment do not differ from one another on overall moral judgement and moral reasoning exhibited in case of eleven items of MJQ. Significant chi-square value was found for eleven item of MJQ. It allows partial rejection of null hypothesis with respect to eleven item of MJQ. It leads to infer that girls perceiving less, moderate and high level of permissiveness differ from one another with respect to item entitled sympathy of a thief friend. Further analysis was done by using Mann Whitney 'U' test. Result is shown in the table 4.142.

Table 4.142 shows that mean ranks for girls perceiving less and moderate permissiveness are 158.86 and 193.13 respectively. The former is lower than latter (Z =- –2.6275, P < .01). It leads us to infer that girls perceiving moderate permissiveness excel girls perceiving less permissiveness, on moral judgement as measured by eleventh item of MJQ. Mean ranks for girls perceiving less and high level of

Table 4.141: Differences among girls perceiving less, moderate and high level of permissiveness in home on moral judgement

Sl. No.	Item Title	Level of Permissiveness			Chi-Sq.	Sign.
		Low[1]	Moderate[2]	High[3]		
A.	Overall moral judgement	215.90	216.15	232.45	.9231	.6303
B.	Various items of moral judgement					
1.	Half cost ticket	202.59	223.23	214.24	1.9241	.3821
2.	Lost examination question paper	212.35	220.42	216.40	.2982	.8615
3.	Mischievous student's group	217.00	216.71	228.60	.6588	.7194
4.	Dilemma of friendship	207.75	214.97	247.13	4.8291	.0894
5.	Obtaining fruits without payment	211.73	217.44	231.10	.9812	.6123
6.	Broken chair for the teacher	227.14	214.95	225.41	.9037	.6364
7.	Act of a ball	227.67	214.84	225.36	.9035	.6359
8.	Unclaimed money	225.97	215.53	224.00	.7358	.6922
9.	Demand for killing by a beautiful girl	221.65	213.14	240.09	2.6449	.2665
10.	Dishonestful honesty	219.06	219.84	211.61	.2654	.8757
11.	Sympathy of a thief friend	185.58	225.89	220.89	6.9377	.0312*
12.	Improper action and friendship	234.26	215.16	216.41	1.8523	.3961

1 N = 72
2 N = 300
3 N = 64
* Significant at .05 level
** Significant at .01 level

Table 4.142: Mean ranks, U-values and Z-values showing differences among girls perceiving less, moderate and high level of permissiveness in home on eleventh item of MJQ

Sl. No.	Level of permissiveness	N	Mean rank	U-value	Z-value	P
1.	Low	72	158.86	8810.0	–2.6275	.0086**
	Moderate	300	193.13			
2.	Low	72	63.22	1923.5	–1.8219	.0685
	High	64	74.45			
3.	Moderate	300	183.26	9372.5	–.3184	.7502
	High	64	178.95			

* Significant at .05 level
** Significant at .01 level

permissiveness are 63.22 and 74.45 respectively. Difference between them is not significant (Z = –1.8219, P > .05). It man that girls perceiving less and high level of permissiveness exhibit similar type of moral judgement. Mean ranks for girls perceiving moderate and high level of permissiveness in home are 183.26 and 178.95 respectively. Mean ranks for groups do not differ from each other (Z = –3184, P > .05). It means that girls perceiving moderate and high level of permissiveness are equal on moral judgement as measured by eleventh item of MJQ.

DISCUSSION

Out of ten dimensions of home environment, five dimensions emerged as significant ones affecting the moral judgement of girls. These dimensions are protectiveness, conformity, nurturance, rejection and permissiveness. Protectiveness, conformity, nurturance and permissiveness dimension of family have positive effect on moral judgement whereas rejection has adversely affected girls moral judgement. Girls perceiving high level of protectiveness excel the girls perceiving low level of protectiveness on moral judgement as measured by two items-nine and twelve, of MJQ. They do not differ from one another on moral adjustment as measured by the rest. Singh, (1983) found significant positive relationship between child's moral judgement and father's attitude of possessiveness. MaCcoby and Martin, (1983) suggest that parental involvement is positively associated with number of aspects of optimal development in children. In our Indian society there is high tendency to have protective attitude towards girls, and this is generally perceived as an indicator of parent's love for girls. This may be the reason that girls perceiving high protection excel girls perceiving less protection on two moral dilemmas. Pulkkien, (1982) found reasons to believe that there is a positive function to be played by continued parental involvement in the child's life and decision, and by continued monitoring well into adolescence. These views lend support to findings with respect to two dilemmas only. The differential effects may be attributed to differences in contents of items.

Girls perceiving moderate conformity in home show more mature judgement than the girls who are perceiving less conformity. Girls perceiving high conformity are similar to girls perceiving moderate as well as low level of conformity in home. These findings hold truth only when viewed in reference to moral judgement as measured by the seventh item of MJQ. It seems that neither less nor high level of conformity is conducive to development of high level of moral judgement. High level of compliance to parents desire and expectations can hinder the growth of independent decision making whereas low level of compliance to parental direction and commands may results in indiscipline. So, moderate level of conformity may provide the environment where children can develop morally. This explanation holds no weight when we consider findings of no significant difference in moral judgement as measured by eleven items of MJQ among girls perceiving high, moderate and low level of conformity in home environment.

Girls perceiving high level of nurturance in home excel girls perceiving low level of nurturance on moral judgement as measured by seventh item of MJQ. Girls perceiving high level of nurturance and girls perceiving moderate level of nurturance have similar level of moral reasoning. Nurturance stands for unconditional love of parents and more parental involvement. According to Kohlberg only warmth and love can not produce high order of moral reasoning. Rather, it depends upon how much role taking is provided by parents. It seems that nurturance has only modest effect on moral judgement as except, seventh item of MJQ, the girls do not differ from one another on moral reasoning. This draws partial support from Hoffman, (1967) who found love oriented discipline to be positively affecting the moral judgement. Sethi and Gupta, (1984) also found that girls, high in moral judgement perceive their mothers to be accepting and loving. The present study, however, has shown that moral judgement as measured by all, except seventh item, is not influenced by nurturance.

Permissiveness seems to have positive effect on moral judgement as measured by eleventh item of MJQ. Girls perceiving moderate and high level of permissiveness excel girls perceiving low level of permissiveness on moral judgement. Parents resorting to permissive style of discipline provide the child opportunities to express their views freely and act according to their desire with no interference by the parents. Study by Baumrind, (1967) shows that permissive parents were warm, at least by comparison with the authoritarian group. When parents are loving and adopt tolerant and accepting attitude towards child's impulses, they may feel that they are secure. This feeling might have contributed to superior level of moral judgement exhibited by girls perceiving moderate and high level of permissiveness on item eleventh of MJQ. These views of Baumrind lend support to the above mentioned significant finding but they contradict the nonsignificant ones. It seems that moral judgement as measured by other items is not susceptible to the effects of lack of permissiveness in home environment.

Rejection appears to have negatively affected moral judgement. Girls perceiving high rejection exhibited lower moral judgement than those perceiving less or moderate rejection in home. This finding holds truth in case of overall moral judgement as well as moral judgement measured by third, ninth and twelfth item of MJQ. It seems that girls perceiving high rejection in home tend to associate with peer group, carrying values that deviate from standard and expectations of society. Girls perceiving high rejection in home environment are denied the right to express their feelings and to become auonomous individual. This may be the reason for lack of independent decision making among rejected girls who may be tempted to show more conformity to peer group decisions. Furthermore, girls perceiving high rejection in home may not be considering mother or father as a model to imitate. So, it seems possible that girls perceiving high rejection in home will exhibit low level moral judgement. This draws partial support from the findings of Sethi and Gupta, (1984) who found perception of rejection in home environment to be negatively related to moral judgement of girls.

The present investigation has shown that different levels of control as perceived by girls do not have differential effect on moral judgement. Singh's, (1983) findings support our findings. He found that father's attitude of dominatingness has nothing to do with moral judgement. Contradictory findings have been reported by Sethi and Gupta, (1984) who found that girls high in moral judgement saw their mother as controlling and enforcing.

Different levels of punishment as perceived by girls in their home environment seems to have no effect on moral judgement of the girls. Punishment is used generally to inhibit the undesired acts of the girls. This technique is generally effective in suppressing lower order, impulsive acts. As the girls belong to age group of 13-14 years they may be reasoning at high level. Some other factors may have moderated the effects of punishment on girls. Hoffman and Saltzstein, (1967) found power assertion to be negatively related to moral judgement. Bandura & Walters, (1963) suggest that punishment is only effective when administered by nurturant adult. Sears, MaCcoby and Levine, (1957) found spanking was only effective when it was administered by warm and affectionate mothers. Hoffman, (1970) concluded that though parent child research indicates power assertion playing a predominant negative role in moral judgement, results of laboratory studies-high intensity and early timing show that power assertion may foster the immediate suppression of pleasure-oriented response tendencies. So, the views and findings of Hoffman and Saltzstein, Bandura and Walters, Sears, et. al. and Hoffman do not lend support to our finding of no difference in effect of deferent level of punishment on girl's moral judgement.

The present study has shown that social isolation and deprivation of privileges do not have effect on moral judgement. Girls perceiving less, moderate and high social isolation or deprivation of privileges or similar to one another on moral judgement. It may be that social isolation and deprivation of privileges are not used by parents who overtly profess warmth and making the child realize that she is loosing something of importance. It is also possible that effect of these disciplinary techniques might have been moderated by other intervening variables e.g. school environment, peer group support and self-awareness.

Different levels of reward have not been found to have any effect on moral judgement of the girls. It is quite possible while providing reward parents may not have chosen appropriate timing, as Bandura and Walters, (1963) suggests that timing of reward is important to reinforce more appropriate behaviour.

Study of Relationship between Stress and Values

RESULTS

It was hypothesized that there exists no significant relationship between stress and values. This hypothesis was tested by computing Kendall coefficient of correlation between overall and four areas of stress and 40 values (R.V.S.E.V.*). Significance of correlation was tested at .01 level and .001 level using one-tailed test. Results have been presented in table 4.143.

The table 4.143 shows correlations between overall stress and various values as measured by R.V.S.E.V. A look at the values of correlations shows that out of 40 correlations only six are significant at .01. This means that all, except six values are not significantly related to overall stress. Values of correlations for a world of peace, happiness, true friendship, wisdom, helpful and polite are –.1339 (P < .01); –.1918 (P <.001); –.1163 (P < .01); –.1140 (P <.01); –.1248, (P < .01); –.1304 (P <.01). They point to existence of negative relationship between overall stress and these values. Non-significant values of correlations point to existence no significant relationship between overall stress and each of the 34 values namely: A comfortable life, an exciting life, a sense of accomplishment, a world of beauty, equality, family security, freedom, inner harmony, mature love, national security, pleasure, salvation, self-respect, social recognition, equity, power, social justice, ambitious, broadminded, capable, cheerful, clean, courageous, forgiving, honesty, imagination, independent, intellectual, logical, loving, obedient, responsible, self-control and self-determination.

Observation of the table 4.144 shows correlation between stress in home and 40 values as measured by R.V.S.E.V. A look at the values of correlations reveal that out of 40 values only 7 are significant. Significant values for a world of beauty, equality, happiness, true friendship,

* R.V.S.E.V. refers to Rokeach Value Survey Extended Version

Table 4.143: Kendall's rank correlation coefficient between overall stress and various values

Sl. No.	Dependent Variable	Value of Correlation
1	2	3
1.	A comfortable life	.0799
2.	An exciting life	–.0167
3.	A sense of accomplishment	–.0803
4.	A world of peace	–.1339*
5.	A world of beauty	–.0602
6.	Equality	–.0843
7.	Family security	.0128
8.	Freedom	.0277
9.	Happiness	–.1918**
10.	Inner harmony	.0438
11.	Mature love	.0402
12.	National security	.0046
13.	Pleasure	–.0333
14.	Salvation	.0166
15.	Self-respect	–.0351
16.	Social recognition	–.0430
17.	True friendship	–.1163*
18.	Wisdom	–.1140*
19.	Equity	–.0691
20.	Power	–.0270
21.	Social justice	–.0899
22.	Ambitious	.0047
23.	Broadminded	.0034
24.	Capable	–.0528
25.	Cheerful	.0178
26.	Clean	.0151

(Table Contd...)

(Table 4.143: Contd...)

1	2	3
27.	Courageous	–.0365
28.	Forgiving	–.0398
29.	Helpful	–.1248*
30.	Honesty	–.0258
31.	Imagination	.0348
32.	Independent	–.0268
33.	Intellectual	–.0727
34.	Logical	–.0356
35.	Loving	–.1012
36.	Obedient	–.0775
37.	Polite	–.1304*
38.	Responsible	–.0806
39.	Self-control	–.0345
40.	Self-determination	–.0172

* Significant at .01 level
** Significant at .001 level

Table 4.144: Kendell's rank correlation coefficient between stress in home and various values

Sl. No.	Dependent Variable	Value of Correlation
1	2	3
1.	A comfortable life	.0364
2.	An exciting life	–.0279
3.	A sense of accomplishment	–.0918
4.	A world of peace	–.1206*
5.	A world of beauty	–.1638**
6.	Equality	–.0684
7.	Family security	.0084
8.	Freedom	.0025
9.	Happiness	–.2119**

(Table Contd...)

(Table 4.144: Contd...)

1	2	3
10.	Inner harmony	.0646
11.	Mature love	.0050
12.	National security	–.0438
13.	Pleasure	–.0574
14.	Salvation	.0274
15.	Self-respect	–.0448
16.	Social recognition	–.0588
17.	True friendship	–.1279*
18.	Wisdom	–.1181*
19.	Equity	–.1172*
20.	Power	–.0492
21.	Social justice	–.0967
22.	Ambitious	.0197
23.	Broadminded	.0005
24.	Capable	–.0422
25.	Cheerful	–.0118
26.	Clean	–.0301
27.	Courageous	–.0302
28.	Forgiving	–.0274
29.	Helpful	–.1055
30.	Honesty	–.0027
31.	Imagination	.0311
32.	Independent	–.0582
33.	Intellectual	–.0736
34.	Logical	–.0516
35.	Loving	–.0894
36.	Obedient	–.0965
37.	Polite	–.1184*
38.	Responsible	–.0744
39.	Self-control	–.0333
40.	Self-determination	–.0264

* Significant at .01 level
** Significant at .001 level

wisdom, equity and polite are .1206 (P <.01); –.1638, (P <.001); –.2119 (P <.001); –.1279 (P<.01); –.1181 (P <.01); –.1172 (P <.01) and –.1184, (P >.01) respectively. It means that values namely: A world of beauty, equality, happiness, true friendship, wisdom, equity and polite, are significantly and negatively related to stress in home. Non-significant values of correlations point to existence of non-significant relationship between stress in home and each of the 33 values namely: A comfortable life, an exciting life, a sense of accomplishment, a world of peace, family security, freedom, inner harmony, mature love, national security, pleasure, salvation, self-respect, social recognition, power, social justice, ambitious, broadminded, capable, cheerful, clean, courageous, forgiving, helpful, honesty, imagination, independent, intellectual, logical, loving, obedient, responsible, self-control and self-determination.

Table 4.145 shows correlations between stress in school and 40 values as measured by R.V.S.E.V. A glance at the table shows that out of 40 correlations given in the table only six are significant. Significant values of correlations for six values namely: A world of peace, happiness, true friendship, wisdom, helpful and loving, are –.1195 (P <.01); –.1574 (P <.01); –.1444 (P <.01); –.1150 (P <.01); –.1528 (P <.01) and –.1216 (P <.01), respectively. It means that values namely: A world of peace, happiness, true friendship, wisdom, helpful and loving are significantly and negatively related to stress in society. Non-significant values of correlations point to existence of negative relationship between stress in society and each of the 34 values namely: A comfortable life, an exciting life, a sense of accomplishment, a world of beauty, equality, family security, freedom, inner harmony, mature love, national security, pleasure, salvation, self-respect, social recognition, equity, power, social justice, ambitious, broadminded, capable, cheerful, clean, courageous, forgiving, honesty, imagination, independent, intellectual, logical, obedient, polite, responsible, self-control and self determination.

Table 4.145: Kendall's rank correlation coefficient between stress in society and various values

Sl. No.	Dependent Variable	Value of Correlation
1	2	3
1.	A comfortable life	.0425
2.	An exciting life	–.0445
3.	A sense of accomplishment	–.0826
4.	A world of peace	–.1195*
5.	A world of beauty	–.0825
6.	Equality	–.0962
7.	Family security	–.0238
8.	Freedom	–.0152
9.	Happiness	–.1574**
10.	Inner harmony	.0278
11.	Mature love	.0114
12.	National security	.0867
13.	Pleasure	–.0507
14.	Salvation	–.0219
15.	Self-respect	–.0339
16.	Social recognition	–.0936
17.	True friendship	–.1444*
18.	Wisdom	–.1150*
19.	Equity	–.0584
20.	Power	–.0422
21.	Social justice	–.0550
22.	Ambitious	.0515
23.	Broadminded	.0083
24.	Capable	–.0461
25.	Cheerful	–.0263
26.	Clean	.0083
27.	Courageous	–.0337
28.	Forgiving	–.0409

(Table Contd...)

(Table 4.145: Contd...)

1	2	3
29.	Helpful	–.1528*
30.	Honesty	–.0744
31.	Imagination	.0220
32.	Independent	–.0477
33.	Intellectual	–.0539
34.	Logical	–.0356
35.	Loving	–.1216*
36.	Obedient	–.0851
37.	Polite	–.1046
38.	Responsible	–.0755
39.	Self-control	–.0534
40.	Self-determination	–.0466

* Significant at .01 level
** Significant at .001 level

Table 4.146 shows correlation between stress and 40 values as measured by R.V.S.E.V. A look at the table reveals that out of 40 correlations only five are significant. Significant value for a comfortable life, a world of peace, happiness, helpful and polite are .1377 (P <.01); –.1468 (P <.01); –.1483 (P <.001); –.1141 (P <.01) and –.1219 (P <.01), respectively. Correlations between stress in school and a comfortable life is positive and reveals existence of positive relationship between the two variables. Significant but negative correlations for a world of peace, happiness, helpful and polite value show that these values are significantly and negatively related to stress in school.

Non-significant values of correlations point to existence of no significant relationship between stress in school and each of the 35 values namely: An exciting life, a sense of accomplishment, a world of beauty, equality, family security, freedom, inner harmony, mature love, national security, pleasure, salvation, self-respect, social recognition, true friendship, wisdom, equity, power, social justice,

Table 4.146: Kendall's rank coefficient of correlation between stress in school and various values

Sl. No.	Dependent Variable	Value of Correlation
1	2	3
1.	A comfortable life	.1377*
2.	An exciting life	–.0130
3.	A sense of accomplishment	–.0565
4.	A world of peace	–.1468*
5.	A world of beauty	–.0274
6.	Equality	–.0955
7.	Family security	.0049
8.	Freedom	.0291
9.	Happiness	–.1483**
10.	Inner harmony	.0380
11.	Mature love	.0269
12.	National security	–.0165
13.	Pleasure	–.0112
14.	Salvation	.0324
15.	Self-respect	–.0287
16.	Social recognition	–.0203
17.	True friendship	–.1004
18.	Wisdom	–.0968
19.	Equity	–.0524
20.	Power	–.0306
21.	Social justice	–.1292
22.	Ambitious	.0028
23.	Broadminded	–.0219
24.	Capable	–.0590
25.	Cheerful	.0317
26.	Clean	.0288
27.	Courageous	–.0393
28.	Forgiving	–.0397

(Table Contd...)

(Table 4.146: Contd...)

1	2	3
29.	Helpful	–.1141*
30.	Honesty	–.0069
31.	Imagination	.0097
32.	Independent	.0146
33.	Intellectual	–.0857
34.	Logical	–.0569
35.	Loving	–.0841
36.	Obedient	–.0508
37.	Polite	–.1219*
38.	Responsible	–.0649
39.	Self-control	–.0293
40.	Self-determination	–.0088

* Significant at .01 level
** Significant at .001 level

ambitious, broadminded, capable, cheerful, clean, courageous, forgiving, honesty, imagination, independent, intellectual, logical, loving, obedient, responsible, self-control and self-determination.

Table 4.148 shows correlation between stress related to self and 40 values as measured by R.V.S.E.V. Observation of the table shows that out of 40 Correlations only one is significant. It was found for happiness. It is –.1472 (P <.001). It means that happiness value is significantly and negatively related to stress related to self.

Non-significant values of correlation point out that no significant relation exists between stress in self and each of the 39 values namely: A comfortable life, an exciting life, a sense of accomplishment, a world of peace, a world of beauty, equality, family security, freedom, inner harmony, mature love, national security, pleasure, salvation, self-respect, social recognition, true friendship, wisdom, equity, power, social justice, ambitious, broadminded, capable, cheerful, clean, courageous, forgiving, helpful, honesty, imagination, independent, intellectual, logical, loving, obedient, polite, responsible, self-control, self determination.

Table 4.147: Kendall's coefficient of correlation between self stress and various values

Sl. No.	Dependent Variable	Value of Correlation
1	2	3
1.	A comfortable life	–.0117
2.	An exciting life	.0270
3.	A sense of accomplishment	–.0520
4.	A world of peace	–.0340
5.	A world of beauty	–.0643
6.	Equality	–.0016
7.	Family security	–.0031
8.	Freedom	.0793
9.	Happiness	–.1472**
10.	Inner harmony	.0144
11.	Mature love	.1097
12.	National security	–.0146
13.	Pleasure	–.0065
14.	Salvation	–.0010
15.	Self-respect	–.0112
16.	Social recognition	.0157
17.	True friendship	–.0153*
18.	Wisdom	–.0555
19.	Equity	–.0048
20.	Power	–.0443
21.	Social justice	.0329
22.	Ambitious	.0943
23.	Broadminded	.0532
24.	Capable	–.0187

(Table Contd...)

(Table 4.147: Contd...)

1	2	3
25.	Cheerful	.0572
26.	Clean	.0181
27.	Courageous	–.0126
28.	Forgiving	–.0310
29.	Helpful	–.0435
30.	Honesty	–.0208
31.	Imagination	.0786
32.	Independent	–.0306
33.	Intellectual	–.0083
34.	Logical	.0560
35.	Loving	–.0507
36.	Obedient	–.0446
37.	Polite	–.0890
38.	Responsible	–.0638
39.	Self-control	.3331
40.	Self-determination	.0208

* Significant at .01 level
** Significant at .001 level

SUMMARY

Overall stress is negatively related to a world of peace, happiness, true friendship, wisdom, helpful and polite values. Stress in home is negatively related to a world of beauty, equality, happiness, true friendship, wisdom, equity and polite values. Stress in society is significantly and negatively related to a world of peace, happiness, true friendship, wisdom, helpful and loving values. Stress in school is positively related to a comfortable life but negatively related to a world of peace, happiness, helpful and polite values. Stress related to self is negatively related to happiness value. To sum up, it can be said that stress is negatively related to happiness.

Study of Relationship between Stress and Moral Judgement

Results

It was hypothesized that "there exists no significant relationship between stress and moral judgement". This hypothesis was tested by computing Kendall Rank Coefficient of correlation between stress overall as well as four areas of stress and (overall as well as twelve items of M.J.Q.) significance of correlation was tested at .01 and .001 level using one-tailed test. Results have been presented in the following tables.

Table 4.148 shows correlation between overall stress and moral judgement—overall moral judgement and moral judgement as measured by twelve items of M.J.Q. Observation of the table reveals that correlation between

Table 4.148: Kendall's coefficient of correlation between overall stress and moral judgement

S. No.	Dependent Variable	Value of Correlation
A.	Overall moral judgement.	–.0912
B.	Various items of moral judgement.	
1.	Half cost ticket	–.0408
2.	Lost examination question paper	–.0557
3.	Mischievous student's group	–.0294
4.	Dilemma of friendship	–.0560
5.	Obtaining fruits without payment	–.0403
6.	Broken chair for the teacher	–.1092
7.	Act of a ball	–.0933
8.	Unclaimed money	–.0266
9.	Demand for killing by a beautiful girl	–.0973
10.	Dishonestful honesty	–.0289
11.	Sympathy of a thief friend	–.0643
12.	Improper action and friendship	–.0267

* Significant at .01 level
** Significant at .001 level

overall moral judgement and overall stress is –.0912. It is not significant at .01 level. It means that overall stress is not related to moral judgement. A look at the values of correlations for moral judgement as measured by various items of MJQ shows that none of the correlation is significant. It shows that overall stress is not related to overall moral judgement. Efforts were also made to study the relationship of moral judgement with stress related to home, school, society and self. Results have been presented in table 4.149 to 4.152.

Observation of the table 4.149 reveals that correlation between overall moral judgement and stress in home is –.0966. It is not significant at .01 level. It means that stress in home is not related to moral judgement. A look at the values of correlations for moral judgement as measured by

Table 4.149: Kendall's coefficient of correlation between stress in home and moral judgement

S. No.	Dependent Variable	Value of Correlation
A.	Overall moral judgement.	–.0966
B.	Various items of moral judgement	
1.	Half cost ticket	–.0111
2.	Lost examination question paper	–.0190
3.	Mischievous student's group	–.0083
4.	Dilemma of friendship	.0478
5.	Obtaining fruits without payment	–.0577
6.	Broken chair for the teacher	–.0473
7.	Act of a ball	–.0436
8.	Unclaimed money	–.0334
9.	Demand for killing by a beautiful girl	–.1560 **
10.	Dishonestful honesty	–.0417
11.	Sympathy of a thief friend	–.1168 *
12.	Improper action and friendship	–.0840

* Significant at .01 level
** Significant at .001 level

various items of MJQ shows that out of twelve correlations only two are significant. It means that moral judgement as measured by various items of MJQ, except, ninth and eleventh item, is not significantly related to stress in home. Significant values for ninth and eleventh item of MJQ are –.1560, (P <.001) and –.1168 (P <.01) respectively. They point to existence of negative relationship between stress in home and moral judgement as measured by ninth and eleventh items of MJQ.

Observation of the table 4.150 shows that correlation between overall moral judgement and stress in society is –.0533. It is not significant at .05 level. It means that stress in school is not related to moral judgement. A look at the values of the correlations for moral judgement as measured

Table 4.150: Kendall's coefficients of correlation between stress in society and moral judgement

S. No.	Dependent Variable	Value of Correlation
A.	Overall moral judgement.	–.0533
B.	Various items of moral judgement.	
1.	Half cost ticket	–.0418
2.	Lost examination question paper	–.0391
3.	Mischievous student's group	–.0761
4.	Dilemma of friendship	.0436
5.	Obtaining fruits without payment	–.0111
6.	Broken chair for the teacher	–.0875
7.	Act of a ball	–.0496
8.	Unclaimed money	.0123
9.	Demand for killing by a beautiful girl	–.0511
10.	Dishonestful honesty	.0238
11.	Sympathy of a thief friend	–.0346
12.	Improper action and friendship	–.0186

* Significant at .01 level
** Significant at .001 level

by various items of MJQ shows that no item of moral judgement is significantly related to stress in society. They point to existence of no relationship between stress in society and moral judgement.

Table 4.151 shows that correlation between stress in school and overall moral judgement is –.0866. It is not significant at .05 level. It means that stress in school is not related to overall moral judgement. Observation of values of correlations for twelve items of MJQ shows that none of the correlation is significant. It points to existence of no relationship between stress in school and moral judgement as measured by various items of MJQ.

Table 4.151: Kendall's coefficient of correlation between stress in society and moral judgement

S. No.	Dependent Variable	Value of Correlation
A.	Overall moral judgement.	–.0866
B.	Various items of moral judgement.	
1.	Half cost ticket	–.0464
2.	Lost examination question paper	–.0504
3.	Mischievous student's group	–.0329
4.	Dilemma of friendship	.0624
5.	Obtaining fruits without payment	–.0385
6.	Broken chair for the teacher	–.1097
7.	Act of a ball	–.1004
8.	Unclaimed money	–.0127
9.	Demand for killing by a beautiful girl	–.1014
10.	Dishonestful honesty	–.0345
11.	Sympathy of a thief friend	–.0476
12.	Improper action and friendship	–.0119

* Significant at .01 level
** Significant at .001 level

Observation of the table 4.152 shows that correlation between stress relates to self and overall moral judgement is –.0642. It is not significant at .05 level. It means that stress related to self is not related to overall moral judgement. Significant values of correlation were found for sixth and seventh items of MJQ. (–.1203, P <.01 and –.1116, P<.01). They point to existence of negative relationship between stress in self and moral judgement as measured by sixth and seventh items of MJQ.

Table 4.152: Kendall's coefficient of correlation between stress related to self and moral judgement

S. No.	Dependent Variable	Value of Correlation
A.	Overall moral judgement.	–.0642
B.	Various items of moral judgement.	
1.	Half cost ticket	–.0316
2.	Lost examination question paper	–.0849
3.	Mischievous student's group	–.0259
4.	Dilemma of friendship	–.0221
5.	Obtaining fruits without payment	–.0236
6.	Broken chair for the teacher	–.1203*
7.	Act of a ball	–.1116*
8.	Unclaimed money	–.0686
9.	Demand for killing by a beautiful girl	.0068
10.	Dishonestful honesty	–.0357
11.	Sympathy of a thief friend	–.0189
12.	Improper action and friendship	–.0222

* Significant at .01 level
** Significant at .001 level

SUMMARY

Overall stress is not related to moral judgement (overall as well as that measured by twelve items of MJQ). Stress in home is not related to overall moral judgement. It is negatively related to moral judgement measured by ninth and eleventh items of MJQ. Stress in society is not significantly related to overall moral judgement as well as moral judgement as measured by twelve items of MJQ. Stress in school is not significantly related to moral judgement overall as well as that measured by twelve items of MJQ stress related to self is not related to overall moral judgement. It is negatively related to moral judgement as measured by sixth and seventh items of MJQ. To sum up it can be said that overall stress in school and society has no relationship with moral judgement. Stress in home is negatively related to moral judgement as measured by the ninth and eleventh items of MJQ stress related to self is negatively related to six and seventh items of MJQ.

Study of Relationship between Home Environment and Values

RESULTS

It was hypothesized that there exists no significant relationship between home environment and values. This hypothesis was tested by computing Kendall rank coefficient of correlation between home environment and various values as measured by R.V.S.E.V. Significance of correlation was tested at .01 and .001 level using one-tailed test. Results have been presented in table 4.153 to 4.162.

Table 4.153 shows correlation between control aspect of home environment and various values as measured by R.V.S.E.V. A look at the values of correlations shows that cut of 40 correlations only six are significant. Values of correlation for values namely: A comfortable life, ambitious, broadminded, capable, courageous and self control, are .1326, (P <.01); .1116, (P <.01); .1325, (P <.01); .1414 (P <.01); .1363 (P <.01) and .1475, (P <.01) respectively. It means that values namely: A comfortable life, ambitious, broadminded, capable, courageous and self-control are significantly and positively related to control aspect of home environment.

Non-significant values of correlations point to the existence of no significant relationship between control aspect of one environment and 34 values namely: An exciting life, a sense of accomplishment, a world of peace, a world of beauty, equality, family security, freedom, happiness, inner harmony, mature love, national security, pleasure, salvation, self-respect, social recognition, true friendship, wisdom, equity, power, social justice, cheerful, clean, forgiving, helpful, honesty, imagination, independent, intellectual, logical, loving, obedient, polite, responsible, self-control, self-determination.

Table 4.153: Kendall's rank correlation between perceived control in home environment and values

Sl. No.	Dependent Variable	Value of Correlation
1	2	3
1.	A comfortable life	.1326 *
2.	An exciting life	.0438
3.	A sense of accomplishment	–.0200
4.	A world of peace	.0556
5.	A world of beauty	–.0313
6.	Equality	–.0063
7.	Family security	.1157
8.	Freedom	–.0386
9.	Happiness	.0752
10.	Inner harmony	.0615
11.	Mature love	.0102
12.	National security	.0456
13.	Pleasure	.0018
14.	Salvation	.0803
15.	Self-respect	.0905
16.	Social recognition	.0782

(Table Contd...)

(Table 4.153: Contd...)

1	2	3
17.	True friendship	.0534
18.	Wisdom	.0683
19.	Equity	.0635
20.	Power	.0851
21.	Social justice	–.0010
22.	Ambitious	.1116 *
23.	Broadminded	.1325 *
24.	Capable	.1414 *
25.	Cheerful	.0363
26.	Clean	.0687
27.	Courageous	.1363 *
28.	Forgiving	.0266
29.	Helpful	–.0249
30.	Honesty	.0257
31.	Imagination	.0725
32.	Independent	.0765
33.	Intellectual	.0843
34.	Logical	.0746
35.	Loving	–.0071
36.	Obedient	.0778
37.	Polite	–.0164
38.	Responsible	.0050
39.	Self-control	.1475 *
40.	Self-determination	–.0198

* Significant at .01 level
** Significant at .001 level

Table 4.154 shows correlation between protectiveness aspect of home environment and various values. Observation of the table reveals that out of 40 correlations, twelve are significant. Significant values of correlations for a world of beauty, family security, happiness, self-respect, social recognition, equity, ambitious, broadminded, capable, cheerful, obedient and self control are .1190 (P <.01); .1857, (P <.001); .1185, (P <.01); .1193, (P <.01); .1431, (P <.01); .1303, (P <.01); .1877, (P <.001); .1422, (P <.01); .1433, (P <.01); .1311, (P <.01); .1746 (P <.001), .1591 (P < .001) respectively. It means that values namely: A world of beauty, family security, happiness, self-respect, social recognition, equity, ambitious, broadminded, capable, cheerful, obedient and self-control are significantly and positively related to protectiveness aspect of home environment.

Table 4.154: Kendall's rank correlation between perceived protectiveness in home environment and various values

Sl. No.	Dependent Variable	Value of Correlation
1	2	3
1.	A comfortable life	.0629
2.	An exciting life	.0446
3.	A sense of accomplishment	–.0012
4.	A world of peace	.0372
5.	A world of beauty	.1190 *
6.	Equality	.0788
7.	Family security	.1857 **
8.	Freedom	.0631
9.	Happiness	–.1185 *
10.	Inner harmony	.0663
11.	Mature love	–.0219
12.	National security	.0593
13.	Pleasure	.0913
14.	Salvation	.0610
15.	Self-respect	.1193 *
16.	Social recognition	.1431 *
17.	True friendship	–.0552

(Table Contd...)

(Table 4.154: Contd...)

1	2	3
18.	Wisdom	.0306
19.	Equity	.1303
20.	Power	.0960
21.	Social justice	.0603
22.	Ambitious	.1877 **
23.	Broadminded	.1422 *
24.	Capable	.1433 *
25.	Cheerful	.1311 *
26.	Clean	.0716
27.	Courageous	.0943
28.	Forgiving	.0678
29.	Helpful	.0259
30.	Honesty	–.0059
31.	Imagination	.0456
32.	Independent	.0206
33.	Intellectual	.0843
34.	Logical	.1000
35.	Loving	–.0261
36.	Obedient	–.1746 **
37.	Polite	.1037
38.	Responsible	.0686
39.	Self-control	.1591 **
40.	Self-determination	–.0735

* Significant at .01 level
** Significant at .001 level

Non-significant values of correlations point to existence of no significant relationship between protectivensss aspect of home environment and 28 values namely: A comfortable life, an exciting life, a sense of accomplishment, a world of peace, equality, freedom, inner harmony, mature love, national security, pleasure, salvation, true friendship, wisdom, power, social justice, clean, courageous, forgiving, helpful, honesty, imagination, independent, intellectual, logical, logical, polite, responsible and self-determination.

Table 4.155 shows correlation between punishment aspect of home environment and various values. Observation of the table reveals that out of 40 values of correlation only two are significant. They are for wisdom (.1162, P <.01) and logical (.1293, P <.01) values. Non-significant values of correlations point out that no significant relationship exists between punishment aspect of home environment and 38 values namely: A comfortable life, an exciting life, a sense of accomplishment, a world of peace, a world of beauty, equality, family security, freedom, happiness, inner harmony, mature love, national security, pleasure, salvation, self-respect, social recognition, true friendship, equity, power, social justice, ambitious, broadminded, capable, cheerful, clean, courageous, forgiving, helpful, honesty, imagination, independent, intellectual, loving, obedient, polite, responsible, self-control and self-determination.

Table 4.155: Kendall's rank correlation between perceived punishment in home environment and various values

Sl. No.	Dependent Variable	Value of Correlation
1	2	3
1.	A comfortable life	.0284
2.	An exciting life	.0079
3.	A sense of accomplishment	–.0050
4.	A world of peace	.0083
5.	A world of beauty	.0180
6.	Equality	.0298
7.	Family security	.0479
8.	Freedom	–.0069
9.	Happiness	–.0622

(Table Contd...)

(Table 4.155: Contd...)

1	2	3
10.	Inner harmony	.0350
11.	Mature love	.0233
12.	National security	.0588
13.	Pleasure	–.0086
14.	Salvation	.0554
15.	Self-respect	.0497
16.	Social recognition	.0552
17.	True friendship	–.0520
18.	Wisdom	.1162 *
19.	Equity	.0803
20.	Power	.0009
21.	Social justice	.0213
22.	Ambitious	.0570
23.	Broadminded	.0569
24.	Capable	.0678
25.	Cheerful	–.0035
26.	Clean	.–.0057
27.	Courageous	–.0025
28.	Forgiving	.0424
29.	Helpful	.0123
30.	Honesty	–.0328
31.	Imagination	.0127
32.	Independent	–.0095
33.	Intellectual	.0028
34.	Logical	.1293 *
35.	Loving	.0080
36.	Obedient	.0056
37.	Polite	.0326
38.	Responsible	.0177
39.	Self-control	.0955
40.	Self-determination	.0574

* Significant at .01 level
** Significant at .001 level

Table 4.156 shows correlation between conformity aspect of home environment and various values. Observation of the table reveals that out of 40 values of correlations, only three are significant. Correlations for equity, ambitious and courageous values are .1347, (P <.01); .1206, (P <.01) and .1290, (P <.01) respectively. They indicate that equity, ambitious and courageous values are significantly and positively related to conformity aspect of home environment.

Table 4.156: Kendall's rank correlation between conformity as perceived by girls in their home environment and various values

Sl. No.	Dependent Variable	Value of Correlation
1	2	3
1.	A comfortable life	.0900
2.	An exciting life	.0052
3.	A sense of accomplishment	.0589
4.	A world of peace	.0721
5.	A world of beauty	.0816
6.	Equality	.0078
7.	Family security	.1076
8.	Freedom	–.0084
9.	Happiness	.0707
10.	Inner harmony	.0490
11.	Mature love	–.0297
12.	National security	.0157
13.	Pleasure	.0766
14.	Salvation	.0727
15.	Self-respect	.0296
16.	Social recognition	.0840
17.	True friendship	–.0128
18.	Wisdom	.0769
19.	Equity	.1347 *

(Table Contd...)

(Table 4.156: Contd...)

1	2	3
20.	Power	.0704
21.	Social justice	.0056
22.	Ambitious	.1206*
23.	Broadminded	.0972
24.	Capable	.0526
25.	Cheerful	.0876
26.	Clean	.0706
27.	Courageous	.1290*
28.	Forgiving	.0495
29.	Helpful	–.0230
30.	Honesty	.0567
31.	Imagination	.0410
32.	Independent	.1004
33.	Intellectual	.0855
34.	Logical	.0907
35.	Loving	.0229
36.	Obedient	.0621
37.	Polite	.0586
38.	Responsible	.0728
39.	Self-control	.0873
40.	Self-determination	.0968

* Significant at .01 level
** Significant at .001 level

Non significant values of correlations point to the existence of no significant relationship between conformity aspect of home environment and 37 values namely: A comfortable life, an exciting life, a sense of accomplishment, a world of peace, a world of beauty, equality, family security, freedom, happiness, inner harmony, mature love, national security, pleasure, salvation, self-respect, social recognition, true friendship, wisdom, power, social justice, broadminded, capable, cheerful, clean, forgiving, helpful, honesty, imagiatnion, independent, intellectual, logical loving, obedient, polite, responsible, self-control and self-determination.

Table 4.157 shows correlation between social isolation aspect of home environment and various values. A look at the table, reveals that out of 40 correlations given for various values, only one (–.1212) is significant at .01. It means that happiness value is negatively and significantly related to social isolation aspect of home environment. The nonsignificant values of correlation shows that social isolation aspect of home environment is not significantly related to the remaining 39 values namely: A comfortable life, an exciting life, a sense of accomplishment, a world of peace, a world of beauty, equality, family security, freedom, inner harmony, mature love, national security, pleasure, salvation, self-respect, social recognition, true friendship, wisdom, equity, power, social justice, ambitious, broadminded, capable, cheerful, clean, courageous, forgiving, helpful, honesty, imagination, independent, intellectual, logical, loving, obedient, polite, responsible, self-control and self-determination.

Table 4.157: Kendall's rank correlation between perceived social isolation in home environment and various values

Sl. No.	Dependent Variable	Value of Correlation
1	2	3
1.	A comfortable life	–.0636
2.	An exciting life	–.0349
3.	A sense of accomplishment	–.0791
4.	A world of peace	–.0805
5.	A world of beauty	–.0758
6.	Equality	–.0797
7.	Family security	–.0146
8.	Freedom	–.0826

(Table Contd...)

(Table 4.157: Contd...)

1	2	3
9.	Happiness	–.1212 *
10.	Inner harmony	–.0877
11.	Mature love	0.164
12.	National security	–.0213
13.	Pleasure	–.0858
14.	Salvation	.0134
15.	Self-respect	–.0710
16.	Social recognition	–.0491
17.	True friendship	–.0091
18.	Wisdom	–.0106
19.	Equity	.0086
20.	Power	–.0319
21.	Social justice	–.0326
22.	Ambitious	.0087
23.	Broadminded	.0375
24.	Capable	–.0127
25.	Cheerful	–.0811
26.	Clean	.0341
27.	Courageous	–.0283
28.	Forgiving	.0141
29.	Helpful	–.0534
30.	Honesty	.0157
31.	Imagination	.0696
32.	Independent	.0105
33.	Intellectual	–.0495
34.	Logical	.0162
35.	Loving	–.0012
36.	Obedient	–.0595
37.	Polite	–.0112
38.	Responsible	–.0684
39.	Self-control	.0428
40.	Self-determination	–.0733

* Significant at .01 level

** Significant at .001 level

Table 4.158 shows correlation between reward aspect of home environment and various values. A look at the table 4.158 shows that out of 40 values of correlations eight are significant. Values of correlation for family security (.1688), wisdom (.1611), power (.1577) and ambitious (.1547) are significant at .001 level. Values of correlation for broadminded, capable, courageous and self-control values. are .1467, .1116, .1460 and .1464 respectively. They are significant at .01 level. So, it can be inferred that family security, wisdom, power, ambitious, broadminded, capable, courageous and self-control values are significantly and positively related to reward aspect of home environment. Non-significant values of correlations show that no significant relationship exists between reward aspect of home environment and each of the 32 values namely: A comfortable life, an exciting life, a sense of accomplishment, a world of peace, a world of beauty, equality, freedom, happiness, inner harmony, mature love, national security, pleasure, salvation, self-respect, social recognition, true friendship, equity, social justice, cheerful, clean, forgiving, helpful, honesty, imagination, independent, intellectual logical, loving, obedient, polite, responsible and self-determination.

Table 4.158: Kendall's rank correlation between reward as perceived by girls in their home environment and various values

Sl. No.	Dependent Variable	Value of Correlation
1	2	3
1.	A comfortable life	.0369
2.	An exciting life	.0745
3.	A sense of accomplishment	.0201
4.	A world of peace	.0209
5.	A world of beauty	.0534
6.	Equality	.0707
7.	Family security	.1688 **
8.	Freedom	.0402

(Table Contd...)

(Table 4.158: Contd...)

1	2	3
9.	Happiness	.0724
10.	Inner harmony	.0649
11.	Mature love	–.0209
12.	National security	.0931
13.	Pleasure	.0330
14.	Salvation	.0154
15.	Self-respect	.0400
16.	Social recognition	.1113
17.	True friendship	–.0162
18.	Wisdom	.1611 **
19.	Equity	.0867
20.	Power	.1577 **
21.	Social justice	.0439
22.	Ambitious	.1547 **
23.	Broadminded	.1467 *
24.	Capable	.1116 *
25.	Cheerful	.0932
26.	Clean	.0444
27.	Courageous	.1460 *
28.	Forgiving	.0365
29.	Helpful	.0164
30.	Honesty	.0603
31.	Imagination	.0397
32.	Independent	.0345
33.	Intellectual	.0857
34.	Logical	.0728
35.	Loving	.0043
36.	Obedient	.0958
37.	Polite	.0460
38.	Responsible	.0907
39.	Self-control	.1464 *
40.	Self-determination	.0920

* Significant at .01 level
** Significant at .001 level

Table 4.159 shows correlations between deprivation of privileges as perceived by girls in their home environment and various values. Contents of the table shows that out of 40 values of correlations six are significant. Significant values of correlation for values namely: A sense of accomplishment, a world of peace, a world of beauty, equality, happiness and wisdom are: –.1283 (P <.01); –1252 (P <.01); –1539, (P <.001); –.1190, (P <.01); –.1853, (P <.001); –.1139 (P <.01) respectively. It means that values namely: A sense of accomplishment, a world of peace, a world of beauty, equality, happiness and wisdom are negatively and significantly related to deprivation of privileges as perceived by girls in their home environment. Non-significant values of correlation shows that no significant relationship exists between deprivation of privileges as perceived by girls on one hand and each of the 34 values namely: A comfortable life, an exciting life, family security, freedom, inner harmony, mature love, national security, pleasure, salvation, self-respect, social recognition, true friendship, equity, power, social justice, ambitious, broadminded, capable, cheerful, clean, courageous, forgiving, helpful, honesty, imagination, independent, intellectual, logical, loving, obedient, polite, responsible, self-control and self-determination.

Table 4.159: Kendall's coefficient of correlation between deprivation of privileges as perceived by girls in their home environment and various values

Sl. No.	Dependent Variable	Value of Correlation
1	2	3
1.	A comfortable life	–.0437
2.	An exciting life	–.0359
3.	A sense of accomplishment	–.1283 *
4.	A world of peace	–.1252 *
5.	A world of beauty	–.1539 **
6.	Equality	–.1190 *
7.	Family security	–.0193

(Table Contd...)

(Table 4.159: Contd...)

1	2	3
8.	Freedom	–.0869
9.	Happiness	–.1853 **
10.	Inner harmony	–.0826
11.	Mature love	–.0336
12.	National security	.0056
13.	Pleasure	–.0865
14.	Salvation	–.0026
15.	Self-respect	–.0738
16.	Social recognition	–.0825
17.	Truc friendship	–.0242
18.	Wisdom	–.1038
19.	Equity	–.1139 *
20.	Power	–.0657
21.	Social justice	–.0607
22.	Ambitious	–.0828
23.	Broadminded	–.0033
24.	Capable	–.0316
25.	Cheerful	–.0863
26.	Clean	–.0663
27.	Courageous	–.0141
28.	Forgiving	.0243
29.	Helpful	–.0975
30.	Honesty	.0116
31.	Imagination	–.0168
32.	Independent	–.1076
33.	Intellectual	–.0814
34.	Logical	–.0179
35.	Loving	–.0449
36.	Obedient	–.0893
37.	Polite	–.1033
38.	Responsible	–.0480
39.	Self-control	–.0188
40.	Self-determination	.0864

* Significant at .01 level

** Significant at .001 level

Table 4.160 shows correlation between nurturance aspect of home environment and various values. Contents of the table 4.161 show that out of 40 values of correlations, only three are significant. Significant values of correlations for power, broadminded and courageous are .1253, .1225 and .1600 respectively. They are significant at .01 level. It means that values namely: Power, broadminded and courageous are significantly and positively related to nurturance in home environment. Non-significant values of correlations point to the existence of no significant

Table 4.160: Kendall's rank correlation between nurturance as perceived by girls in their home environment and various values

Sl. No.	Dependent Variable	Value of Correlation
1	2	3
1.	A comfortable life	.0292
2.	An exciting life	.0715
3.	A sense of accomplishment	–.0362
4.	A world of peace	–.0104
5.	A world of beauty	.0810
6.	Equality	.0914
7.	Family security	.0863
8.	Freedom	.0647
9.	Happiness	.1028
10.	Inner harmony	.0775
11.	Mature love	–.0389
12.	National security	.0396
13.	Pleasure	.0108
14.	Salvation	.0320
15.	Self-respect	.0726
16.	Social recognition	.0372
17.	True friendship	.0342

(Table Contd...)

(Table 4.160: Contd...)

1	2	3
18.	Wisdom	.0274
19.	Equity	.0436
20.	Power	.1253 *
21.	Social justice	.0277
22.	Ambitious	.1098
23.	Broadminded	.1225 *
24.	Capable	.0692
25.	Cheerful	.0430
26.	Clean	.0207
27.	Courageous	.1600 **
28.	Forgiving	.0714
29.	Helpful	.0397
30.	Honesty	.0488
31.	Imagination	.0395
32.	Independent	.0028
33.	Intellectual	.0145
34.	Logical	.0601
35.	Loving	.0368
36.	Obedient	.0950
37.	Polite	–.0410
38.	Responsible	.0378
39.	Self-control	.0957
40.	Self-determination	.0748

* Significant at .01 level
** Significant at .001 level

relationship between nurturance in home environment and 37 values namely: A comfortable life, an exciting life, a sense of accomplishment, a world of peace, a world of beauty, equality, family security, freedom, happiness, inner harmony, mature love, national security, pleasure, salvation, self-respect, social recognition, true friendship, wisdom, equity, social justice, ambitious, capable, cheerful, clean, forgiving, helpful, honesty, imagination, independent, intellectual, logical, loving, obedient, polite, responsible, self-control and self-determination.

Table 4.161 shows relationship between rejection aspect of home environment and various values. Observation of the table 4.161 shows that out of 40 value of correlations given in the table, twenty two are significant. Significant values of correlations for a sense of accomplishment a world of peace, a world of beauty, equality, freedom, happiness, inner harmony, salvation, self-respect, social recognition, wisdom, equity, social justice,

Table 4.161: Kendall's rank correlation between perceived rejection in home environment and various values

Sl. No.	Dependent Variable	Value of Correlation
1	2	3
1.	A comfortable life	–.0452
2.	An exciting life	–.1027
3.	A sense of accomplishment	–.1223 *
4.	A world of peace	–.1582 **
5.	A world of beauty	–.1770 **
6.	Equality	–.2366 **
7.	Family security	–.0958
8.	Freedom	–.2029 **
9.	Happiness	–.1690 **
10.	Inner harmony	–.1340 *
11.	Mature love	.0029
12.	National security	–.0190
13.	Pleasure	–.0537
14.	Salvation	–.1366 *
15.	Self-respect	–.1345 *
16.	Social recognition	–.1342 *
17.	True friendship	–.0810
18.	Wisdom	–.1397 *

(Table Contd...)

(Table 4.161: Contd...)

1	2	3
19.	Equity	–.1289 *
20.	Power	–.0972
21.	Social justice	–.1616 **
22.	Ambitious	–.1613 **
23.	Broadminded	–.1663 **
24.	Capable	–.1397 *
25.	Cheerful	–.0802
26.	Clean	–.0693
27.	Courageous	–.0458
28.	Forgiving	–.1233 *
29.	Helpful	–.1018
30.	Honesty	–.0087
31.	Imagination	–.0565
32.	Independent	–.2191 **
33.	Intellectual	–.1253 *
34.	Logical	–.0770
35.	Loving	–.0918
36.	Obedient	–.1451 *
37.	Polite	–.1250 *
38.	Responsible	–.1310 *
39.	Self-control	–.0726
40.	Self-determination	–.0632

* Significant at .01 level
** Significant at .001 level

ambitious, broadminded, capable, forgiving, independent, intellectual, obedient, polite and responsible are –.1223, (P <.01); –.1582, (P <.001); –.1770, (P <.001), –.2366, (P <.001); –.2029, (P <.001); 0.1690, (P <.001); –.1340, (P <.01); –.1366, (P <.01); –.1345 (P <.01), –.1342, (P <.01); –.1397, (P <.01); –1289 (P <.01); .1616, (P < .001); –.1613, (P <.001); –1163, (P <.001); –.1397, (P <.01); –.1233, (P <.01); –.2191, (P <.01); –.1253, (P <.01); –.1451, (P <.01);

–.1250, (P <.01); –.1310 (P <01) respectively. It means that a sense of accomplishment, a world of peace, world of beauty, equality, freedom, happiness, inner harmony, salvation, self-respect, social-recognition, wisdom, equity, social justice, ambitious, broadminded, capable, forgiving, independent, intellectual, obedient, polite and responsible values are significantly and negatively related to rejection aspect of home environment.

Non-significant values of correlations show that no significant relationship exists between rejection aspect of home environment and 18 values namely: A comfortable life, an exciting life, family security, mature love, national security, pleasure, true friendship, power, cheerful, clean, courageous, helpful, honesty, imagination, logical, loving, self-control and self-determination.

Table 4.162 shows correlation between permissiveness aspect of home environment and values. Contents of the table 4.162 reveal that out of 40 values of correlations given in the table, only two are significant at .01 level. They are for an exciting life, (.1132) and clean (–.1185). It means that permissiveness aspect of home environment is positively related to an exciting life value while clean value is negatively related to permissiveness aspect of home environment. Non-significant values of correlations show that no significant relationship exists between permissiveness aspect of one environment and 38 values namely: A comfortable life, a sense of accomplishment, a world of peace, a world of beauty, equality, family security, freedom, happiness, inner harmony, mature love, national security, pleasure, salvation, self-respect, social recognition, true friendship, wisdom, equity, power, social justice, ambitious, broadminded, capable, cheerful, courageous, forgiving, helpful, honesty, imagination, independent, intellectual, logical, loving, obedient, polite, responsible, self-control and self-determination.

Table 4.162: Kendall's rank correlation between perceived permissiveness in home environment and various values

Sl. No.	Dependent Variable	Value of Correlation
1	2	3
1.	A comfortable life	.0268
2.	An exciting life	.1132 *
3.	A sense of accomplishment	–.0049
4.	A world of peace	–.0824
5.	A world of beauty	–.0530
6.	Equality	–.0116
7.	Family security	–.0696
8.	Freedom	–.0076
9.	Happiness	.0975
10.	Inner harmony	.0338
11.	Mature love	.0197
12.	National security	–.0334
13.	Pleasure	.0022
14.	Salvation	–.0759
15.	Self-respect	.0812
16.	Social recognition	.0332
17.	True friendship	–.0376
18.	Wisdom	.0324
19.	Equity	.0524
20.	Power	.0734
21.	Social justice	.0100
22.	Ambitious	.0634
23.	Broadminded	.0471
24.	Capable	–.0068
25.	Cheerful	.0356
26.	Clean	–.1185 *

(Table Contd...)

(Table 4.162: Contd...)

1	2	3
27.	Courageous	.0288
28.	Forgiving	–.0846
29.	Helpful	–.0509
30.	Honesty	–.0492
31.	Imagination	–.0032
32.	Independent	.0321
33.	Intellectual	.0135
34.	Logical	.0491
35.	Loving	–.0115
36.	Obedient	–.0302
37.	Polite	–.0398
38.	Responsible	–.0612
39.	Self-control	.0281
40.	Self-determination	.0088

* Significant at .01 level
** Significant at .001 level

SUMMARY

Analysis of data as reported earlier has shown that control, as perceived by girls in their home environment, is positively related to a comfortable life, broadminded, capable, courageous and self-control values. Protectiveness, as perceived by girls, is positively related to a world of beauty, family security, happiness, self respect, social recognition, equity, ambitious, broadminded, capable, cheerful, obedient, and self-control values. Punishment as perceived by the girls in their home environment is positively related to wisdom and logical values. Conformity, as perceived by the girls is positively related to equity, ambitious and courageous values. Girls perceiving of social isolation in their home environment is negatively related to happiness value. Reward, as perceived by girls in their home environment is related to family security, wisdom, power, ambitious, broadminded, capable, courageous and self control values. Girls perception of deprivation of privileges is negatively related to a sense of accomplishment, a world of peace, a world of beauty, equality, happiness and wisdom values. Girls positively related to power, broadminded and courageous values. Rejection, as perceived by girls in their home environment is negatively related to a sense of accomplishment, a world of peace, a world of beauty, equality, freedom, happiness, inner harmony, salvation, self-respect, social-recognition, wisdom, equity, social justice, ambitious, broadminded, capable, forgiving, independent, intellectual, obedient, polite and responsible values. Permissiveness as perceived by girls in their home environments is positively related to an exciting life but negatively related to clean value.

Study of Relationship between Home Environment and Moral Judgement

Results

It as hypothesized that "There exists no significant relationship between home environment and moral judgement". This hypothesis was tested by computing Kendall's rank coefficient of correlation between home environment and overall moral judgement as well as measured by various items of MJQ. Significance of correlation was tested at .01 and .001 level using one-tailed test. Results have been presented in table 4.163 to 4.172.

Table 4.163 shows correlation between home environment and moral judgement. Contents of the table 4.163 shows that value of correlation between control aspect of home environment and overall moral judgement is .0527 which is not significant at .01 level. It means that control aspect of home environment is not significantly related to moral judgement.

Table 4.163: Kendall's rank correlation between control as perceived by girls in their home environment and various values

S. No.	Dependent Variable	Value of Correlation
A.	Overall moral judgement.	.0527
B.	Various items of moral judgement.	
1.	Half cost ticket	–.0039
2.	Lost examination question paper	.0546
3.	Mischievous student's group	.0471
4.	Dilemma of friendship	.0080
5.	Obtaining fruits without payment	.0128
6.	Broken chair for the teacher	.0225
7.	Act of a ball	.0877
8.	Unclaimed money	–.0183
9.	Demand for killing by a beautiful girl	.0671
10.	Dishonestful honesty	.0485
11.	Sympathy of a thief friend	.0088
12.	Improper action and friendship	–.0085

A look at the values of correlations for moral judgement as measured by various items of MJQ also shows that none of the values is significant at .05 level. It means that moral judgement as measured by all items is not significantly related to control aspect of home environment.

Table 4.164 shows that correlation between overall moral judgement and protectiveness aspect of home environment is .1100. It is not significant at .01 level. It means that protectiveness aspect of home environment is not significantly related to overall moral judgement. Observation of the values of correlations for moral judgement as measured by various items of MJQ shows that out of twelve correlations only one is significant. It

Table 4.164: Kendall's rank correlation between protectiveness as perceived by girls in their home environment and moral judgement

S. No.	Dependent Variable	Value of Correlation
A.	Overall moral judgement.	.1100
B.	Various items of moral judgement.	
1.	Half cost ticket	.0063
2.	Lost examination question paper	.0751
3.	Mischievous student's group	.1085
4.	Dilemma of friendship	–.0162
5.	Obtaining fruits without payment	.0249
6.	Broken chair for the teacher	.0076
7.	Act of a ball	.0527
8.	Unclaimed money	.0585
9.	Demand for killing by a beautiful girl	.1476*
10.	Dishonestful honesty	.0799
11.	Sympathy of a thief friend	.0355
12.	Improper action and friendship	.1063

means that moral judgement as measured by all, except ninth item of MJQ, is not significantly related to protectiveness aspect of home environment. Significant values of correlation for ninth item is .1476 (P <.01). It points to existence of positive relationship between protectiveness aspect of home environment and moral judgement as measured by ninth item of MJQ.

Table 4.165 shows that correlation between punishment, as perceived by girls in their home environment and their overall moral judgement is .0625 which is not significant at .01 level. It means that

Table 4.165: Kendall's rank correlation between punishment as perceived by girls in their home environment and moral judgement

S. No.	Dependent Variable	Value of Correlation
A.	Overall moral judgement.	.0625
B.	Various items of moral judgement.	
1.	Half cost ticket	.0151
2.	Lost examination question paper	.0646
3.	Mischievous student's group	–.0431
4.	Dilemma of friendship	.0181
5.	Obtaining fruits without payment	–.0368
6.	Broken chair for the teacher	.0738
7.	Act of a ball	.0692
8.	Unclaimed money	.0829
9.	Demand for killing by a beautiful girl	.0074
10.	Dishonestful honesty	.0363
11.	Sympathy of a thief friend	.0623
12.	Improper action and friendship	.0624

punishment administered by parents and perceived so by girls, is not related to overall moral judgement. Examination of the values of correlation for various items of MJQ shows correlations are not significant at .01 level. This allows to infer that punishment as perceived by girls in their home environment is not significantly related to moral judgement as measured by various items of MJQ.

Observation of the table 4.166 reveals that correlation between conformity as perveived by girls and their overall moral judgement is .0510 which is not significant at .01 level. It means that girls perception of conformity in their

Table 4.166: Kendall's coefficient of correlation between girls perception of conformity in home environment and their moral judgement

S. No.	Dependent Variable	Value of Correlation
A.	Overall moral judgement	.0510
B.	Various items of moral judgement	
1.	Half cost ticket	–.0486
2.	Lost examination question paper	.0387
3.	Mischievous student's group	.0186
4.	Dilemma of friendship	.0345
5.	Obtaining fruits without payment	.0244
6.	Broken chair for the teacher	.0148
7.	Act of a ball	.0459
8.	Unclaimed money	.0724
9.	Demand for killing by a beautiful girl	.0573
10.	Dishonestful honesty	.0054
11.	Sympathy of a thief friend	.0019
12.	Improper action and friendship	.0605

homes is not related to overall moral judgement. A look at the values of correlation for moral judgement as measured by various items of MJQ reveals that out of twelve correlations none is significant at .01 level. It means that moral judgement as measured by various items of MJQ is not significantly related to girls perception of conformity in their home environment.

Table 4.167 shows that correlation between overall moral judgement and girls perception of social isolation in their homes is –.0377 (P <.01). It reveals existence of no relationship between overall moral judgement and social isolation as used by parents. Values of correlation given for various items of MJQ. are not significant at .01 level. They show that girls perception of social isolation in their homes is not related to moral judgement as measured by various items of MJQ.

Table 4.167: Kendall's coefficient of correlation between girls perception of social isolation in their homes and moral judgement

S. No.	Dependent Variable	Value of Correlation
A.	Overall moral judgement.	–.0377
B.	Various items of moral judgement.	
1.	Half cost ticket	–.0937
2.	Lost examination question paper	–.0224
3.	Mischievous student's group	–.0463
4.	Dilemma of friendship	–.0425
5.	Obtaining fruits without payment	–.0403
6.	Broken chair for the teacher	.0463
7.	Act of a ball	–.0012
8.	Unclaimed money	–.0220
9.	Demand for killing by a beautiful girl	–.0304
10.	Dishonestful honesty	–.0190
11.	Sympathy of a thief friend	–.0207
12.	Improper action and friendship	–.0283

Contents of the table 4.168 reveal that correlation between overall moral judgement and girls perception of reward in their homes is .1153. It is significant at .01 level. It means that girls' perception of reward in their homes is positively related to overall moral judgement. A look at the values of correlations for moral judgement as measured by various items of MJQ reveals that out of twelve correlations given, only one is significant at .01 level. It indicates that moral judgement, as measured by eleven items of MJQ is not significantly related with girls perception of reward in their homes. Value of correlation for eighth item of MJQ is .1143 (P <.01). It points to the existence of positive relationship between moral judgement as measured by eighth item of MJQ and girls perception of reward in their homes.

Table 4.168: Kendall's coefficient of correlation between girls perception of reward in their homes and moral judgement

S. No.	Dependent Variable	Value of Correlation
A.	Overall moral judgement.	.1153*
B.	Various items of moral judgement.	
1.	Half cost ticket	.0276
2.	Lost examination question paper	.0765
3.	Mischievous student's group	.1000
4.	Dilemma of friendship	.0681
5.	Obtaining fruits without payment	.0249
6.	Broken chair for the teacher	.0447
7.	Act of a ball	.0573
8.	Unclaimed money	.1143*
9.	Demand for killing by a beautiful girl	.0723
10.	Dishonestful honesty	.0051
11.	Sympathy of a thief friend	.0842
12.	Improper action and friendship	.0631

Table 4.169 shows that correlation between overall moral judgement and deprivation of privileges in home environment as perceived by girls is –.0557. It is not significant at .01 level. It means that overall moral judgement is not related to deprivation of privileges as

perceived by girls in their home environment. A look at the values of correlation given for various items of MJQ reveals that none of them is significant at .01 level. It means that deprivation of privileges in home environment as perceived by girls is not significantly related to moral judgement as measured by various items of MJQ.

Table 4.169: Kendall's coefficient of correlation between girls perception of deprivation of privileges and moral judgement

S. No.	Dependent Variable	Value of Correlation
A.	Overall moral judgement.	–.0557
B.	Various items of moral judgement.	
1.	Half cost ticket	–.0073
2.	Lost examination question paper	–.0134
3.	Mischievous student's group	–.0439
4.	Dilemma of friendship	–.0406
5.	Obtaining fruits without payment	–.0344
6.	Broken chair for the teacher	.0384
7.	Act of a ball	–.0180
8.	Unclaimed money	–.0243
9.	Demand for killing by a beautiful girl	–.0899
10.	Dishonestful honesty	–.0447
11.	Sympathy of a thief friend	–.0291
12.	Improper action and friendship	–.0341

Observation of table 4.170 shows that value of correlation between overall moral judgement and nurturance in home environment as perceived by girls is .1387 which is significant at .01 level. It means that nurturance as perceived by girls in their home environment is significantly and positively related with overall moral judgement. Out of twelve correlations given in the table for moral judgement as measured by various items of MJQ only two are significant at .01 level. It means that moral judgement as measured by all except seventh and ninth item of MJQ, is not significantly related to nurturance in home environment. Values of correlation for seventh and ninth items are .1154, (P <.01) and .1458 (P <.01). They point to the existence of positive relationship between nurturance in home environment as perceived by the girls and moral judgement as shown for seventh and ninth item of MJQ.

Table 4.170: Kendall's coefficient of correlation between girls perception of nurturance in home and moral judgement

S. No.	Dependent Variable	Value of Correlation
A.	Overall moral judgement.	.1387*
B.	Various items of moral judgement.	
1.	Half cost ticket	.0580
2.	Lost examination question paper	.0926
3.	Mischievous student's group	.0690
4.	Dilemma of friendship	.0696
5.	Obtaining fruits without payment	.1082
6.	Broken chair for the teacher	.0414
7.	Act of a ball	.1154*
8.	Unclaimed money	.0743
9.	Demand for killing by a beautiful girl	.1458*
10.	Dishonestful honesty	.0022
11.	Sympathy of a thief friend	.0549
12.	Improper action and friendship	.0244

Table 4.171 shows that value of correlation between overall moral judgement and rejection as perceived by girls is –.1533 (P <.001). It means that rejection in home

environment as perceived by girls is negatively related to overall moral judgement. Further examination of the table reveals that out of the twelve values of correlations given in the table for moral judgement as measured by twelve items of MJQ eight are not significant at .01 level. It means that moral judgement as measured by first eight items of MJQ is not significantly related to girls perception of rejection in their home. Values of correlation for ninth, tenth, eleventh and twelfth items of MJQ are –.1723 (P <.001); –.1436 (P <.001), –.1160 (P<.01) and –.1263 (P <.01) respectively. It means that moral judgement as measured by ninth, tenth, eleventh and twelfth items of MJQ is negatively related to girls perception of rejection in their home environment.

Table 4.171: Kendall's coefficient of correlation between girls perception of rejection in their home environment and moral judgement

S. No.	Dependent Variable	Value of Correlation
A.	Overall moral judgement.	–.1533**
B.	Various items of moral judgement.	
1.	Half cost ticket	–.0764
2.	Lost examination question paper	–.0737
3.	Mischievous student's group	–.1047
4.	Dilemma of friendship	–.0879
5.	Obtaining fruits without payment	–.0325
6.	Broken chair for the teacher	–.0225
7.	Act of a ball	.0119
8.	Unclaimed money	–.0290
9.	Demand for killing by a beautiful girl	–.1723**
10.	Dishonestful honesty	–.1436**
11.	Sympathy of a thief friend	–.1160*
12.	Improper action and friendship	–.1263*

Table 4.172 shows correlation between overall moral judgement and girls' perception of permissiveness in their home environment is not (.0225, P>.01) significant. Out of the twelve values of correlations given in the table for various items of MJQ none is significant at .01 level. So, it can be inferred that girls' perception of permissiveness in their home environment is not significantly related to moral judgement.

Table 4.172: Kendall's coefficient of correlation between girls perception of permissiveness in their home environment and moral judgement

S. No.	Dependent Variable	Value of Correlation
A.	Overall moral judgement.	.0225
B.	Various items of moral judgement.	
1.	Half cost ticket	.0246
2.	Lost examination question paper	.0116
3.	Mischievous student's group	.0334
4.	Dilemma of friendship	.0925
5.	Obtaining fruits without payment	.0254
6.	Broken chair for the teacher	.0269
7.	Act of a ball	.0200
8.	Unclaimed money	.0105
9.	Demand for killing by a beautiful girl	.0555
10.	Dishonestful honesty	.0324
11.	Sympathy of a thief friend	.0569
12.	Improper action and friendship	.0749

SUMMARY

Analysing of data has shown that overall moral judgement is not significantly related to control, punishment conformity, social isolation, deprivation of privilege and permissiveness. Protectiveness in home environment as perceived by girls is not related to overall moral judgement but is significantly and positively related to ninth item of MJQ. Girls perception of reward in their home environment is positively related to overall moral judgement. Moral judgement as measured by eighth item of MJQ is positively and significantly related to girls perception of reward in their home environment. Girls perception of nurturance in their home environment is positively related to overall moral judgement. Moral judgement as measured by seventh and eighth item of MJQ are positively related to girl's perception of nurturance in their home environment. Rejection as perceived by girls is negatively related to overall moral judgement. It is also significantly and negatively related to moral judgement as measured by eighth, ninth, eleventh and twelfth items of MJQ.

5

Findings, Implications and Suggestions

The present study was undertaken to investigate the effect of stress and home environment on moral judgement and values of girls and study the relationship of stress and home environment two values and moral judgement. Data was collected from 436 girls studying in IXth Class in four schools situated in Allahabad city with the help of four tools namely: (i) Stress Scale for Students (ii) Home Environment Inventory (iii) Rokeach Value Survey extended by Ng. et. al., (1982) and (iv) Moral Judgement Questionnaire. Data was analysed by using Kruskal Wallis one way ANOVA. Mann Whiteny U-test and Kendall rank correlation. The previous chapter embodied the analysis and interpretation of data. The findings, their educational implication and suggestion for further study has been described in this chapter.

Findings

Effects of Stress on Values

(a) Effects of overall stress on values

As compared to girls experiencing low overall stress, girls experiencing moderate overall stress give less importance to happiness value. As compared to girls experiencing less stress, highly stressed girls give more importance to mature love. Girls experiencing less and high stress give equal importance to equity value.

(b) Effects of stress in home on values

As compared to girls experiencing low stress in home, moderately stressed girls give less importance to happiness and pleasure values but give more importance to imagination value. Both less and moderately stressed girls are equal on world of beauty, wisdom, and helpful values. As compared to girls experiencing high stress, moderately stressed girls give more importance to world of beauty of and happiness values. They give equal importance to pleasure, wisdom, helpful and imagination values. In comparison to less stressed girls, girls experiencing high stress give less importance to world of beauty, happiness, pleasure, wisdom and helpful values but they equal importance to imagination value.

(c) Effect of stress in society on values

As compared to girls experiencing low stress in society, moderately stressed girls give less importance to equality, happiness, true friendship, wisdom, forgiveness and helpful values. In comparison to highly stressed girls, moderately stressed girls give more importance to happiness value but both give equal importance to equality, true friendship, wisdom, forgiveness and helpful values. As compared to girls experiencing low level of stress, highly stressful girls give less importance to equality, happiness, true friendship, wisdom and helpful values but they give equal importance to forgiveness value.

(d) Effect of stress in school on values

As compared to girls experiencing low stress in school, moderately stressed girls give less importance to an exciting life, broadminded, capable values but give more importance to mature love values. Both moderately and highly stressed girls give equal importance to an exciting life, mature love, broadminded and capable values. As compared to less stressed, highly stressed girls give more importance to mature love but less importance to capable values. They give equal importance to an exciting life and broadminded values.

(e) Effect of stress in self on values

As compared to girls experiencing low stress related to self, moderately stressed girls give more importance to mature love and ambitious values but they give equal importance to happiness value. Both moderately and highly stressed girls give equal importance to

EFFECT OF STRESS ON MORAL JUDGEMENT

(a) As compared to girls experiencing low/moderate overall stress girls experiencing high overall stress exhibit inferior level moral judgement as measured by sixth and ninth item of MJQ. Girls experiencing different levels of overall stress do not differ on moral judgement as measured by all except sixth and ninth items of MJQ.

(b) Girls experiencing less and moderate stress in home do not differ on moral judgement as measured by ninth item of MJQ. Both moderately and highly stressed girls exhibit similar type of moral judgement as measured by this item. Girls experiencing less stress in home excel girls experiencing high stress on moral judgement as measured as measured by item ninth of MJQ.

(c) Girls experiencing less and moderate stress in society exhibit similar type of moral judgement as measured by sixth item of MJQ. As compared to highly stressful girls, girls experiencing less stress excel on moral judgement as measured by item sixth of MJQ.

(d) As compared to girls experiencing moderate stress in school, less stressful girls excel on moral judgement as measured by item ninth of MJQ. Both moderately and highly stressful girls in

society or equal on moral judgement. Less stressful girls in society excel highly stressful girls on moral judgement as measured by ninth item of MJQ.

(e) Girls experiencing moderate and less stress related to self are equal on moral judgement as measured by sixth items of MJQ. Girls experiencing moderate stress in self excel girls experiencing high stress in self on moral judgement. As compared to girls experiencing high stress, less stressed girls excel in moral judgement, measured by sixth item of MJQ. Girls experiencing less and moderate stress in self do not differ on moral judgement as measured by seventh item of MJQ. Moderately stressed girls excel highly stressed girls on moral judgement measured by seventh item of MJQ. Both less and highly stressed girls do not differ on moral judgement as measured by seventh item of MJQ.

Effect of Home Environment on Values

(a) Girls perceiving less and moderate control do not differ on national security and courageous values. Girls perceiving moderate control give more importance to obedient value. Girls perceiving moderate and high control in their home environment do not differ on obedient and courageous values whereas girls perceiving high control give more importance to national security value. Girls perceiving high control give more importance to courageous value than those who perceive less control. Girls perceiving less and high control give equal importance to national security and obedient values.

(b) Girls perceiving moderate protectiveness give more importance to family security, broadminded and cheerful values than the girls perceiving less protectiveness. They give equal importance to a world of peace, a world of beauty, happiness, social recognition, equality, power, ambitious, capable, intellectual, logical, obedient, self-control and self-determination values. In comparison to girls perceiving moderate protection in their home environment, girls perceiving high protection give more importance to a world of peace, a world of beauty, happiness, social-recognition, equity, ambitious, broadminded, capable, intellectual, logical, obedient and self-determination values, but they give equal importance to family security, power, cheerful and self-control values. As compared to girls perceiving less protectiveness, girls perceiving high protectiveness give more importance to world of peace, world of beauty, family security, happiness, social-recognition, equity, power, ambitious, broad-minded, capable, cheerful, logical, obedient, self-control and self-determination values but are equal on intellectual values.

(c) Girls perceiving moderate punishment in their home environment give more importance to wisdom value then those who perceive less punishment. Girls perceiving moderate and high punishment give equal importance to wisdom value. As compared to girls perceiving less punishment, girls perceiving high punishment give more importance to wisdom value.

(d) As compared to girls perceiving less conformity, girls perceiving moderate conformity give more importance to happiness and equity values whereas they are equal on family security; clean and courageous values. In comparison to girls perceiving high conformity in their home environment, girls perceiving moderate conformity give less importance to family security and clean values whereas they give equal importance to

happiness, equity and courageous values. As compared to girls perceiving less conformity, girls perceiving high conformity give more importance to family security, happiness, equity, clean and courageous values.

(e) As compared to girls perceiving less social isolation, girls perceiving moderate social isolation give less importance to equality value. They give equal importance to a comfortable life and happiness values. In comparison to girls perceiving moderate social isolation in their home, girls perceiving high level of social isolation give less importance to a comfortable life and happiness values but they do not differ on equality value. As compared to girls perceiving less social isolation, girls perceiving high level of social isolation give less importance to a comfortable life, equality and happiness values.

(f) In comparison to girls perceiving less reward, girls perceiving moderate reward in their home environment give more importance to wisdom, power, ambitious and courageous values but give equal importance to inner-harmony, social recognition, broadminded and self-control values. As compared to girls perceiving moderate level of reward, girls perceiving high level of reward give more importance to inner-harmony, social recognition and broadminded values whereas they give equal importance to wisdom, power, ambitious, courageous and self-control values. In comparison to girls perceiving less reward, girls perceiving high reward in their home give more importance to social-recognition, wisdom, power, ambitious, broad minded, courageous and self-control values.

(g) In comparison to girls perceiving less deprivation of privileges, girls perceiving moderate level of deprivation of privileges in their home give less importance to a world of beauty, happiness, social recognition and polite values. As compared to girls perceiving moderate level of deprivation of privileges, girls perceiving high level of deprivation of privileges give less importance to happiness value but they do not differ on a world of beauty, social recognition and polite values. In comparison to girls perceiving less deprivation of privileges, girls perceiving high level of deprivation of privileges give less importance to a world of beauty and happiness values whereas they are equal on social recognition and polite values.

(h) Girls perceiving high and moderate level of nurturance give more importance to ambitious, broadminded, courageous and forgiving values than those perceiving less nurturance. Moderately nurtured girls give more importance to self-control value than those perceiving less nurturance. Girls perceiving less and moderate level of nurturance in home give equal importance to self-control value.

(i) As compared to girls perceiving less rejection in home environment, girls perceiving high level of rejection assign less importance to a world of peace, a world of beauty, equality, freedom, happiness, inner-harmony, salvation, self-respect, social recognition, wisdom, equity, social justice, ambitious, broadminded, capable, cheerful, forgiving, helpful, independent, intellectual, polite and responsible values. Girls perceiving moderate and high level of rejection give equal importance to a world of peace, happiness, inner-harmony, salvation, self-respect, equity, capable, cheerful and helpful values. Girls perceiving moderate rejection give more importance to a world of beqauty, equality, freedom, social recognition, wisdom, social justice, ambitious, broadminded,

forgiving, independent, intellectual, polite and responsible values than the girls perceiving high rejection in home. Girls perceiving less rejection in home environment give more importance to a world of peace, equality, happiness, inner-harmony, salvation, self-respect, equity, broadmined, capable, cheerful values than those who perceive moderate rejection.

(i) Girls perceiving high level of permissiveness give more importance to happiness value than girls perceiving moderate or low level of permissiveness. Social justice value is preferred by girls perceiving moderate permissiveness. Girls perceiving high and low level of permissiveness give equal importance to social justice value. Girls perceiving high level of permissiveness do not differ from those perceiving moderate level of permissiveness with respect to the importance they give to polite value. Value polite is preferred by girls perceiving less permissiveness.

Effect of Home Environment on Moral Judgement

(a) Girls perceiving different level of control in their home environment do not differ on their moral judgement.

(b) Girls perceiving high level of protectiveness excel on moral judgement as measured by item 9. and 12 of moral judgement than their counterparts perceiving less and moderate level of protectiveness in their home.

(c) Girls perceiving moderate level of conformity excel girls perceiving less conformity on moral judgement as measured by seventh item of MJQ. Girls perceiving high level of conformity do not differ from girls perceiving moderate or low level of conformity on moral judgement measured by seventh item of moral judgement.

(*d*) Girls perceiving different levels of social isolation, reward, punishment or deprivation of privileges in their home environment do not differ on moral judgement.

(*e*) Girls perceiving high level of nurturance in home excel girls perceiving less nurturance on moral judgement as measured by seventh item of MJQ. Girls perceiving moderate and high nurturance do not differ in their moral reasoning as measured by the item entitled 'act of a fall'.

(*f*) Girls perceiving less and moderate rejection in home environment differ on overall moral judgement as well as on moral judgement as measured by third, ninth and tenth item of the MJQ. Girls perceiving moderate rejection excel girls perceiving high rejection while girls perceiving less rejection excel girls perceiving high level of rejection on overall moral judgement as well as on moral judgement as measured by third, ninth and tenth items of MJQ.

(*g*) Girls perceiving high level of permissiveness excel girls perceiving less permissiveness in home on moral judgement as measured by eleventh item of MJQ. Girls perceiving moderate permissiveness excel girls perceiving less permissiveness and are equal to girls perceiving high permissiveness in home on moral judgement as measured by eleventh item titled as 'sympathy of a thief friend'.

RELATIONSHIP BETWEEN STRESS AND VALUES

(*a*) Overall stress is negatively related to a world of peace, happiness, true friendship, wisdom, helpful, and polite values.

(b) Stress in home is negatively related to a world of peace, a world of beauty, happiness, true friendship, wisdom, equity and polite values.

(*c*) Stress in society is negatively related to a world of peace, happiness, true friendship, wisdom, helpful, and loving values.

(*d*) Stress in school is positively related to comfortable life but is negatively related to a world of peace, happiness, helpful and polite values.

(*e*) Stress in self is negatively related to happiness value.

Relationship Between Stress and Moral Judgement

(*a*) Overall stress in not related to moral judgement.

(*b*) Stress in home is negatively related to moral judgement as measured by ninth and eleventh items of MJQ.

(*c*) Stress in school is not related to moral judgement.

(*d*) Stress in society is not related to moral judgement.

(*e*) Stress in self is negatively related to moral judgement as measured by sixth and seventh items of MJQ.

Relationship Between Home Environment and Values

(*a*) Control aspect of the home environment as perceived by girls is positively related to comfortable life, family security, ambitious, broadminded, capable, courageous and self-control values.

(*d*) Girl's perception of protectiveness in their home environment is positively related to a world of beauty, family security, happiness, self-respect, social recognition, equity, ambitious, broadminded, capable, cheerful, obedient and self-control values.

(c) Punishment as perceived by girls in their home environment is positively related to wisdom value.

(*d*) Girl's perception of conformity in their home environment is positively related to equity, ambitious and courageous values.

(e) Social isolation as perceived by girls in their home environment is negatively related to happiness value.

(f) Reward as perceived by girls in their home environment is positively related to family security, wisdom, power, ambitious, broadminded, capable, courageous and self-control values.

(g) Deprivation of privileges as perceived by girls in their home environment is negatively related to a sense of accomplishment, world of peace, a world of beauty, equality, happiness, wisdom values.

(h) Nurturance as perceived by girls in their home environment is positively related to power, broadminded and courageous values.

(i) Rejection as perceived by girls in their home environment is negatively related to 'a sense of accomplishment, a world of peace, a world of beauty, equality, freedom, happiness, inner-harmony, salvation, self-respect, social recognition, wisdom, equity, social justice, ambitious, broadminded, capable, forgiving, independent, obedient, polite, responsible values.

(j) Permissiveness as perceived by girls in their home environment is positively related to 'an exciting life' value but it is negatively related to 'clean' value.

RELATIONSHIP BETWEEN HOME ENVIRONMENT AND MORAL JUDGEMENT

(a) Control aspect of home environment is not related to moral judgement.

(b) Protectiveness as perceived by girls in their home environment is positively related to moral judgement as measured by ninth item of the MJQ.

(c) Girl's perception of punishment is not significantly related to their moral judgement.

(*d*) Conformity as perceived by girls in their home environment is not related to moral judgement..

(*e*) Social isolation as perceived by girls in their home environment is not related to their moral judgement.

(*f*) Reward as perceived by girls in their home environment is positively related to overall moral judgement and moral judgement as measured by eighth item of MJQ.

(*g*) Girl's perception of deprivation of privileges is not related to moral judgement.

(*h*) Nurturance as perceived by girls in their home environment is positively related to overall moral judgement and moral judgement as measured by item seventh and ninth of the MJQ.

(*i*) Girl's perception of rejection in their home environment is negatively related to overall moral judgement. It is also negatively related to moral judgement as measured by four items of MJQ-ninth, tenth, eleventh and twelfth.

(*j*) Girl's perception of permissiveness is not significantly related to moral judgement.

Implications of the Findings

We have values and morality, so we are human beings but for development, maintenance and enhancement of values and morality certain conditions are indispensable. If girls are under stress and home environment is not congenial, the development of values and moral reasoning can be adversely affected. This study was undertaken to find out the effect of stress and various dimensions of home environment on values and moral judgement among girls. Findings have been described in the earlier section. Now an attempt will be made to think about the educational implications of various findings.

Implications for the Parents

Family is a basic and universal institution and survival of society depends upon the continued existence of the family and parental role. Patenting aims at providing best type of family climate for socialization of child as well as for the development of personality and real self. Socialization occurs through internationalization of values. Every human value, as English and English, (1958) have noted is a "social product" that has been transmitted and preserved in successive generations through one or more society's institution. Family has been regarded as one of the major institution through which values are maintained, enhanced and transmitted. Parent-child interactions are, undoubtedly, the source of the children's primary value systems. There are ample reasons to believe that many secondary needs and generalized values are established early in pre-school years and as the child's social life is broadened in scope parental influence tends to wane in importance. However, role of family and parent-child relationship maintains its central importance even throughout adolescence (Coleman, 1980; Siddique & D' Arcy, 1984).

Results of this study reveal that climate of the home plays an important role in development of values. Congenial and supportive environment, where the parent-child relationship is based upon natural love and respect for each other, is likely to help in the development of values like world of peace, a world of beauty, family security, happiness, social recognition, equity, power, ambitious, broadminded, capable, cheerful, logical, intellectual, obedient, courageous, self-control and self-determination values. Strained parent-child relationship where girls perceive themselves to be isolated, deprived and rejected, the child is likely to experience a feeling of fragmentation, indecision, and social and interpersonal isolation. This may lead to the development of psycho-social disorders such as anxiety, despair, depersonalization, meaninglessness, loneliness, a feeling of anonymity and pessimism. Such a hazardous climate is very likely to have adverse effect on values. This study has revealed that perception of high level of social isolation, deprivation of privileges and rejection in home environment adversely affect the development of values like a comfortable life, a world of peace, a world of beauty, equality, freedom, happiness, inner harmony, salvation, self-respect, social recognition, wisdom, equity, social justice, ambitious, broadminded, capable, cheerful, forgiving, helpful, independent, intellectual, polite and responsible values. So, parents must try to ensure creation of a home environment characterized by less use of rejection, social isolation and deprivation of privileges.

Development of moral judgement demands internalization of socially sanctioned prohibitions and mandates. This process of internalization is facilitated largely through the efforts of socialization. children's experiences determine the extent to which they acquire internal resources for controlling egoistic impulses and behaving morally. There are certain parental behaviours which may help perpetuate children's initial sense of opposition between their desires and external demands, whereas others may provide them with the inner resources—both cognitive and motivational—for changing their views about these demands and adopting them as internal guides to their own behaviour.

Results of this investigation provide guidelines to parents about the type of family climate which can be slightly more conducive for the moral development of children. The study reveals that supportive and affectionate environment of the family helps in developing self control and child's inner resources like self-esteem or concern for others. Parent should provide for moral orientation characterized by independence of external sanctions so that children may operate in real life regardless of presence or absence of surveillance. Study also shows that when the home environment is full of rejection and parents try to discipline the child through authoritarian, power-asserting, fear inducing method of punishment, they are likely to provide for moral orientation based on fear of external detection. It is the family on which the child depends for emotional and physical support. Parents should provide adequate social support and help their children in coping with stressful life events. They should reason and be sympathetic towards adolescent, who might be facing crisis. By providing an environment full of protectiveness, nurturance and reward, parents may help in resolving the crisis in positive way, and provide for their search for 'identity'.

Implications for the Teacher

Teacher plays a significant role in development of a child. As a friend, philosopher and guide, he helps the child in achieving the ultimate aim of self-actualization. It is their social duty to provide an environment which would cater to the needs of students. Stimulating socio-emotional environment can lead to high level of satisfaction, performance, goal attainment and health whereas less than optimal match between individual's needs and the class room environment may be accompanied by dissatisfaction, goal blockage, performance and health deficits, and stress. At this critical juncture, the teacher is supposed to act as gardener. With their nurturant and sympathetic attitude, they should try to lessen the gap between the teacher and the taught. Teachers with their personal influence should try to foster trust and confidence among their students and help them in coping with stress. It is evident from the findings of this study that stress in school is detrimental to the development of values and moral judgement as measured by ninth item of MJQ. Values serve as guide to behaviour. Values and attitude change can be nurtured by providing occasions which demand involvement, decision and action. Skinner tells us that values come by practice and reinforcement. Findings of this study will help the teacher to select students who are exposed to inappropriate home environment that inhibits the development of values. Then, they can try to make up for the deficiency in development of values.

Teachers can also facilitate moral judgement of children by adopting inductive techniques of discipline rather than managing the child through power assertive technique. They can help in developing moral values by providing appropriate reading material i.e., biographies and views of great man. Most important thing he can do is to provide an appropriate model which the students can observe and imitate. For a harmonious and well integrated development of child, cooperation between home and school is indispensable. In meetings of parent-teacher association, teachers can try to convince parents about the facilitative and harmful effects of various home environment conditions.

Implications for Counsellors

Every one wants to lead happy and contented life. Stress arises when demands exceed the capabilities of the person. Girls may find themselves unable to adjust to their environment. Cognitive and behavioural problems including health deficit arise as a result of stress. They require help in solving these problems. Counsellor can help girls in understanding their problems and finding out appropriate ways to reach a solution. After having identified girls who exhibit deficiencies in development of values and moral judgement, Counsellors, may study the stressors experienced by students and their home environment. This will help him in locating the problem. Findings of this study can help the counsellor in doing this task of locating the sources of poor development of values and moral deterioration. Counsellor's suggestions and rational persuasions can provide insight problem faced by girls and help them in solving problems. He can advice parents not to adopt authoritarian attitude towards adolescents. Findings of this study have shown that stress in home, school society and self adversely affects the development of values namely: a world of peace, happiness, pleasure, wisdom, helpful, equality, true friendship, forgiving, an exciting life, broadminded and capable values.

Counsellors, while attempting to locate the causes of girl's problems, should study their perception of home environment. Findings of this study can help the counsellors in their task. It has been found that social isolation, deprivation of privileges and rejection as perceived by girls in their home environments adversely affect the development of values namely: A comfortable life, equality, happiness, a world of beauty, social recognition, a world of peace, freedom, inner harmony, salvation, self-respect, equity, social justice, ambitious, broadminded, capable, cheerful, forgiving, helpful, independent, intellectual, polite and responsible values. It also shows that girls who perceive rejection in their home are unable to reach higher level of moral reasoning. These findings imply that parents should use social isolation, deprivation of privileges and rejection less frequently.

Counsellors can use findings of this study to convince the parents about the detrimental effects of their authoritarian and rejecting behaviour on the development of values and moral judgement. They can persuade the parents to provide a supportive environment full of protection, conformity, nurturance and reward. Findings of this study reveal that these aspects of home environment help in the development of values and moral judgement.

Suggestions for the Further study

This study was conducted on girls only. The findings are not applicable for boys. So, there exists a need to study values and moral judgement of boys with respect to their stress and home environment. Besides this, the following problems may also be studied by further researchers

(a) Moral judgement and values of children experiencing different levels of stress and studying in different grades in schools of different level of stress and studying in different grades in schools of different managements and organizational climate.

(b) Influence of educational choice and choice for co-curricular activities and schools on moral judgement and values of girls belonging to different religious groups.

(c) Development of values and moral judgement among girls in relation to their socio-economic status, intelligence, personality and adjustment.

(d) Interaction effect of home environment and stress on development of values and moral judgement.

(e) Effect of availability of role models and identifications on development of moral judgement.

(f) Similarities Between values of parents and children.

(g) Influence of peer-group interaction on values and moral judgement.

(h) Development of values and moral judgement among highly stressful students belonging to different castes and economic status.

(i) Coping behaviours adopted by students experiencing high/moderate/low stress in home/school/society/self areas.

Delimitations

The major delimitations of the study are as follows:

(a) R.V.S. Extended Version was used for measuring values. This test allows for rating procedure where each value is treated on its own, and would be less likely to confront the respondent with the task of searching through his priorities to establish his own value system.

(b) Home Environment Inventory measures ten dimensions of socio-emotional climate as perceived by students. These dimensions are control, protectiveness, punishment, conformity, social isolation, reward, deprivation of privileges, nurturance, rejection and permissiveness.

(c) Only girls studying in urban schools in IXth grade have been included in the sample.

(d) Stress scale measures stress in four areas i.e., home, school, society and self.

(e) Moral dilemmas included in the Moral Judgement Questionnaire measure moral judgement as exhibited in giving justifications for one's own response in a situation.

Bibliography

1. Acock, A.C., and Bengtson, V.L. 1976. On the relative influence of mothers or fathers: A co-variance analysis of political and religious socialization. In Feather, N.T., 1980. Values in adolescence. In Adelson, J. (Ed) *Hand Book of Adolescent Psychology* Vol. V. New York: Wiley.
2. Andrews, G., Tennant, C., Hewson, D., and Vaillant, G.E. 1978. Life event stress, social support, coping style and risk psychological impairment. *The Journal of Nervous and Mental Disease,* 166, 307-315.
3. Ahrentzen, S., Gregory, M.J., Skorpanich, M.A. and Evans, G.W. 1982. School environment and stress. In Evans, G.W. (Ed), *Environmental Stress*. Cambridge University Press.
4. Allport, G.W., Vernon, P.E., & Lindzey, G. 1960. *A study of values.* Boston: Houghton Mifflin.
5. Antonovsky, A. 1972. Breakdown: A needed fourth step in the conceptual armamentarium of modern medicine. In Hamilton, V. & Warburton, D.M. 1979. *Human Stress and Cognition: An Information Processing Approach.* New York: Wiley.
6. Andreasen, N.I.C., Noyes, R., Jr. and Hartford, C.E. 1972. Factors influencing adjustment of burn patients during hospitalization. *Psychosomatic Medicine,* 34, 517-525.
7. Ansari, A.A., Udupa K.N., & Agarwal. P. 1979. Trait of anxiety in relation to achievement motive in certain stress disorders. *Indian Journal of Clinical Psychology.* 6, 185-189.
8. Ariel, K.S. 1988. *Impact of Stress and Personality on Scientific Creativity of Adolescent Girls.* Med. Dissertation. University of Allahabad.

9. Atkinson. J., & Feather, N. 1966. *A Theory of Achievement Motivation.* New York: Wiley.

10. Baldwin. A.L. 1955. *Behaviour and Development in Childhood.* New York: The Dreyden Press.

11. Bandyopadhyay, R. 1981. *Growth and Development of Moral Judgement in Children,* Ph.D. Psy., Cal. University.

12. Bandura, A., 1962. Social learning through imitation. In M.R. Jones (Ed.), *Nebraska Symposium on Motivation.* Lincoln: University of Nebraska Press.

13. Bandura, A. 1965. Influence of models reinforcement contingencies on the acquisition of limitative responses. *Journal of Personality & Social Psychology.,* 589-595.

14. Bandura, A. 1968. Social learning theory of identificationary processes. In goslin, D., & Glass, D.C. (Ed). *Handbook of Socialization Theory and Research.* Chicago: Rand Mcnally.

15. Bandura, A. 1977. Self-efficacy: toward a unifying theory of behavioural change. *Psychological Review,* 84, 191-215.

16. Bandura, A., & Macdonald, F.J. 1963. Influence of social reinforcement and the behaviour of models in shaping children's moral judgements. *Journal of Abnormal & Social Psychology.,* 67, 274-281.

17. Bandura, A., & Walters, R.H., 1963. *Social Learning and Personality Development.* New York: Holt, Rinehart, & Winston.

18. Baumrind, D. 1967. Child care practice anteceding 3 patterns of preschool behaviour. In Grolnick, W.S. & Ryan, M. 1989. Parent style associated with children's self-reliance and competence in school. *Journal of Educational Psychology.* 8: No. 2, 143-154.

19. Baumrind, D. 1975. Early socialization and adolescent competence. In Dragastin, S.E., and Elder Jr, G.H. (Eds.), *Adolescence in the Life Cycle: Psychological Change and Social Context,* New York: Wiley.

20. Baum, A., & Valins, S. 1977. Architecture and social behaviour: Psychological studies of social density. In Evans, W.G., 1982 (Ed). *Environmental Stress.* Cambridge University Press.

21. Baker, G.W. & Chapman, D.W. 1962. Man and society in disaster. In Appley, M.H. & Trumbull, R. 1986 (Ed.). *Dynamics of Stress: Physiological, Psychological & Social Perspective.* New York: Plenum.

22. Berkman, L. 1977. Social networks, host resistance, and mortality: a follow-up study of Alameda country residents. In Hamilton. V. & Warburton. D.M. 1979 (Ed). *Human Stress and Cognition: An Information Processing Approach.* New York. John Wiley & Sons.

23. Beech, R.P. & Schoeppe, A. 1974. Development of value systems in adolescents. *Developmental Psychology.* 10, 644-656.

24. Bearison, D.J. & Cassel, T.Z. 1975. Cognitive decentration and social codes: Communication effectiveness in young children from differing family context. *Developmental Psychology,* 11, 29-36.

25. Bengtson, V.L., and Starr, J.M. 1975. Contrast and consensus: A generational analysis of youth in the 1970's. In Havighurst, R.J., and Dreyer, P. H. (Eds.), *Youth.* Chicago: University of Chicago Press.

26. Bhargawa, I. 1986. *Development of Moral Judgement Among Children at Concrete and Formal Operational Stages and its Relationship with the Variable of Home and Educational Environment,* Ph. D. Edu., Pan. University.

27. Bhargava, S.C. Sharma, S.N. & Agarwal, B.V. 1982. Stress of life events and coronary heart disease. *Indian Journal of Clinical Psychology,* 9. 51-52.

28. Block, J.H. 1972. Generational continuity and discontinuity in the understanding of societal rejection. *Journal of Personality and Social Psychology.* 22, 333-345.

29. Block. J., Hann. N., & Smith, M.B., 1969. Socialization correlates of student activism. In Hoffman, M.L., 1980. Moral development in adolescence. In Adelson. J., (Ed) *Handbook of Adolescent Psychology* Vol. V. New York. John Wiley & Sons Inc.

30. Bramel, D. 1968. Dissonance, expectation and the self. In Rokeach. M. 1973. *The Nature of Human Values.* New York, Free Press.

31. Buch, M.B. 1988. *Survey of Education.* N.C.E.R.T.

32. Buunk, B.P. & Hoorens, V. (1992). Social support and stress: The role of social comparison and social exchange processes. *British Journal of Clinical Psychology.* Vol. 31, 445-457.

33. Burnam, N.A., Pennebaker, J.W., & Glass, D.C. 1973. Time consciousness, Achievement striving and the type A coronary-prone behaviour pattern. *Journal of Abnormal Psychology.* 84, 76-79.

34. Buunk, B.P. & Schaufeli, W.B. 1992. In Buunk. B.P. & Hoorens. Social support and stress. The role of social comparison and social exchange processes. *British Journal of Clinical Psychology.* 31, 445-457.

35. Bulman, R.J. & Wortman, C.B. 1977. Attributions of blame and coping in the 'real world': Severe accident victims react to their lot. *Journal of Personality and Social Psychology,* 35, 351-363.

36. Burger, G.R. & Armentrout, J.A. 1971. A factor analysis of 5th and 6th grader's reports of parental child-rearing behaviour, *Developmental Psychology,* 4,483.

37. Burrera, M. & Garrison, J.C. 1992. Family and peer social support as specific correlates of adolescents depressive symptoms. *Journal of Abnormal Child Psychology,* Vol, 20, (1), 1-16.

38. Burton, R.V. 1972. Cheating related to maternal pressures for achievement. In Hoffman M.L. 1980. Moral development in adolescence. In Adelson. J. (Ed.). *Handbook of Adolescent Psychology* Vol. V. New York. John Wiley & Sons.

39. Byrne, D. 1971. *The Attraction Paradigm.* New York: Academic Press.

40. Caldwell, B.M., & Bradley, R.H. 1975. The relation of infant's home environment to mental test performance from six to thirty six months; A Longitudinal analysis: *Child Development,* 46. pp. 71-76.

41. Campbell, E.Q. 1969. Adolescent socialization. In Goslin, D.A., (Ed.). *Handbook of Socialization Theory and Research.* Chicago: Rand McNally.

42. Carstairs, G.M., and Kapur, R.L. 1976. *The Great Universe of Kota: Stress, Change and Mental Disorders in an Indian Village.* London: Hogarth Press.

43. Cassel, J. 1967. The contribution of the social enviroment to host resistance. *American Journal of Epidemiology,* 104, 107-123.

44. Chalmers, B.E. 1981. A şelective review of stress: some cognitive approaches taken a step further. In Apply, M.H., & Trumble, R, 1986 (Ed.). *Dynamics of Stress: Psychological, Psychological and Social Perspective.* New York. Plenum.

45. Chatterjee, S.B. 1978. Effect of environmental stress on the human mind and its role in psychosomatic illness. In Pandey, J. 1988. *Psychology in India: The State of Art.* Vol. 1. New Delhi. Sage Publications.

46. Chaturvedi, M.K. 1983. *Human Stress and Stressors: A sociological study.* New Delhi. Cosmo Publications.

47. Chakraborty, P.K., Shah, A.V., & Parikh H.K. 1983. Psychiatric factors in ulcerative colitis. *Indian Journal of Psychiatry.* 25, 219-222.

48. Christopher, B. 1979. Control of emotions, remote stress, and the emergence of breast cancer. *India Journal of Clinical Psychology.* 6, 213-220.

49. Chattopadhyay, P.K., and Das, M. 1983, Stressful life events and psychopathological episodes. *Indian Journal of Clinical Psychology,* 10, 227-231.

50. Cobb, S. 1976. Social support as a moderator of life stress. *Psychosomatic Medicine.* 38, 300-314.

51. Coby, G., Kamp, E., Paul, M. & William, A.A., 1991. Anxiety, depression and perception of early parenting: A meta analysis. *Clinical Psychological Review.* Vol. II (5). 667.

52. Coddington, R. 1972. The significance of ļife events as etiological factors in the diseases of children: A study of normal population. *Journal of Psychosomatic Research,* 16, 205-213.

53. Cohen, S. & Wills, T.A. 1985. Stress, social support and the buffering hypothesis. *Psychological Bulletin,* 98, 310-357.

54. Coleman, J. 1980. Friendship and the peer group in adolescence. In Adelson, J. (Ed.), *Handbook of Adolescent Psychology.* New York: Wiley.

55. Cooper, C.L., & Payne, R. 1978. *Stress at Work.* New York: John Wiley.

56. Cooper, C.L. & Payne, R. 1980. *Current Concerns in Occupational Stress.* New York: John Wiley.

57. Cox, T. 1978. *Stress.* London: MacMillan.

58. Cox, T. & Mackay, C. 1981. A transactional approach to occupational stress. In Corlett, E.N. & Richardson, J. (Ed.). *Stress, Work Design, Productivity,* pp. 91-113. New, York: Wiley.

59. Coyne J.C. 1976. Depression and the response of others. *Journal of Abnormal Psychology,* 85, 186-193.

60. Coyne, J.C. & Downey, G. 1991. Social factors and psychopathology: Stress, social support and coping processes. *Anual Review of Psychology,* 42, 401-429.

61. Coyne, J.C. & Lazarus, R.S. 1980. Congnative style, stress perception, and coping. In Kutash, C.L. & Schlesinger, L.B. (Eds.), *Handbook on Stress and Anxiety: Contemporary Knowledge, Theory, and Treatment.* San Francisco: Jossey-Bass.

62. Dimsdale, J.E. 1974. The coping behaviour of Nazi Concentration Camp survivors. In Hamilton, V. & Warburton, D. 1979 (Ed.). *Human Stress and Cognition: An Information Processing Approach.* New York. Wiley.

63. Diwedi, S. 1980. *Social Class and Their Value System.* Med. Dissertation. Allahabad University.

64. Douvan, E. & Adelson, J. 1966. *The Adolescent Experience.* New York: Wiley.

65. Epstein, Y. 1981. Crowding, stress and human behaviour. In Evan, G.W. 1982. (Ed.). *Environmental Stress.* Cambridge University Press.

66. Feather, N.T. 1959. Subjective Probability and decision under uncertainty. *Psychological Review,* 66, 150-164.

67. Feather, N.T. 1962. The study of persistence. *Psychological Bulletin,* 59, 94-115.

68. Feather, N.T. 1970. Educational choice and students attitudes in relation to terminal and instrumental values. *Australian Journal of Psychology,* 22, 127-144. *Society.* 1975. The Free Press.

69. Feather, N.T. 1972. Value similarity and school adjustment. *Australian Journal of Psychology.* 24, 193-208.

70. Feather, N.T. 1974. Coeducational values, and satisfaction with school. *Journal of Educational Psychology,* 26, 199-216.

71. Feather, N.T. 1975. *Values in Education and Society.* New York, The Free Press.

72. Feather, N.T. 1978. Family resemblances in conservatism: Are daughters more similar to parents than sons are? *Journal of Personality,* 46, 460-278.

73. Feather, N.T., and Collins, J.M. 1974. Differences in attitude in values of students in relation to programe of study at a college of advance education. *Australian Journal of Education,* 18, 16-29.

74. Feather, N.T., and Hutton, M.A. 1974. Value systems of students in Paupa New Guinea and Australia. *International Journal of Psychology.* 9, 91-104.

75. Feather, N.T., and Rudzitis, A. 1974. Subjective assimilation among Latvian adolescents: Effect of ethnic schools and perceptions of value system. *International Migration,* 12, 71-87.

76. Feg, C.C., 1992. Life stress and psychological adjustment among American, Asian American and Asian foreign graduate students: The mediating role of objective social networks. *Dissertation Abstract International.* Sept. pp., 755-756.

77. Feuer, L. 1969. *The Conflict of Generations.* New York: Basic Books.

78. Frankenhaeuser, M. & Gardell, B. 1976. Underload and overload in working life: Outline of a multidisciplinary approach. *Journal of Human Stress.* 2(3) 35-56.

79. Fried, M. 1963. Grieving for a lost home. In Evans, G.W. 1982 (Ed.). *Environmental Stress.* Cambridge University Press.

80. Friedman, S.B., Chodoff, P. Mason, J.W. and Hamburg, D.A. 1963. Behavioural observations on parents anticipating the death of a child. In Hamilton, V.,

Warburton, D. (1979). *Human Stress and Cognition: An Information Processing Approach.* New York: Wiley.

81. Garg, R.R. 1983. *Children's Perceptions of Parental Disciplinary Practice and its Relation to Development of Personality Needs, Moral Judgement and Problem-solving Ability.* Ph.D. Psy., Agra University.

82. Garrett, H.E. 1979. *Statistics in Psychology and Education.* Vakils, Feffer and Simons LTD.

83. Gottlieb, B. 1985. Theory into practice: Issues that surface in Planing interventions which mobilize support. In I.G. Sarason & Sarason, B.R. (Eds.). *Social Support: Theory, Research and Application.* Boston: Martinus Nijhoff.

84. Greene, W.A. 1966. The psychosocial setting of development of leukemia and lymphoma. In Evans, G.W. 1982 (Ed.). *Environmental Stress.* Cambridge University Press.

85. Gupta, L.N., & Srivastava, D. 1983. Life events and course of a physical illness. *Indian Journal of Psychiatry.* 25, 317-321.

86. Hackett, T.P. & Weisman, A. D. 1964. Reactions to the imminence of death. In Grosser, G.H., Wechsler, H. & Greenblatt, M. (Eds.). *The Threat of Impending Disaster,* Cambridge, Mass.: MIT Press. 300-311.

87. Hamburg, D.A., Hamburg, B. and DeGoza 1953. Adoptive problems and mechanisms in severely burned patients. *Psychiatry,* 16, 1-20.

88. Hamburg, D.A., & Adams, J.E. 1967. A perspective on coping: Seeking and utilizing information skin major transitions. *Archives of General Psychiatry,* 17, 277-284.

89. Hamilton, V. 1979. Personality and stress. In Hamilton, V. & Warberton, D.M. (Eds.). *Human Stress and Cognition: An Information Processing Approach.* New York. John Wiley & Sons.

90. Harburg, E., Erfrut, J.C., Chaperi, E., Nauenstien, L.F., Schull, W.F., & Schork, M.A. 1973. Sociological stressor areas and black-white blood pressure: Detroit. *Journal of Chronic Diseases,* 26, 295-611.

91. Hatfield, E., Trumpmann, J., Sprecher. S., Utne, M. & Hay, J. 1984. Equity and intimate relations: Recent

research. In W.Icks (Ed.), *Compatible and Incompatible Relationships*. pp. 1-27. New York: Springer-Verlag.

92. Hiller K. & Swindle, R.V. 1983. Social networks, perceived social support, and coping with stress. In Felner, R.D., Jason, L.A., Moritsugu, J. and Farver, S.S. (Eds.). *Preventive Psychology: Research and Practice in Community Intervention,* pp. 87-107. New York, Pergamon Press.

93. Hinkle, L.E. 1974. The concept of stress in biological and social sciences. In Peston Jee, D.M. 1992. *Stress and Coping. The Indian Experience.* New Delhi. Sage Publications.

94. Hoffman, M.L. 1963. Parent discipline and the child's consideration for others. *Child Development.* 34.

95. Hoffman, M.L. and Saltzstein, H.D., 1967. Parent discipline and the child's moral development. *Journal of personality and Social Psychology.,* 5, 45-57.

96. Hoffman, M.L. 1970. Moral development. In Mussen, P.H. (Ed.). *Carmichael's Manual of Child Psychology* (Vol. 2). New York: Wiley.

97. Hoffman M.L. 1976. Empathy, role-taking, guilt, and development of altruistic motives. In Linkona, (Ed.). *Moral Development: Current Theory and Research.* New York: Holt, Rinehart & Winston.

98. Hoffman, L.W. 1977. Changes in family rules, socialization and sex differences. *American Psychologist,* 32, 644-657.

99. Hoffman, M.L. 1978. Toward a theory of empathetic arousal and development. In Lewis, M. & Rosenblum, L. (Eds.), *The development of Affect.* New York: Plenum.

100. Hoffman, M.L. 1980. Moral development in adolescence. In Adelson, J. (Eds.), *Handbook of Adolescent Psychology.* New York: John wiley & Sons.

101. Hofstede, G. 1980. Culture's Consequences: International differences in work-related values. In Berry. J.W., Poortinga, Y.H., Sega, M.H., Dasen, P.R., 1992 (Ed.). *Cross Cultural Psychology: Research and Application:* Combridge University press.

102. Holmes, T.H., & Masuda, M. 1974. Life changes and illness susceptibility. In Dohrenwend, B.S., &

Dohrenwend, B.P. (Eds.). *Stressful Life Event: Their Nature and Effects.* New York: Wiley.

103. Holroyd. K.A. & Lazarus, R.S. 1982. Stress, coping, and somatic adoption. In Goldberger, L. & Breznitz (Ed.). *Handbook of Stress: Theoretical and Clinical Aspects.* New York: The Free Press.

104. Horn, J.L. & Knott, P.D., 1971. Activist youth of the 1960s: In Hoffman, 1980: Moral development in adolescence. In Adelson. J, (Ed.) *Handbook of Adolescent Psychology.* Vol. V. New York: Wiley.

105. Horwitz, M. 1976. *Stress Response Syndromes,* New York: Aronson.

106. Hyman, I.A., Zelikoff, W. Clarke, J. 1988. Psychological and Physical abuse in the schools: A paradigm for understanding post-traumatic stress disorder in children and youth. Special Issue: Progress in traumatic stress research. *Journal of Traumatic Stress.* Vol. 1, (2), 243-267.

107. Janis, I. 1974. Vigilance and decision making in personal crises. In Hamburg, D.A., Coelho, C.V. and Adams, J.E. (Eds.). *Coping and Adaptation.* New York: Basic Books.

108. Janis, I., & Mann, L. 1977. *Decision Making.* New York: The Free Press.

109. Jennings, M.K., and Niemi, R.G. 1974. *The Political Character of Adolescent.* Princeton, N.J.

110. Kahn, R.L. and French, J.R.P. 1970. Status and conflict: Two themes in the study of stress. In McGrath, J.E. (Ed.). *Social and Psychological Factors in Stress.* New York: Holt, Rinehart and Winston.

111. Kaplan, B., Cassel, J., and Gore, S. 1977. Social support and health. *Medical Care,* 15, No. 5 Supplement, 47-58.

112. Kasl, S. V. & Cobb., S. 1970. Blood pressure changes in men undergoing job loss: A preliminary report. *Psychosomatic Medicine,* 32, 19-38.

113. Khorana, S. 1983. A study of psychological factors and psychotherapy in ulcerative colitis. *Indian Journal of Clinical Psychology,* 10, 257-262.

114. Kluckhohn, C. 1951. Values and value orientations in theory of action. In Partsons, T. and Shils, E.A. (Ed.).

Towards a Journal Theory of Action. Cambridge: Harvard University Press.

115. Kluckhohn, F.R. & Strodtbeck, F.L. 1961. *Variations in Value Orientations.* Evanston, 11.: Row, Peterson.

116. Kohlberg. L. 1958. In Thomes, R.M. 1985 (Ed.). *Comparing Theories of Child Development.* New York: Wadsworth Publishing Company.

117. Kohlberg, L. 1981. *Essays on Moral Development.* New York. Harper & Row.

118. Kohlberg. L. 1984. *The Psychology of Moral Development:* The nature and validity of moral stages. San Francisco: Harper and Row.

119. Kraut, R.E. & Lewis, S.H. 1975. Alternate models of family influence on student political ideology. *Journal of Personality and Social Psychology.* 31, 791-800.

120. Larocco, J.M. and Jones, A.P. 1978. Co-worker and leader support as moderators of stress-strain relationship in work situations. *Journal of Applied Psychology.* 63, 229-634.

121. Lazarus, R.S. 1966. *Psychological Stress and the Coping Process.* New York: McGraw-Hill.

122. Lazarus, R.S., & Cohen, J.B. 1977. Environmental stress. In Altman, I., & Wohlwill, J.F. (Eds.). *Human Behaviour and the Environment: Current Theory and Research* (Vol. 2, pp. 89-128). New York: Plenum press.

123. Lazarus, R.S., & Lavnier, R. 1978. Stress related transactions between person and environment. In Pervin, L.A., & Lewis, M. (Eds.). *Perspectives in Interactional Psychology.* New York: Plenum.

124. Lefcourt, H.M. 1976. *Locus of Control, Current Trends in Theory and Research.* Hillsdale, N.J.: Lawrence Erlbaum.

125. Leventhal, H. 1970. Findings and theory in the study of fear communications. In Berkowitz, (Ed.). *Advances in Experimental and Social Psychology:* Vol, 5 pp. 120-186. New York: Academic Press.

126. Luther, S.S., & Quinlan, D.M. 1993. Personal images in two cultures: A study of women in India and America. *Journal of Cross-Cultural Psychology.*

127. Maccoby, E. and Martin, J. 1983. Socialization in the context of the family: Parent child interaction. In Hetherington, I.M. & Mussen, P.H. (series Ed.), *Handbook of Child Psychology,* Vol. IV, Socialization, Personality and Social Development. New York: Wiley.

128. Mechanic, D. 1962. *Students under stress.* Glencoe, III.: Free Press.

129. MaGrath, J.E. 1970. *Social and Psychological factors in stress.* New York: Holt, Rinehart and Winston.

130. Moore, M. (1975). Rating versus ranking in the Rokeach value survey: An Israeli Comparison. *European Journal of Social Psychology.* 5, 405-408.

131. Misra, K.S. (1981). *Effects of Children's Perception of Home and School Environment on their Scientific Creativity.* Ph.D. Edu., University of Rajasthan.

132. Naidu, R.K. 1983, December. *A developing programme of stress research.* Paper presented at the seminar on stress. Anxiety and mental health, University of Allahabad, Allahabad.

133. Ng.S.H. (1981). *Choosing between the ranking and rating procedures in the cross-cultural comparison of values.* Unpublished manuscript, Department of Psychology, University of Otago.

134. Ng, S.H., Hossain, A., Ball, P., Bond M.H., Hayashi, K., Lim, S.P., O. Dricoff, M.P., Sinha. D., Yang, K.S. 1982. Human values in nine countries. In Roth, R., Sinha, D., and Sinha J.P.B., (Ed.). *Diversity and Unity in Cross-Cultural Psychology.* Holland Swets and Zeitginger B.V. Lisse.

135. Nuckolls, K.B, Cassel, J. and Kaplan, B.H. 1972. Psychosocial assets, life crisis, and the prognosis of pregnancy. *American Journal of Epidemiology,* 95, 431-441.

136. Pandey, N. 1990. *Studies on differential vulnerability to stress: The impact of detachment on health.* Doctoral dissertation. Dept. of Psy. Allahabad University.

137. Pareek. U., 1981. *Role stress scale.* Research report. Ahmedabad. Indian Institute of Management.

138. Parker, G., Tupling, H, & Brown. L.B. 1979. A parental bonding instrument. In MaCcoby, E. & Martin. J. 1983. Socialization in the context of the family Parent Child interaction. In Hetherington, I.M., Mussen, P.H. (series Ed.), *Handbook of Child Psychology,* Vol. IV, Socilization, personality and social development. New York: Wiley.

139. Parkes, C.M. 1972. *Bereavement.* New York: International Universities Press.

140. Parmesh, C.R. (1970). *A study of Creativity in relation to extroversion, emotionality, body image and values.* Doctoral Dissertation. Madras University.

141. Parsons, T.M. 1968. On the concept of value-commitments. In Williams, R.M. 1979. In Rokeach, M. (Ed.). *Understanding Human Values; Individual and Societal.* New York. Free Press.

142. Pattnaik, A. (1987). *A study of relationship between Home environment and values of secondary girl students.* M.Ed. dissertation. Dept. of Education, Allahabad University.

143. Pearlin, L.I. 1975. Sex roles and depression. In Datan, N. and Ginsberg, L.H. (Eds.), *Life-span developmental Psychology: Normative Life Crisis.* New York: Academic Press.

144. Piaget, J. (1932). *The moral judgement of the child.* New York: Harcourt, Brace. Pulkkinen, L. 1982. Self-control and continuity from childhood to adolescence. In Baltes, P.B. & Brim, O.G. (Eds). *Life-span development and behaviour* (Vol. 4). New York: Academic Press.

145. Punetha, D., Giles, H., and Young, L. (1987). Ethnicity and immigrant values: Religion and Language choice: *Journal of Language and Social Psychology.*

146. Ramanujam, B.K. 1993. Towards maturity problems of identity seen in the Indian Clinical setting. In Kakkar, S. (Ed.). *Identity and adulthood.* Oxford University Press. New Delhi.

147. Rangaswami, K. 1983. Personality, life events and alcoholism. *Indian Journal of Clinical Psychology.* 10, 179-182.

148. Rankin, W.L. and Grube, J.W. (1980). A comparison of ranking and rating procedures for value system

measurement. *European Journal of Social Psychology.* 10, 233-246.

149. Roberto, K.A. & Scott, J.P. (1986). Equity Considerations in the friendship of older adults. In Buunk, B.P.& Hoorens, V. 1992. Social support and stress. The role of social comparison and social exchange processes. *The British Journal of Clinical Psychology.* 31 445-457.

150. Rokeach, M. 1964. The three christs of Ypsilanti. In Rokeach, M. 1973. *The nature of human values.* New York: Free Press.

151. Rokeach, M. (1973). *The nature of human values.* New York: Free Press.

152. Rotter, J.B. 1966. Generalized expectancies for internal versus external control of reinforcement. *Psychological Monographs,* 80, Whole No. 609.

153. Saraswathi, T.S. (1978). *Perceived Maternal Disciplinary Practices and Their Relation to Development of Moral Judgement,* Dept. of Child Development, MSU, (ICSSR financed).

154. Sarason, B.R., Sarason, I. G. and Pierce, G.R. 1990. *Social support: An Interactional view.* New York: Wiley.

155. Saxena, S., Mohan. D., Dube. S., Sundaram, K.R. and Chawla, P.L. 1983. Stressful life events in psychiatric outpatients: A controlled study. *Indian Journal of Psychiatry,* 25, 129-133.

156. Scarr, S. & McCartney, K. 1983. How people make their own environment: A theory of genotype environment effects, *Child Development.* 54, 424-435.

157. Schwartz, S.H. and Bilsky, W. (1987). Towards a universal psychological structure of human values. *Journal of Personality & Social Psychology,* 53, 550-562.

158. Schwartz. S.H. and Bilsky, W. (1990). Toward a theory of the universal content and structure of values: Extensions and cross-cultural replications. *Journal of Personality and Social Psychology,* 58, 878-891.

159. Schafer, E.S. 1965. Children's reports of parental behaviour: An inventory. *Child Development,* 36, 413-424.

160. Schachter, S. (1959). *The Psychology of affiliation.* Stanford calif: Stanford University Press.

161. Schulz, R. 1976. Effects of control and predictability on the physical and psychological well-being of institutional aged. *Journal of Personality and Social Psychology*. 33. 563-573.

162. Sears, R.R., MaCcoby, E.E. and Levin. H. (1957). *Patterns of child rearing*. Evanston Row. Paterson & Company.

163. Selye, H. 1936. *In Selye's guide to stress research*. 1980, Vol. 1. New York. Van Vostrand Reinhold Company.

164. Seyle, H. 1956. *The stress of life*. New York McGraw Hills.

Selye, H. 1976. *The stress of life*. (revised, ed) New York: McGraw Hills.

165. Sethi, A.S. and Gupta,. D. (1984). Moral judgement level and perceived maternal child rearing attitudes of boys and girls. *Journal of Psychology Researches*. Vol. 28; No. 2, 102-106.

106. Sethumadhavan, P. 1992. *Sense of responsibility and the effects of stress experience,* Doctoral dissertation Dept. of Psy. Allahabad University.

167. Sharma, S. 1972. Changes in state and trait anxiety scores with the approaching examination. *New Trends in Education,* 4, 10-13.

168. Siddique, C. & 'D' Arch, C., (1984). Adolescence stress and Psychological well-being. In Shirley, F. & James, R., 1988 (Ed.). *Handbook of life stress: Cognition and Health*. New York. Wiley.

169. Siegel, S. (1956). *Non-parametric statistics for the behavioural sciences*. New York: McGraw-Hill.

170. Signman, M. and Erdynast, A.,(1988). Interpersonal understanding and moral judgement in adolescents with emotional and cognitive disorder. *Child Psychiatry and Human Development*. Vol. 19.

171. Simons, R.G., Rosenberg, F. & Rosenberg, M., 1973. Disturbances in self image at adolescence. In Pal, S.K., Malhotra. S. & Misra, K.S., 1986 (Ed.). *Trends and Thoughts in Education* Vol. III Stress. Dept. of Education, Allahabad.

172. Sims, J.H. and Baumann, D.D. 1974. The torando threat: Coping styles of the North and South. In Evans. G.W. 1982. *Environmental Stress*. Cambridge University Press.

173. Singh, R.S. (1983). *Children's Moral Judgement in Relation to Prolonged Deprivation and Parental Attitudes,* Ph.D. Edu., Gor. University.

174. Singh, A.J., and Kang, S.A. 1977. Study of adjustment of college students in relation to anxiety. *Indian Educational Review,* 12(3), 109-111.

175. Singer, J.E., Lundberg, U.& Frankenhaeuser, M. 1978. Stress on the train: A study of urban commuting. In Baum, A., Singer, J.F. and Valins, S. (Ed.). *Advances in Environmental Psychology,* (Vol. 1). Hillsdale, N.J.: Erlbaum.

176. Sinha, D. 1962. Cultural factors in emergence of anxiety. *Eastern Anthropologist.* 25 (1). 10. 21-31.

177. Solnit, A.J. 1972. Youth and the Campus: The search for a social conscience. In Hoffman, M.L. 1980. Moral development in adolescence. In Adelson J. (Ed.) *Handbook of Adolescent Psychology.* New York. Wiley.

178. Spielberger, C.D., Gonzalesz, H.P., Taylor, C.J., Algaze, B., and Anton, W.D. 1978. Examination stress and test anxiety. In Spielberger, C.D. and Sarason, I.G. (Eds.). *Stress and anxiety* (Vol. 5, PP. 167-191). New York: Hemisphere.

179. Srivastava, J.R. and Singh, S.B. 1979. The basis of Psychosomatic disorder in children. *Child Psychiatry Quarterly,* 12, 25-32.

180. Syme, S.L. and Berkman, L.F. 1976. Social class, susceptibility and sickness. *American Journal of Epidemiology,* 104, 1-8.

181. Teichimann, Y. 1973. Emotional comparison and affiliation. *Journal of Experimental Social Psychology,* 9, 591-605.

182. Thoits, P.A. 1986. Social support as coping assistance. *Journal of Consulting and Clinical Psychology,* 58, 360-370.

183. Tripathi, R.C., Caplan, R.D., and Naidu, R.K. 1986. Accepting advice: A modifier of social support's effect on well-being. *Journal of Social and Personal Relationships,* 3, 213-228.

184. Troll, L., Neugarten, B.L., and Krains, R.J. 1969. Similarities in values and other personality

characteristics in college students and their parents. In Feather, N.T. 1980. Values in adolescence. In Adelson, J:, (Ed). *Hand book of Adolescent Psychology* Vol. V. New York Wiley.

185. Udupa, K.N. 1980. Role of Stress in Cancer. Indian Journal of Cancer, 17, 7-10.

186. Vanyperen, N.W., and Buunk, B.P. 1990. A longitudinal study of equity and satisfaction in intimate relationships. *European Journal of Social Psychology.* 20, 287-309.

187. Venkoba, R.A. and Nammalvar, N. 1976. Life changes and depressive disease. *Indian Journal of Psychiatry,* 18, 293-304.

188. Visotsky, H.M., Gross, M.E. and Lebovits, B.Z. 1961. Coping behaviour under extreme stress. *Archives of General Psychiatry,* 5, 423-448.

189. Vogel, W., Raymond, S. and Lazarus, R.S., 1959. Intrinsic motivation and psychological stress. *Journal of Abnormal and Social Psychology,* 58, 225-233.

190. Walter, E.G., Walter, W. and Bercheid, E. 1978. *Equity: Theory and Research.* Boston: Allyn and Bacon.

191. Weiner, I. 1980. Psychopathology in adolescence. In Adelson, J. (Ed). *Handbook of Adolescent Psychology,* New York: Wiley.

192. Williams, R.M. 1968. Values. In Sills, E. (Ed.), *International Encyclopedia of Social Sciences,* New York, Macmillan.

193. Williams, R.M. 1979. Change and stability in values and value systems: A sociological perspective. In Rokeach, M. (Ed.), *Understanding Human Values: Individual and Societal.* New York. Free Press.

194. Zimbrdo and Formica 1963. In Hamilton, V. and Warburton, D.M., 1979. (Ed.). *Human Stress and Cognition: An Information Processing Approach.* New York, John Wiley & Sons.

195. Zavalloni, M. 1980. Values. In Triandis, H.C., and Brislin, R.W. (Ed.), *Handbook of Cross-Cultural Psychology.* Boston: Allyn and Bacon.

Index